CURRICULUM AND THE SPECIALIZATION OF KNOWLEDGE

This book presents a new way for educators at all levels – from early years to university – to think about curriculum priorities. It focuses on the curriculum as a form of specialized knowledge, optimally designed to enable students to gain access to the best knowledge available in any field.

Based on papers jointly written by the authors over the last eight years and specially revised for this volume, the book draws on the sociology of knowledge and in particular the work of Émile Durkheim and Basil Bernstein, opening up the possibilities for collaborative interdisciplinary enquiry with historians, philosophers and psychologists.

Although primarily directed at researchers, university teachers and graduate students, its arguments about specialized knowledge have profound implications for policy makers.

Michael Young is Professor of Education at the UCL Institute of Education, London.

Johan Muller is Emeritus Professor of Education in the School of Education at the University of Cape Town, South Africa.

CURRICULUM AND THE SPECIALIZATION OF KNOWLEDGE

Studies in the sociology of education

Michael Young and Johan Muller

Routledge
Taylor & Francis Group

LONDON AND NEW YORK

First published 2016
by Routledge
2 Park Square, Milton Park, Abingdon, Oxon OX14 4RN

and by Routledge
711 Third Avenue, New York, NY 10017

Routledge is an imprint of the Taylor & Francis Group, an informa business

© 2016 Michael Young and Johan Muller.

British Library Cataloguing in Publication Data
A catalogue record for this book is available from the British Library

Library of Congress Cataloging in Publication Data
A catalog record for this book has been requested

ISBN: 978-1-138-81491-2 (hbk)
ISBN: 978-1-138-81492-9 (pbk)
ISBN: 978-1-315-74713-2 (ebk)

Typeset in Bembo
by Cenveo Publishers Services

For Penny, Alice and Elinor

CONTENTS

ACKNOWLEDGEMENTS

The authors would like to thank the following colleagues who, in different ways, have all lent their encouragement.

Stephanie Allais, Helena Araujo, Paul Ashwin, John Beck, Cyril Cannon, Charmian Cannon, Jenni Case, Nico Cloete, Christine Counsell, Zain Davis, Jan Derry, Paula Ensor, Roger Firth, Alison Fuller, Jeanne Gamble, Amparo Tome Gonzalez, Gerald Grace, David Guile, Michael Hand, Suzy Harris, Dennis Hayes, Ursula Hoadley, Wayne Hugo, Karen Jensen, Peter Kallaway, Ben Kotzee, David Lambert, Hugh Lauder, Shirley Lawes, Peliwe Lolwana, Ingrid Lunt, Peter Maassen, Toby Marshall, Ana Morais, Antonio Flavio Moreira, John Morgan, Richard Noss, Tim Oates, David Perks, John Polesel, Kim Quy, Elizabeth Rata, Michael Reiss, Luciola Santos, David Scott, Yael Shalem, Suellen Shay, Paul Standish, Nick Taylor, Lorna Unwin, Penny Vinjevold, Philippe Vitale, Leesa Wheelahan, Geoff Whitty, Chris Winch, Claudia Gallian, Tian Xu and Lyn Yates.

We would also like to pay tribute to our colleagues Rob Moore, Jack Keating and Pete Medway who sadly died while this book was in preparation.

We would like to thank Lynne Teixeira for her careful and accurate help in putting the manuscript together.

We would like to express our appreciation to Anna Clarkson and her colleagues at Routledge for the support for our work over many years.

This work is based on research supported in part by the National Research Foundation of South Africa (UID 85813). The Grant holder acknowledges that opinions, findings and conclusions or recommendations expressed are those of the authors.

PREVIOUSLY PUBLISHED MATERIAL

The authors would like to thank the publishers for permission to draw on previously published material.

Chapter 2 was originally published as:
M. Young and J. Muller (2007) 'Truth and truthfulness in the sociology of educational knowledge', *Theory & Research in Education*, 5(2), pp. 173–201.

Chapter 3 was originally published as:
M. Young (2012) 'Education, globalisation and the "voice" of knowledge' in H. Lauder, M. Young, H. Daniels, M. Balarin and J. Lowe (eds), *Educating for the Knowledge Economy? Critical Perspectives*, London: Routledge, pp. 114–28.

Chapter 4 was originally published as:
M. Young (2010) 'Alternative education futures for a knowledge economy', *European Education Research Journal*, 9(1), pp. 1–12.

Chapter 5 was originally published as:
M. Young and J. Muller (2010) 'Three educational scenarios for the future: lessons from the sociology of knowledge', *European Journal of Education*, 45(1), pp. 11–27.

Chapter 7 is also to be published as:
J. Muller (in press) 'The future of knowledge and skills in science and technology higher education', *Higher Education*. DOI: 10.1007/s10734-014-9842-x.

Chapter 8 was originally published as:
M. Young (2009) 'What are schools for?' in H. Daniels, H. Lauder, J. Porter and S. Hartshorn (eds), *Knowledge, Values and Education Policy: A Critical Perspective*, London: Routledge, pp. 10–18.

Chapter 9 was originally published as:

M. Young and J. Muller (2013) 'On the powers of powerful knowledge', *Review of Education*, 1(3), pp. 229–50.

Chapter 10 was originally published as:

M. Young (2013) 'Overcoming the crisis in curriculum theory: a knowledge-based approach, *Journal of Curriculum Studies*, 45(2), pp. 101–18.

Chapter 12 is also to be published as:

J. Muller (in press) 'The body of knowledge' in P. Vitale and B. Exley (eds), *Pedagogic Rights and Democratic Education: Bernsteinian Explorations of Curriculum, Pedagogy and Assessment*, London: Routledge.

Chapter 13 was originally published as:

J. Muller and M. Young (2014) 'Disciplines, skills and the university', *Higher Education*, 67(2), pp. 127–40.

Chapter 14 was originally published as:

J. Muller (2014) 'Every picture tells a story: epistemological access and knowledge', *Education as Change*, 18(2), pp. 255–69.

Chapter 15 was originally published as:

M. Young and J. Muller (2014) 'From the sociology of professions to the sociology of professional knowledge' in M. Young and J. Muller (eds), *Knowledge, Expertise and the Professions*, London: Routledge, pp. 3–17.

SECTION 1
Setting the scene

1

INTRODUCTION

This book brings together papers in the sociology of education that we have worked on jointly and separately over the last decade. It is about the increasing importance of knowledge in education and its role not only in the school curriculum, but also in the curriculum of universities and programmes for the education of future members of professions and other occupations. We argue for a sociological approach to the knowledge which extends beyond schooling; this is not only because higher and professional education programmes have a major role in shaping the school curriculum, but because their curricula deserve study in their own terms.

The growing importance of ideas such as the knowledge society and the knowledge economy prefigures the likely possibility that most employment in future societies will depend on knowledge-based (rather than on solely skill-based or routine-based) work. In responding to this problem, this book attempts to modernize curriculum theory and the research that follows by moving from our earlier work on curricula for schools, colleges and universities to developing an approach to 'knowledge about knowledge' in education and, in particular, the differentiated and specialized forms it takes.

Our point of departure as sociologists of education is to draw on the classical sources of the sociology of knowledge – specifically those theorists who have not always been given the importance they warrant in the wider discipline but have a unique salience to the problem of knowledge faced by educators. In this book, we draw on concepts from the sociology of knowledge to grasp the changing knowledge landscape and its implications for what all pupils need if they are to become productive and fulfilled citizens in today's globalized world.

Research on the curriculum has been dominated since its inception in the USA at the turn of the last century by the problems faced by school administrators, curriculum specialists and head teachers (see Chapter 10). We do not under-emphasize the problems that schools face; they provide the unique and often sole opportunity for the vast majority of young people to acquire knowledge that takes them beyond their experience. However, our focus on the curriculum as a form of specialized knowledge geared specifically to its transmission leads us to two issues largely neglected by curriculum theory. The first is that school curricula are significantly shaped, not only by the universities as sources of specialized disciplinary knowledge, but by their role in preparing students for entry into universities and professional programmes. The second issue largely neglected by curriculum theory is that schools are not the only institutions that have curricula and therefore face curriculum problems. Thus in both Sections 2 and 4 of this book, we extend our discussion to university and professional education curricula.

In introducing this collection of our joint and single-authored papers, it is important to explain its origins and to say something about what we hope it will achieve. For some time we were both separately thinking of editing a collection of our recent papers into a book. However, it soon became clear to each of us that five of the papers we would both want to include were jointly authored. Second, we also became aware that several of our single-authored papers had arisen out of our ongoing discussions. Furthermore, although our intellectual biographies as sociologists of education have been rather different, and we have pursued our scholarship in two very different countries, many of our individual papers address issues that concern us both. It was these issues together with our experience of a successful collaboration on an earlier book (Young and Muller 2014) that led us to decide to bring our single- and joint-authored papers together in a single book. An advantage of doing so is that, while we share basic theoretical assumptions, the papers we include in this book vary significantly in their theoretical explicitness. This means, we hope, that the chapters will be read not only 'for themselves', but also as informing each other and in some cases forming a dialogue that suggests new questions to readers. It is for this reason that we decided to leave unchanged the paragraphs where there is repetition in the interests of maintaining the coherence of the individual chapters that have been previously published. We hope that those who read the book sequentially will bear with us.

The book aims to be a specific contribution to the sociology of education and to developing and broadening that strand of the sub-discipline which traces its roots back to Emile Durkheim, the first sociologist of education, and his leading contemporary interpreter, Basil Bernstein. The papers we have included were written between 2006 and 2014 and although they do not appear in the sequence in which they were written, the collection as a whole represents shifts in our own thinking, and in the development of the field. Furthermore in many cases they were written as specific interventions in policy debates in England and South Africa.

Our previous books (Muller 2000; Young 2008; Young and Lambert 2014) together with the influential texts of the late Rob Moore (2004; 2009) with whom we had both written, amongst others, were a critical response to earlier attempts by sociologists of education to make the question of knowledge a central issue for the sub-discipline. The jointly-written Chapter 2, 'Truth and truthfulness in the sociology of educational knowledge', can be understood best as a 'transition paper'. It sets out to summarize the previous essentially epistemological debates in the sociology of education around truth and relativism and, at the same time, to suggest a way beyond them (see also Chapter 9 in this volume). It reprises these debates by drawing comparisons between Durkheim's response to the early pragmatist ideas of Dewey and William James and the critiques by Moore and others of the social constructivism of the 1970s New Sociology of Education. The chapter builds on Moore's argument that the sociality of knowledge not only explains its bias, but can also explain its objectivity. We explore this idea through a discussion of Durkheim's lectures to future teachers and their interpretation by Basil Bernstein, and also suggest how the ideas of the social philosopher of knowledge Ernst Cassirer may offer a way forward.

By the time Chapter 2 was written, the idea that all knowledge is in some sense 'socially constructed' but at the same time can have an emergent reality of its own, was reasonably widely accepted in the sociology of education, at least, 'in theory'. The question the sociology of education was left with was 'what follows?' The remaining sections represent our attempts to answer that question.

Section 2 includes a series of chapters that engage with current policies and their assumptions, not just by presenting critiques, but also with emerging attempts to develop alternatives. The shift from Chapter 2 can be represented as a shift in the focus of the sociology of knowledge from a concern with the epistemological question of truth to the question 'how do we undertake enquiries into "knowledge about knowledge"'? The earlier work summarized in Chapter 2 provides us with the basis for moving beyond the sociology of knowledge's historical concern with the debate about relativism to questions about how knowledge is differentiated and specialized in its production and in curricula.

This sets our sociological approach on a collision course with policy developments which were increasingly playing down the importance of knowledge per se and giving priority to forms of generic and skills-based curriculum stipulations. Section 2 also engages with changes in curriculum policy, most notably in England as a new subject-based National Curriculum was launched in 1988.

The chapters in Section 3 examine the potential of the sociology of education as a basis for curriculum theory and engage with the idea of 'powerful knowledge', its potential and limitations, while Section 4 takes the argument into the universities and the professions.

Section 1: Setting the scene

The jointly-written Chapter 2 tackles the most fundamental question for any sociology of education that takes the question of knowledge seriously. Does it inevitably lead to a relativism that for all its emancipatory optimism leaves it powerless to offer any constructive alternatives? In answering this question it revisits the questions we were concerned with in the middle of the last decade. If we want to argue that the curriculum should represent an entitlement of all children to knowledge, what grounds do we have for claiming that there is 'better', more reliable, more worthwhile knowledge that all children should have a right to? Furthermore, how do we rebut the conclusion of the mainstream tradition of the sociology of knowledge that knowledge is always an expression of circumscribed activities and interests, and that therefore it makes no sense to enquire as to whether there is objectively 'better' knowledge?

Global policies for the expansion of education have been based on the assumption that they will deliver increasingly knowledgeable citizens for a society in which knowledge-based jobs will play an ever-increasing role. On the other hand, the concept of knowledge that is implied in the term 'knowledge-based', in the idea of a 'knowledge society' and in the kind of curriculum that it is assumed such a future society will require remains largely taken for granted. Furthermore, insofar as the issue of knowledge is discussed in the policies of international organizations and increasing numbers of governments, it is assumed to be generic and takes a form that can be expressed in learning outcomes. We take up these issues in Chapter 3 of Section 2.

Section 2: Knowledge and curriculum futures

Chapter 3, 'Education, globalization and the "voice" of knowledge', was written by Michael Young as a contribution to an Economic and Social Research Council (ESRC) seminar series at the University of Bath on the Knowledge Economy and Education. It builds on the theoretical tradition in the sociology of knowledge from Durkheim to Bernstein and takes forward the argument that the principles of a knowledge-based curriculum have to be based on a concept of knowledge that (a) treats it as emergent from the context of its production and (b) is located in the conditions for the production of new knowledge.

The succeeding chapters in Section 2 explore the implications of the first of these conditions. Chapter 4, 'Alternative education futures for a knowledge society', was initially written by Michael Young as a keynote address at the European Conference on Educational Research (ECER) in 2009. It focuses on three trends in European educational policy, all of which express the broad theme of genericism. It examines how this is manifest in (a) national qualification frameworks, (b) policies based on the idea of learning outcomes and (c) the assumption that the speed of knowledge growth implies a curriculum that can rely on generic skills and underplay the importance of specialist disciplinary content and concepts.

Chapter 5, 'Three educational scenarios for the future: lessons from the sociology of knowledge', was written jointly as a contribution to the project Beyond Current Horizons led by Carey Jewitt. It develops this analysis further by positing three scenarios distinguished in terms of their assumptions about knowledge. The trends analysed in Chapter 4 are located in this analysis as exemplifying an 'over-socialized' concept of knowledge (scenario 2), an over-reaction to the static and elitist features of the curriculum model it sought to replace (scenario 1). The chapter ends with a preliminary sketch of a third possible future (scenario 3).

Chapter 6, 'Curriculum and the question of knowledge: the legacy of Michael Gove and beyond', was initially presented by Michael Young at a symposium at the

ECER in Porto in September 2014. Drawing again on the 'three futures' model, which we develop in Chapter 5, the chapter turns to the reforms of the former Conservative-led coalition government which was replaced by a Conservative government following the General Election in May 2015. While starting from a critique of Future 2 developments that has some similarities to that developed in Chapter 4 of this book, these reforms present a radically different alternative to that based on an attempt to return to a modernized version of Future 1. While welcoming the fact that the Coalition's policies have brought the question of knowledge to the centre of the curriculum policy agenda, the chapter is critical of its backward-looking concept of knowledge and its failure to locate knowledge in contemporary concerns about the conditions for innovation and the production of new knowledge.

Chapter 7, 'The future of knowledge and skills in science and technology higher education', which concludes the section, was written by Johan Muller in response to an invitation to provide a 'think piece' for a group of science and technology higher educators, and extends Chapter 6's focus on Future 2 developments in the upper secondary curriculum in relation to science and technology courses in higher education. Its specific focus is on the teaching and learning initiatives in universities that are often referred to as academic development in South Africa. As an example of a Future 2 development these initiatives do not seek to replace the existing undergraduate curriculum but to improve access to it by providing additional support for disadvantaged learners who face problems in engaging with the specialist knowledge of traditional Future 1 university curricula. While supporting these attempts to broaden access to university curricula, the chapter builds on recent philosophical analyses to suggest that they under-specify the curriculum basis of their support, in particular in the case of science and technology curricula. It concludes that a re-specification of the role of academic development will be needed if universities are to improve the progression of students who lack the prior knowledge that traditional higher education students depend on.

Section 3: The idea of powerful knowledge

Section 3 addresses directly the notion that has become known as 'powerful knowledge'. It opens with Chapter 8, 'What are schools for?' written by Michael Young as a response to a position paper by the philosopher of education, John White, that took the view that considerations of curriculum should start with the aims of education rather than with knowledge. The central argument is that a dynamic notion of knowledge, underpinned by the key distinction between 'knowledge of the powerful', and 'powerful knowledge' must be the starting point for considering the purposes of schools. The chapter concludes by stressing the importance, for any curriculum, of the differentiation of knowledge, principally the differentiation between everyday and specialized knowledge.

Chapter 9 which follows, 'On the powers of powerful knowledge', was jointly authored to respond to various criticisms of the emerging notion of powerful knowledge and to lend it greater sociological substance. It starts by deriving resources from three key classical theorists, Durkheim, Vygotsky and Bernstein. It goes on to consider, and rebut, the criticism that powerful knowledge is modelled on, and applies only to, the natural sciences and technology. It begins to address the dilemmas of specialization and its implications for social justice and returns to the concerns about the objectivity of both the natural and social sciences first raised in Chapter 2. The chapter concludes by exploring different meanings of 'power' in relation to knowledge and their implications for the curriculum.

Chapter 10, 'Overcoming the crisis in curriculum theory', was initially presented by Michael Young at the Portuguese-Brazilian Association for Curriculum Studies in 2012, and was a response to the concern that curriculum theory had lost contact with its object of enquiry. The chapter begins by presenting a brief history of the development of curriculum theory, and the critical response by Michael Apple and others to instrumental views of the curriculum as instruction that developed principally in the USA. It argues that in its critique of the idea of the curriculum as instruction, curriculum theory, and the critical pedagogy tradition associated with it, lost sight of the curriculum as a primary source of access to knowledge. It draws on themes in the previous two chapters to spell out what a knowledge-based approach might mean for the curriculum. It concludes with a concrete example of a school in England that began to implement the idea of a knowledge-based approach, and reflects on the practical, political and epistemological problems that such an approach may lead to.

The final chapter in this section, Chapter 11 'The promise and the pathos of knowledge', was written by Johan Muller for a panel keynote presentation on the occasion of the inauguration of the South African Educational Research Association in 2013. It has since been substantially revised. The paper responds to a principal political criticism of the idea of powerful knowledge, and indeed of all forms of specialized knowledge, which is that it is inevitably partisan, instrumental and technicist, discriminating against those from different cultural and class backgrounds. The paper revisits the wellsprings of specialized knowledge in moral and religious thought, a connection it appears to lose in the secularization of knowledge in the nineteenth and twentieth centuries. It concludes by reflecting on the dark as well as the light side of specialized knowledge, and speculates that it may just be that a moral core – albeit secularized – still subsists in submerged form in secular concerns about equality and social justice in the distribution of educational goods.

Section 4: Universities, professions and specialized knowledge

Section 4 carries the book's argument forward into the sphere of higher education and the knowledge base of the professions. The idea that knowledge structure is simply a higher or lower pile of propositions, as in the classical positivist picture of Nagel (1982), for instance, is extended. The prompting to do this is an attempt to grasp the complexity of specialized professional knowledge and the attendant problem of how to represent it coherently in a curriculum. Following in the steps of

Gilbert Ryle and, more recently, Christopher Winch, the chapters in this section seek to unwrap the various kinds of specialized knowledge that go to make up professional expertise. This takes us beyond propositional knowledge as the sole model for knowledge, and involves coming to terms with the various forms of inferential and practical knowledge that undergird the infrastructure of professional judgement. These too are to be understood as epistemic domains with properties of 'epistemic ascent' – that is, with requirements for sequencing and progression stipulated in curricula. This does not mean that all forms of procedural knowledge are specialized, but some forms indubitably are.

This section opens with Chapter 12, 'The body of knowledge', written by Johan Muller for the 7th Basil Bernstein symposium. It represents an attempt to counter what the paper calls 'skills talk', which refers to the strategy of stipulating the curriculum in terms of what learners are able to do rather than what they should know. We ask: what is it learners must know when they can do something expertly? After a brief examination of the 'know that/ know how' distinction of Ryle and the inferentialism of Robert Brandom, the chapter returns to Bernstein and finds his concept of 'grammaticality' serviceable for thinking about the knowledge and how it links general theory to particular cases. The chapter ends with a consideration of the relation of the openness of a professional knowledge base to innovation and the strength of the professional social base – their robustness as a profession.

Chapter 13, 'Disciplines, skills and the universities', was jointly co-authored in response to an invitation from Paul Ashwin to contribute to a special issue of *Higher Education*. It too is concerned with 'skills talk' in higher education as well as with the challenge to traditional modes of research by the so-called 'mode two' argument, locating them both in a general drift to 'relevance' which has challenged universities and the knowledge they purvey to respond to worldly calls to show their 'relevance' for everyday concerns. By reviewing how disciplines originally arose in the medieval university, and reprising Bernstein's account of singulars and regions, the paper shows how both responses to 'relevance' – 'skills talk' and 'mode two' – pose a threat not only to disciplines as traditionally conceived (to 'singulars'), but to the very notion of specialized knowledge on which the contemporary university rests.

The penultimate Chapter 14, 'Every picture tells a story: epistemological access and knowledge', was written by Johan Muller in response to an invitation by the 'teaching and learning' educators in South Africa (called 'education developers' there) to address the issue of knowledge in higher education. The chapter uses the device of the notion of 'epistemological access', that is increasingly used by these education developers to enquire into what exactly 'access to university' affords access to. The chapter asks whether 'epistemological access' belongs to a 'practice-based' or a 'knowledge-based' view, and concludes that at its best it belongs to an expanded idea of knowledgeable expertise which unites forms of propositional and practical knowledge into a composite notion of expertise, or expert professional knowledge, thus trying to combine the best features of a 'practice-based' and a 'knowledge-based' view, a strategy harking back to the strategy discussed above in Section 2, namely our attempt to combine the strengths of scenarios 1 and 2 in a yet-to-be-fully-formulated scenario for Future 3.

The final chapter in this section and in the book, 'Towards the sociology of professional knowledge', was jointly written as a first substantive chapter in a collection on professional knowledge edited by the authors. The chapter continues the concern with locating the principal features of professional knowledge by transcending the polarization between a 'practice-based' view, represented here by Donald Schön, and a traditional 'knowledge-based' view explored through the lens of Basil Bernstein. The chapter broadens the terms of debate by locating it in the traditional sociological study of professions which, with the exception of Andrew Abbott, has by and large confined its examination to the social relations of professions at the expense of the knowledge relations; that is, to their social base, not their knowledge base. The chapter concludes with the insight reached in the preceding chapter, that bodies of professional knowledge are composed of different specialized knowledge forms, along with their relation to their field of practice in which expertise must operate. This returns our concerns to the sphere of effective and intelligent action, or knowledgeable practice.

2

TRUTH AND TRUTHFULNESS IN THE SOCIOLOGY OF EDUCATIONAL KNOWLEDGE

> ... endless forms most beautiful and most wonderful.
>
> (From the last sentence of Darwin's *The Origin of Species*)

> There is only knowledge, period. It is recognizable not by its air of holiness or its emotional appeal but by its capacity to pass the most demanding scrutiny of well-informed people who have no prior investment in confirming it. And a politics of sorts, neither leftist nor rightist, follows from this understanding. If knowledge can be certified only by a process of peer review, we ought to do what we can to foster communities of uncompromised experts. That means actively resisting guru-ism, intellectual cliquishness, guilt-assuaging double standards, and, needless to say, disdain for the very concept of objectivity.
>
> (Crewes 2006: 5)

Introduction

In his book *Truth and Truthfulness* (Williams 2002), Bernard Williams identifies the 'commitment to truthfulness' as a central tendency in current social thought that can be traced back to the Enlightenment and now stretches from philosophy and the humanities to 'historical understanding, the social sciences and even to the interpretations of discoveries and research in the natural sciences' (ibid.: 1). He describes this tendency as 'an eagerness to see through appearances to the real structures and motives that lie behind them' (ibid.: 1). However, he sees this 'commitment to truthfulness' as increasingly paralleled by a no less pervasive 'scepticism about truth itself', 'whether there is such a thing [as truth] ... whether it can be more than relative or subjective or something of that kind' (ibid.: 1). His argument is that the latter inexorably corrodes the former.

The two tendencies, towards truthfulness and against the idea of truth, are not for Williams, as for many, just a contradiction or tension that as sociologists or philosophers we have to live with. Rather he sees an acceptance of the notion of truth as the condition for a serious commitment to truthfulness. This chapter takes Williams' claim as a starting point for re-examining what kind of activities the sociology of knowledge (in educational studies, and more generally), is engaged in, bearing in mind that in most forms it has been an almost paradigmatic case of endorsing a scepticism about the truth.

Williams compares the sociology of knowledge with muck-raking journalism with which it has some similarities. Both seek truthfulness, but more often are little more than forms of debunking. Muck-raking journalism and some strands of the sociology of knowledge have little doubt about what truth is or where it lies – it is in identifying the corruption of the powerful. This is the basis for the kind of moral self-righteousness and absolute certainty that we find in campaigning journalists such as John Pilger. Some sociologists of education have tried to resolve the tension between truth and truthfulness in similar ways, often by assuming that their identification with the powerless or with a particular disadvantaged group brings them automatically closer to the truth. Such positions are often referred to as 'standpoint' theories,[1] even if the grounds for claiming that a standpoint can be the basis for a theory are far from clear. Though superficially attractive, such solutions, Williams argues, serve only to deflect us from facing the really difficult questions about knowledge and truth that we cannot avoid if sociology is to offer more than – as some postmodernists claim – a series of stories (Mendick 2006).

Williams also points out that the end of the 'science wars' and the 'culture wars' and the gradual collapse of any credibility that postmodernism had as a social theory (Benson and Stangroom 2006) has not led to a new commitment to exploring the inescapable links between truth and truthfulness. More commonly, he suggests, the outcome has been 'an inert cynicism … [which] runs the risk of sliding … through professionalization, to a finally disenchanted careerism' (Williams, ibid.: 3.)

In this chapter we focus largely on the sociology of knowledge as it has developed within educational studies. This is partly because this is the context within which we have worked. However, locating the question of knowledge in educational debates raises more fundamental questions for social theory that are not always recognized. As Durkheim and Vygotsky (and more recently Basil Bernstein) recognized, just as every theory of education implies a theory of society, educational theories always imply a theory of knowledge (Young 2006).

As sociologists of education, we are, as Floud and Halsey (1958) pointed out long ago, creatures of the rise of mass education and the range of attempts to resolve its particular contradictions. As an aspect of modernization, mass education faced and still faces what might be described as the fundamental pedagogic issue – overcoming the discontinuity (sometimes expressed as a conflict) between the formal, codified, theoretical and, at least potentially, universalizing knowledge of the curriculum that students seek to acquire and teachers to transmit, and the informal, local, experiential and everyday knowledge that pupils (or students) bring to school.

When most of the small proportion of each cohort who attended school shared the underlying cultural assumptions of those designing and delivering the formal curriculum, this discontinuity was barely acknowledged. Nor was it seen as a problem, at least by policy makers, in the earlier stages of industrialization when schools prepared the majority for unskilled work and knowledge acquisition was seen as only important for a minority. However, the clash between the democratizing, universalizing goals of mass education and the reality of selection, failure and early leaving that was the reality of schooling for the majority in most countries was never going to remain unnoticed for long. Mass schooling was not achieving the social justice and equality goals set for it by the emerging democratic movements, or fulfilling adequately the growing demand from a globalizing labour market for higher levels of knowledge and skills.

This was the context in the 1960s, when the sociology of education was 're-established'[2] in the UK, as a sub-discipline of sociology, and not, as it had tended to be, an aspect of social mobility and stratification studies. At that time, the central problematic of the sociology of education became, and has largely remained, the discontinuity between the culture of the school and its curriculum and the cultures of those coming to school. It was partly as a critique of existing approaches to access and equality, and partly to focus on the deeper cultural and political issues that underpinned the persistence of educational inequalities, that Bourdieu and Bernstein developed their early work on cultural capital, language codes and educability (Bourdieu and Passeron 1977; Bernstein 1971). One outcome of their ideas was that a focus on the sociology of the curriculum became a key element in what became known as the 'new sociology of education' (Young 1971).

Despite starting with the theoretical goal of reorienting the sociology of education towards the question of knowledge, the sociology of the curriculum in the 1970s took on many of the characteristics that Williams identified with muckraking journalism rather than with social science. It knew the truth – the link between power and knowledge – and set out to show how this truth manifested itself in the school curriculum.[3]

It is not our intention to dismiss the new sociology of education's 'commitment to truthfulness' or its attempt to 'go deeper' and explore the links between curriculum organization and the wider distribution of power.[4] Reminding educationalists that the curriculum, and indeed knowledge itself, is not some external given but a product of historical human activities – part of our own history – was an important task at the time and remains so. However, it would be foolish to deny that many of those working in the sociology of the curriculum at the time identified, albeit not always explicitly, with the prevailing scepticism about truth and knowledge itself (Jenks 1977). This led many to question the idea that a curriculum committed to the idea of truth could 'truthfully' be the aim of the sociology of educational knowledge. As a consequence, the 'new' sociology of education that began, in Williams' terms, with a radical commitment to truthfulness, undermined its own project by its rejection of any idea of truth itself.

The aim of this chapter is to reflect on and explore the issues that Williams raises in the particular case of the sociology of education. The first section considers two questions. First, what went wrong with the sociology of knowledge in educational studies and the social constructivist approach with which it was associated? Second, what might be the basis of an alternative to social constructivism that retains a commitment both to truthfulness and to the idea of truth itself? The next section begins to suggest how an alternative might be developed by drawing on the work of the French sociologist and educationalist, Emile Durkheim. The issues that Durkheim posed in relation to the rise of pragmatism before World War I (Durkheim 1983) have extraordinary echoes in the dilemmas posed by the 'new sociology of education' in the 1970s. We then revisit Basil Bernstein's development of Durkheim's ideas. We show that despite Durkheim's remarkable insights and the highly original conceptual advances made by Bernstein, both remain trapped in the belief that the natural sciences remain the only model for objective knowledge and knowledge growth. This discussion paves the way for the next section, when we draw on the work of Ernest Cassirer and propose a sociological approach to knowledge in terms of his idea of symbolic forms. Finally, we return to our starting point: how far can a social realist approach to knowledge in educational studies that draws on Cassirer's idea of 'symbolic objectivity' come to terms with the tension between truth and truthfulness that was articulated so clearly by Bernard Williams and was left unresolved, even unaddressed, by the 'new' sociology of education of the 1970s?

We started by showing, via Bernard Williams, that if a commitment to truth is paired with scepticism about truth, the latter inevitably corrodes the former. We end by arguing that sociology of education must realign itself with realism, either of a naturalistic kind (after Durkheim 1983 and perhaps Moore 2004), that relies on the natural sciences for its model of objectivity, or a formalist kind (after Cassirer and, although less clearly, after Bernstein). Nor need there be that kind of choice. The primary choice, we will argue, is between objectivity and anti-objectivity. There was a time when the idea of objectivity in the social sciences seemed to be aligned with oppression, and the route to an acceptable objectivity politically blocked. The time is ripe, we argue, to consolidate and develop the considerable advances made by current developments in the sociology of education that demonstrate the case of its potential objectivity (Nash 2005).

Social constructivism in the sociology of education; what went wrong?

Our answer to the question 'what went wrong?' begins by accepting the premise that the 'new sociology of education' and its social constructivist assumptions were an important, albeit a seriously flawed attempt to establish a sociological basis to debates about the curriculum. It undoubtedly represented an advance on the uncritical acceptance in England of the idea of liberal education (Hirst and Peters 1970) and on the technicist tradition of curriculum theorizing prevalent in the USA at the time (Apple 1975). It created considerable interest within educational studies, as well as much opposition; however, it did not provide a reliable basis for an alternative curriculum. Nor did it provide an adequate theory of how, in practice, the curriculum was changing. Why was this so?

First, it is important to recognize the extent to which the sociological approach to knowledge and the curriculum which emerged in the 1970s, and the social constructivist ideas which underpinned it were neither new nor isolated developments. This was true in two senses. First, despite its claims to novelty at the time, the apparently radical idea that all knowledge is in some sense a product of human activities and that this leads at least implicitly and sometimes explicitly to scepticism about the possibility of objective knowledge, was not itself new. It can be traced back to the sophists and sceptics in Ancient Greece, and found a new lease of life in Vico's challenge to the emergent hegemony of natural science in the early eighteenth century (Berlin 2000), and it survives to this day among those, like Richard Rorty, whom Bernard Williams refers to as the 'truth deniers' (Williams 2002). It is also true that very similar sets of ideas could be found at the time in every discipline within the social sciences and the humanities. In other words, we are dealing as much with the context of the time as with the content of this supposedly 'new' sociology of education.

If there was anything new about the 'new sociology of education', it was the educational contexts in which the idea of 'social constructivism' was applied, and the particular conclusions that were drawn from the assumption that the educational realities of curriculum and pedagogy were socially constructed and could be changed by teachers – almost at will (Gorbutt 1972). The 'decisionism' this displayed is typical of all cognate constructivisms.

For social constructivists, how we think about the world, our experience, and any notion of 'how the world is', are not differentiated. It follows that the idea that reality itself is socially constructed had two closely related implications as it was interpreted in the sociology of education. First, it provided the basis for challenging any form of givenness or fixity, whether political, social, institutional, or cultural. It was assumed that challenging givenness was as applicable to science or knowledge in general as to the social rules, conventions and institutions that had traditionally been studied by sociologists.[5] Second, it was able to treat all forms of givenness as arbitrary and, given different social arrangements, potentially changeable. It followed that in so far as a form of givenness persisted it was assumed to express the interests (political, cultural or economic) of some groups *vis à vis* others. The intellectual battle was between those, the social constructivists, who saw their task as exposing the apparent givenness of reality for 'what it really was' – a mask to obscure the deeper reality of arbitrariness and interests – and those who opposed them by defending as given what was 'in reality' arbitrary. The distinction between 'constructivists' and 'realists' is inevitably an over-simplification.[6] The primary difference between them was that the constructivists claimed that the only reality was that there was no reality beyond our perceptions. What with hindsight is puzzling is the combination of indeterminism – everything is arbitrary, and determinism – everything can be changed, that this led to.

Within the 'broad church' of social constructivism in educational studies, a range of different perspectives were drawn on that had little in common and sometimes directly contradicted each other. At different times, different theorists and traditions were recruited. Within the sociology of education, at least from the early 1970s, the dominant perspectives from which the idea of social constructivism was drawn were the social phenomenology and ethnomethodology of Schutz, Merleau Ponty and Garfinkel, the symbolic interactionism of Mead and Blumer, the eclectic social constructivism of Berger and Luckmann, the cultural anthropology of Robin Horton (and later Clifford Geertz), the neo-Weberian sociology of Pierre Bourdieu, and albeit slightly uneasily, the critical Marxism of the Frankfurt School. For Bourdieu, for example, the unmasking of arbitrariness was sociology's core problematic. What these writers had in common, or were interpreted as having in common, was a form of sociological reductionism. As everything was social, sociological analysis could be applied to and account for anything and everything – even though sociologists often disagreed about what the social was. In the 1980s these theoretical traditions were extended to include (and, for many, were replaced by) discourse and literary theories. The latter drew on writers such as Derrida, Foucault and Lyotard who treated the social as just another text, a discourse, or in the case of the latter, a language game. The reductionist logic, however, was the same.

Education was in a sense a special, or even, one might say, an ideal case for social constructivist ideas. This partly reflected the relative theoretical weakness of educational studies and hence its openness to (or inability to resist) any new theory that came along. However, the sociology of the curriculum and the idea that educational realities were socially constructed had a quite specific appeal in the often authoritarian, bureaucratic and always hierarchical world of schooling. It easily led to challenges to existing forms of school knowledge, subjects and disciplines and their familiar expression in syllabuses (Keddie 1971; Whitty and Young 1976). More fundamentally, social constructivism challenged and exposed what it saw as the arbitrariness of the most basic categories of formal education such as intelligence, ability and attainment (Keddie 1971; 1973) and even of the institution of school itself. If social constructivism could show that all such categories, rules and institutions were arbitrary, this also made them potentially open to change, even if social constructivism could not say how or to what. The links between social constructivist ideas and the political left or at least parts of it, were hardly surprising, although more often than not expedient.

Why did these ideas gain such a stranglehold in educational studies, and why later were they so easily criticized and rejected? Did this pattern of initial support but later rejection indicate some flaw in the basic idea of reality being 'socially constructed', or did the idea contain, as Marx said of Hegel, a 'rational kernel' that somehow got lost? Why were these ideas particularly seductive and, as with hindsight we can see, particularly disastrous for educational studies and the sociology of the curriculum in particular?

Two different kinds of response to such questions can be given. One is an external or contextual argument. It is familiar, relatively uncontroversial and can be dealt with briefly. It is relevant only to the extent to which it reminds us of the non-unique aspect of particular intellectual fields and that the sociology of education is no exception. Two kinds of external or contextual factors are worth mentioning that shaped ideas in the sociology of education – one social and one cultural. The first was the massive expansion and democratization of higher education, the parallel expansion and diversification of the social sciences and humanities, and the assumption, at least in educational studies, that these new types of knowledge could be used to transform what was widely recognized as an inefficient and unequal education system. These developments, magnified since the 1980s by globalization and the emphasis on markets in every sphere of life, created a quite new context for intellectual work in education that had considerable affinity with the new, relativist and supposedly more democratic ideas about knowledge. This new context for educational studies brought in new and sometimes already radicalized students and new lecturers and provided fertile ground for a range of cultural changes which all played a role in shaping the sociology of education. These included a much wider critical and, for a time, highly politicized academic climate, an affinity with populist ideas, a sometimes uncritical respect for the cultures of subordinate and minority groups and those from non-western societies, and a parallel scepticism about the academy and all forms of authority, including science and other forms of specialist knowledge. All these developments drew on and were implicitly or explicitly supportive of social constructivist ideas (Benson and Stangroom 2006).

It is the internal issues – developments within the intellectual field of educational studies – that we want to concentrate on in this chapter. From early in the 1970s, social constructivist ideas were challenged, usually by philosophers (e.g. Pring, 1972) but sometimes by other sociologists (Gould 1977; Demaine 1981). However, it was relatively easy for the 'new sociologists' to dismiss these critics by labelling them as reactionary,[7] reformist or 'social democratic'[8] (Young and Whitty 1977).

In developing a less superficial response to its critics, social constructivism in educational studies only had two ways to go, at least within the terms it set itself as a radical theory. One direction was towards a politics that linked constructivist ideas to the privileging of subordinate (as opposed to ruling class or official) knowledge. Subordinacy could refer to the working class and be linked to Marxism, to women and be linked to feminism or to non-white groups and what later became known as post-colonial or subaltern studies. In a response that was quite specific to the sociology of education, identification with subordinacy was linked to a celebration of the culture of those who were rejected by and failed at school. Their language and their resistance to formal learning were seen as at least potentially supportive of a new more radical working class consciousness (Willis 1977).[9] The other direction for social constructivism was towards postmodern versions of a Nietzschean nihilism and the denial of any possibility of progress, truth or knowledge. Not only were such interpretations of Nietzsche somewhat dubious, as Bernard Williams shows (Williams 2002: ch. 1); they offered little that was substantive to educational studies beyond a continuing, if largely empty role for theory (or theorizing, as it became known).[10]

To summarize our argument so far – social constructivism provided teachers and students of education with a superficially attractive but ultimately contradictory set of intellectual tools. On the one hand, it offered the possibility of intellectual emancipation and freedom through education – we, as teachers, students or workers have the epistemological right to develop theories and to criticize and challenge scientists, philosophers, and other so-called experts and specialists. Furthermore, in some unspecified way, this so-called freedom was seen as contributing to changing the world. This emancipation from all authoritative forms of knowledge was linked by many to the possibility of achieving a more equal or just world, which for some but not all meant socialism. On the other hand, by undermining any claims to objective knowledge or truth about anything, social constructivism, at least in some of the ways it was (and could legitimately) be interpreted, denies the possibility of any better understanding, let alone of any better world. For obvious reasons, however, this denial tended to be ignored by educational researchers, at least most of the time.

The double-bind that combined emancipation and its impossibility was particularly problematic in education. If not only the selection of knowledge in the curriculum, but even the rankings, reporting and everyday judgements made by teachers about pupils were treated as arbitrary, continuing to be a teacher (let alone an educational researcher), became deeply problematic, except in 'bad faith'. Furthermore, such ideas have left their mark in today's fashionable language of facilitation, group work and 'teaching is a conversation'. All these pedagogic strategies can be seen as strands of an attempt to suppress hierarchy, or at least render it invisible (Muller 2006). This new 'language of practice' or activity in educational studies, increasingly linked to the 'promise' of e-learning, mobile phones and the internet, is now with us and has close affinities with the language of the market. It is of course supported by many who know nothing of the original sociological critiques of pedagogic authority.

Why did such ideas persist, and why are they resurrected again and again as if they were new? It is not because they are true, unless a fundamental contradictoriness and the consequent impossibility of knowledge can be the truth. Nor, as in the case of new ideas in physics and chemistry, can it be that the idea of reality being socially constructed is so powerful that it has been used to change the world in ways that no one can deny. At best, social constructivism reminds us that however apparently given and fixed certain ideas or institutions appear to be, they are always the product of actual human activities in history. They do not have their origins solely in the material world external to us, nor can we find their origins, as Descartes thought, in our heads. In Cassirer's terms, as we will see later in this chapter, ideas and institutions are 'expressive'; that is, they are part of social action that is both of the objective social world, but suffused by subjective meanings which frequently push at the bounds of any objective categories. At worst, social constructivism has provided an intellectual legitimacy for criticizing and challenging any institution, any hierarchy, any form of authority and any knowledge as arbitrary. The superficial political correctness and at times the idiocy that this position leads to has been a heavy price to pay for the small 'moment' of emancipation that is expressed in the truth that reality is socially constructed. One response to this latter observation, widely if not always explicitly admitted, has been to reject the enterprise of the sociology of education and more particularly sociology as it is applied to the curriculum. This was the response of the political right, who labelled it as left wing ideology (Gould 1977). A more pragmatic and technocratic version of this position has since been adopted by most teacher training programmes and an increasing number of higher degrees in educational studies in the UK today. Programmes of initial teacher education or professional development that include the systematic study of the sociology of education are increasingly rare. This rejection of the sociology of knowledge was also, with rather more justification, the position taken by the group of natural scientists who waged the science wars (Sokal 1998)[11] and who had, by the 1990s, become massively impatient with the patent circularity of constructivism. It is not unlikely that the latter provided the intellectual justification for the policy consequences of the former.

A more positive alternative, in our view, is to begin by remembering something that was too easily forgotten in the heady days of the 1970s, and often still is. That is that sociology itself, like all social life, institutions, knowledge and even science, has a history. We need, it follows, not only to see society and education historically, but to recall the history of sociology and the sociology of education and to recognize that debates within one generation of sociologists always need to be extended to be debates with earlier generations.

The social constructivists were wrong, we have argued. However, as we shall see, like the pragmatists such as James and Dewey at the beginning of the last century, and with whom they had much in common, they were not wholly wrong. They were right to emphasize the socio-historical character of knowledge (and therefore the curriculum) as against the prevalent view of its givenness. Their flaws, we can see in retrospect, were (i) in not spelling out the limits of the theory and (ii) in giving substance to their opening claim. The theory remained, therefore, largely rhetorical. Let us take one example. It is one thing to claim that such an apparently solid idea like that of a liberal education is a social construct, and therefore no more than an exercise of domination. It is quite another to document liberal education as a historically changing phenomenon – very different for Eliot, Leavis and C.P. Snow from what it had been for Arnold and Newman.

Social constructivism was fundamentally wrong in the conclusions that it drew about knowledge and the curriculum. The social character of knowledge is not a reason for doubting its truth and objectivity, or for seeing curricula as no more than politics by other means. Its social character is (even more truthfully) the only reason that knowledge can claim to truth (and objectivity) (Collins 1998) and therefore for preferring some curriculum principles to others. To begin to see where this idea leads, we will turn to Durkheim's argument in his far too little-known lectures published as *Pragmatism and Sociology* (Durkheim 1983).

The remarkable thing about Durkheim's lectures is that in the pragmatism of James (and to a lesser extent, Dewey), Durkheim confronted almost identical problems to those introduced by the sociology of education in the 1970s. He knew that pragmatism was an advance on the rationalism and empiricism of the time, just as social constructivism was an advance on the view of the curriculum and knowledge that treated it as an a-social given. At the same time he also saw that pragmatism's form of 'humanizing' or socializing knowledge and truth, if left unqualified, led to far worse problems than those it claimed to overcome. The next section draws heavily on Durkheim (1983) to suggest a basis for how we might develop an alternative to social constructivism for the sociology of education.

From social constructivism to social realism: some lessons from Durkheim

There are significant but not complete parallels between our engagement in this chapter with the social constructivist ideas that became part of the sociology of education in the 1970s and Durkheim's engagement with the pragmatist ideas that were sweeping French intellectual life 60 years earlier. However, our interest in finding an alternative to social constructivism is somewhat different from Durkheim's concerns about pragmatism. As many writers have commented (most notably, Lukes 1972), Durkheim was writing at a time of great social upheaval in France that had been triggered in large part by militant opposition to the powers of the Catholic Church. He saw pragmatism, with its antagonism to any notion of objective rationality and its linking of truth to its consequences as adding to the disorder and providing no basis for the consensus that for him underpinned any just social order. His primary concern therefore was to develop an objective basis for the moral values that could constitute a new consensus. Ideas of truth and knowledge were important to Durkheim not primarily for themselves, but on account of their moral role. He saw them as binding people together as members of society. Without denying the moral role of knowledge and truth, our concern is rather different. It is with the intellectual basis of the curriculum and the nature of knowledge and the way the former was undermined and the latter avoided by the relativist implications of social constructivism.

Both pragmatist and social constructivist approaches to knowledge arose as responses to the weaknesses of existing epistemologies – both rationalist and empiricist. Both the latter led to static and dualist assumptions about knowledge and its relationship to the world. In trying both to overcome this dualism and to 'humanize' knowledge by locating it 'in the world', Durkheim argued that pragmatism (and by implication, social constructivism) treats concepts and the world of experience as part of one seamless reality. In other words, they assume that knowledge is undifferentiated from human experience. In contrast, for Durkheim, the humanness of knowledge can only be located in society and in the necessity of concepts being both 'of the world' (a world that includes both society and the material world) and differentiated from our experience of it. The social was 'objective' for Durkheim at least in part because it excluded the subjectivities of the ego and, for him, the 'profane' world of individual action and experience.

Durkheim agrees with the pragmatists in not treating knowledge or truth as in some way independent of human society and history. However, this does not mean, as James assumed, that truth is subjective – or no different from people's feelings and sensitivities. Truth and knowledge have a givenness, but it is a givenness that is historical and social. We create knowledge, Durkheim argues, just as we create institutions; not in any way but in relation to our history, and on the basis of what former generations have discovered or created.

Perhaps surprisingly for someone so concerned with consensus, it is Durkheim, rather than the pragmatists with their obsession with problem solving, who, by recognizing the tension between knowledge as a social given and this givenness being historically formed, provides the basis for a social theory of innovation. The body of work in the sociology of science inaugurated by Robert Merton (1973) makes this plain. Furthermore, it was in the differentiation between the 'sacred' as an internally consistent world of concepts and the 'profane' as a vague and contradictory continuum of procedures and practices, that Durkheim found the social basis of science and the origins of speculative thought (Muller 2000).

Another parallel between pragmatism and social constructivism is exemplified in Durkheim's argument about how pragmatism resorts to an instrumental theory of truth, what he referred to as 'logical utilitarianism'. Knowledge was true for the pragmatists if it satisfied a need. Similarly, social constructivism, although not explicitly concerned with satisfying needs, emphasizes the situatedness of all knowledge, and therefore locates it in practice (hence we have the origins of what became known as 'the practice turn' in social theory). Furthermore, social constructivism has also associated itself with the importance of knowledge 'being socially relevant' – a utilitarianism thinly veiled beneath a moral correctness. As Durkheim pointed out, satisfying a need could never account for the essential impersonality of truth that is not related to any specific individual, standpoint, interest or need.

A related problem with pragmatism for Durkheim was that if the truth can only be verified by its consequences – i.e. a posteriori – it always depends on what may (or may not) happen. As he points out, something cannot logically be judged true on the basis of what may happen; that is like relying on hope or 'wishful thinking', a tendency that has bedevilled much Marxist writing. To claim that because something works, it is true, is to confuse (or blur) two distinct categories – truth and utility. If something is true because it works, this either relies on an implicitly subjective and a priori criterion of 'what works' or it points to the need for a complex consideration of what working means and for whom, and on its own tells us little. Durkheim argued that truth must be a priori – not a priori in the Kantian sense, which makes it rigid and abstracted from human life, but a priori in the social sense – it is prior and it relies on what society has demonstrated to be true. Likewise for social constructivists, knowledge and truth are located in who the knowers are and in their interests.[12] Just as with pragmatism we are left with consequences, so with social constructivism we are left only with interests. In both cases, both truth and knowledge disappear.

Durkheim's strongest objection to pragmatism was that it neglected what he saw as the unique character of truth – its external, constraining, obligatory and, for him, moral force. When applied to social constructivism, Durkheim's insight emphasizes the limits that the social (for him society) imposes on our ability to socially construct reality. It is those limits – the boundaries, as Bernstein would put it – that free us to search for the truth. To paraphrase Durkheim, we feel the pressure of the truth on us – we cannot deny it, even if we do not like it. Satisfying a need or relating to an interest are ultimately subjective criteria and can never be adequate as criteria of truth. Sometimes the truth does exactly the opposite to satisfying a need and does not seem to be in one's interest; however that does not stop it from being true.

Let us summarize this section so far. We have argued that in his critique of pragmatism Durkheim offers us at least the beginning of an alternative to social constructivism that retains the idea that knowledge has a social basis but does not reduce the idea of 'the social' to interest groups, activities or relations of power. At the same time, in his sacred/profane distinction which underpins the separation of objective concepts from practical subjective reality, and in his recognition of the continuity in modern societies of both mythological and scientific truths, his theory recognizes the crucial importance of the social differentiation of knowledge.

Finally, there remains the issue which we touched on earlier. For Durkheim, the social is the moral; it is about values. In so far as knowledge (and the curriculum) are social, they too for Durkheim are primarily moral issues. This makes it difficult to use his framework to explore questions of knowledge content and structure that are avoided by the reductionist implications of social constructivism. Is Durkheim right in equating the social with the moral, even when it comes to the question of knowledge? Or can we envisage a non-moral concept of the social? We think the answer to the latter question must be yes; furthermore, a cognitive as well as a moral concept of the social is essential if we are to develop an alternative to social constructivist sociologies of knowledge (Moore and Young 2001; Schmaus 1994).

Durkheim seems to focus more on the shared values on which the objectivity of knowledge depends rather than the nature of the knowledge itself. A clue to this feature of Durkheim's work may be found in his indebtedness to the Kantian tradition of a priori-ism. In his short book with his nephew Marcel Mauss (Durkheim and Mauss 1967), Durkheim makes clear that it is not knowledge in the sense of what we know about the world that he is concerned with, but the foundations of that knowledge – how it is possible. In other words, he is interested in the social basis of notions such as logic and cause, without which knowledge would not be possible. For Durkheim the objectivity of morality and logic have the same basis, society.

Paul Fauconnet, in his introduction to Durkheim's *Education and Sociology* (Durkheim 1956), offers an interpretation of Durkheim's sociology of education which gives more attention to his intellectual (or cognitive) concerns. In commenting on Durkheim's rejection of pragmatism's utilitarian concept of education, he writes that:

> the transmission [of knowledge] through the teacher to the pupil, the assimilation by the child of a subject seemed to him [Durkheim] to *be the condition of real intellectual formation* ... [our emphasis]. One does not recreate science

through one's own personal experience, because [science] is social not individual; one learns it.

(Durkheim 1956: 48)

So much for ideas like 'pupil as scientist' (or theorist) popularized by constructivists (e.g. Driver 1982). Fauconnet continues:

Forms [of the mind] cannot be transmitted empty. Durkheim, like Comte, thinks that it is necessary to learn about things, to acquire knowledge.

(Durkheim 1956: 48)

For us, therefore, despite Durkheim's stress on the moral basis of society, issues of the structure and content of knowledge must lie at the heart of the sociology of the curriculum. Although Fauconnet notes that Durkheim prepared lectures on specialist pedagogies, in mathematics, physics, geography and history, no texts survive. Durkheim leaves us, therefore, with only some very general propositions about the social basis of the foundations of knowledge and its differentiation. However, it is precisely the issue of differentiation, so crucial to a sociology of the curriculum, that the English sociologist Basil Bernstein addressed in his early papers on classification and framing, and in a paper published towards the end of his life, in which he introduces the distinction between vertical and horizontal knowledge structures. It is therefore to Bernstein's ideas that we turn in the next section.

Bernstein's typology of vertical and horizontal knowledges

This section begins with a brief description of Bernstein's ideas on the differentiation of knowledge. He intervened decisively in the discussion about the form of symbolic systems (or knowledge) and set out to delineate the 'internal principles of their construction and their social base' (Bernstein 2000: 155). As is by now well known, he distinguishes between two forms of discourse, horizontal and vertical, and within vertical discourse, between two kinds of knowledge structure, hierarchical and horizontal.

For Bernstein, knowledge structures differ in two ways. The first way is in terms of what may be called verticality. Verticality has to do with how theory develops. In hierarchical knowledge structures, it develops through the integration of propositions, towards ever more general sets of propositions. It is this trajectory of development which lends hierarchical knowledge structures their unitary triangular shape. In contrast, horizontal knowledge structures are not unitary but plural; they consist of a series of parallel and incommensurable languages (or sets of concepts). Verticality in horizontal knowledge structures occurs not through integration but through the introduction of a new language (or set of concepts) which constructs a 'fresh perspective, a new set of questions, a new set of connections, and an apparently new problematic, and most importantly a new set of speakers' (Bernstein 2000: 162). Because these 'languages' are incommensurable, they defy incorporation into a more general theory.[13] The level of integration, and the possibility for knowledge progress in the sense of greater generality and hence wider explanatory reach, is thus strictly limited in horizontal knowledge structures.

Before we proceed to discuss grammaticality, the second form of knowledge form variation, it is worth making a few observations on verticality. The first is that it artfully incorporates and recapitulates the fierce dispute in the philosophy and sociology of science between the logical positivists and the non-realists. Bernstein is implicitly asserting that the logical positivists (or realists) were right, but only in respect of hierarchical knowledge structures, and that the non-realists (Kuhn and those who followed him) were likewise right, but only in respect of horizontal knowledge structures. In other words, encoded into Bernstein's principle of verticality are the terms of the debate in the philosophy of science.

Second, we note that horizontal knowledge structures span a surprisingly broad range; they include not only sociology and the humanities but logic and mathematics. The anomaly is that in the latter exemplars of horizontal knowledge structures, we have a form of verticality that is almost equivalent to that obtained in hierarchical knowledge structures. The germane question then becomes, not so much what hinders progression in all horizontal knowledge structures, but rather what internal characteristics distinguish those horizontal knowledge structures such as the social sciences that proliferate languages from those like mathematics where language proliferation is constrained. It was in search of a sociological answer to this question and to provide an alternative to Bourdieu's sociological reductionism (see Bernstein 1996), that Bernstein began, by setting out his distinction between vertical and horizontal knowledge structures.

We turn now to the second form of knowledge variation, grammaticality. We have suggested that verticality has to do with how a theory develops internally (what Bernstein later referred to as its internal language of description). In contrast, grammaticality has to do with how a theory deals with the world, or how theoretical statements deal with their empirical predicates (what he later referred to as its external language of description in Bernstein 2000). The stronger the grammaticality of a language, the more stably it is able to generate empirical correlates and the more unambiguous, because they are more restricted, are the field of referents. The weaker the grammaticality, the weaker is the capacity of a theory to stably identify empirical correlates and the more ambiguous, because it is much broader, becomes the field of referents. Thus knowledge structures with weak grammars are deprived of a principal means of generating progress (or new knowledge), namely empirical disconfirmation. As Bernstein puts it, 'Weak powers of empirical descriptions remove a crucial resource for either development or rejection of a particular language and so contribute to its stability as a frozen form' (Bernstein 2000: 167–8). To summarize, whereas grammaticality determines the capacity of a theory to progress through worldly corroboration, verticality determines the capacity of a theory to progress through explanatory sophistication. Together, we may say that these two criteria determine the capacity a particular knowledge structure has to progress.

However, for all its rigour and suggestiveness, this analysis merely starts the ball rolling, so to speak. What it provides is a survey of the range of variation, but even the charitable must admit that the poles remain clearer than the intermediate zones of the range. This is partly because the precise nature of and relation between verticality and grammaticality is unclear. A plausible surmise could be the following. Verticality is a categorical principle; it consigns knowledge structures to either a theory-integrating or a theory-proliferating category. On the other hand, grammaticality is an ordinal principle, constructing a continuum of grammaticality within each category, or perhaps across the entire spectrum. Although at one point Bernstein depicts grammaticality as a feature only of horizontal knowledge structures (Bernstein 2000: 168), at another point he refers to physics, his paradigm of verticality, as having a 'strong grammar' (Bernstein 2000: 163). What this means is that Bernstein at times uses the 'grammar' metaphor to refer to the internal language, though mostly it refers to the external language.

However, even if we grant the surmise, anomalies persist, none more so than in the case of mathematics. In Bernstein's account, mathematics is a horizontal knowledge structure with a strong grammar. However, the principal criterion of strong grammaticality – how the theory deals with the world, doesn't quite fit. As Bernstein (2000: 163) concedes, mathematics does not progress by empirical corroboration, like physics does. It is a deductive system, and its grammar appears to be a purely internal one. This depicts mathematics as a knowledge structure with a strong internal but weak external language of description – the latter categorizing it as similar in type to the social sciences. However, the history of mathematics suggests this picture is far from adequate. As Penrose argues in his remarkable book *The Road to Reality* (Penrose 2006), time and time again, mathematical concepts at extraordinary levels of abstraction (one of his examples is the patterning of prime numbers) and with no apparent relationship to the material world, turn out to be integral to our understanding of both the structure of the universe and the structure of matter (see also Cassirer 1943). Such examples are not evidence of a 'weak external language of description', but maybe of the need for a more developed sense of what grammaticality involves. Perhaps, as Kay O'Halloran (2006) suggests, mathematics is the language the empirical sciences must use to generate verticality in their internal languages. If that is so, then its lack of an external language ceases to be strange.

The difference between sociology and mathematics is strikingly brought out by Moore and Maton's (2001) example of the epistemic continuity displayed in the story of the proof of Fermat's last theorem:

> What is so striking about this story is its sheer scale in historical time and in geographical and cultural space. It tells a story of a mathematician in late-twentieth century England effectively communicating with a French judge at the court of Louis X1V, and through him with Babylonians from three millennia ago. It represents an epistemic community with an extended existence in time and space, a community where the past is present, one in which, when living members die, will be in turn the living concern of future members.
>
> *(Moore and Maton 2001: 172)*

Things could not look more different in sociology.[14] By contrast, mathematics also shares this temporal feature with literature. Gyorgy Markus (2003) has remarked that the 'tradition' in the arts is 'ever expanding' and 'of great depth in time' (op. cit.: 15), a feature he contrasts to science which has a 'short-term' tradition, because it is ever 'evolving' (ibid.). Which knowledge form is nearer to which? Maths and science in one sense; and maths, literature and perhaps sociology in another? The fact is, which forms comprise the middle of the knowledge range is not clear at all. Is geography closer to physics than to biology, for example, and how would we know? Would we count their respective numbers of languages? It is certainly the case that empirical study would help to shed light on the theory, but it is also likely that the theory stands in need of some elaboration.

Towards a logic of the social and human sciences

As we saw in the previous section, Bernstein develops a language of description for dealing with variations in knowledge structure that provides us with tools for discussing variation that are so far unmatched in sociology, with the possible exception of Randall Collins (Collins 1998). Bernstein's main intent was to develop a way of discussing how different symbolic ensembles become socially distributed. In so doing, he had also to confront the age-old question as to how knowledge progresses. The conciseness of the concepts of verticality and grammaticality have taken us a considerable way towards those goals. And yet, the long shadow of physicalist idealism falls over this attempt, as it does over practically all other attempts in the history of philosophy and social thought. When the chips are down, Bernstein's model for knowledge progression is ineluctably that of physics, or more precisely as Cassirer expresses it, that of the mathematical sciences of nature. Here the recurrent problem for sociology rears its head again: is there only one ideal form of objectivity, namely that of physics? Or is there another?

Bernstein certainly strives to distinguish the form of progression in hierarchical knowledge structures from that in horizontal knowledge structures. But the difficulty is apparent in the name he gives to the latter. These progress, says Bernstein, by developing parallel theoretical languages, that is, horizontally. It is not hard to see that while this might account for how knowledge elaborates, it cannot account for how it grows. The pathos of this description is sharpened when we consider it in the light of Bernstein's own strenuous attempts to develop a more vertical and robust language of description for sociology. Yet according to his own account of how sociological knowledge develops, his attempt can at best contribute another parallel language. It is not expressly said in these terms, but it is hard to avoid the conclusion that, unless and until sociology can stiffen its vertical spine and develop more powerful worldly corroborations – that is, become more like physics – sociological knowledge will not progress.

We return inevitably to the dilemma that we raised earlier (Muller 2006). We argued that Bernstein characterizes hierarchical knowledge growth in a way that parallels the accounts of the logical positivists, and horizontal knowledge growth after the accounts of Kuhn and the constructivists. This effectively rules out the possibility of growth or progress in the social sciences. We are thus left with a position that is uncomfortably close to the relativism of pragmatism and constructivism, a position that Bernstein in his larger intents certainly did not align himself with. As we saw at the beginning of this chapter, for Bernard Williams the two views – a commitment to verticality or truthfulness, on the one hand, and scepticism about its realization, on the other – do not co-exist happily. The latter must inexorably corrode the former.

At least the outlines for a route out of this impasse can be gleaned from another of Bernstein's favourite sources, Ernst Cassirer (Durkheim being the first). Cassirer wrote in the period between the two World Wars, at a time when natural science, especially physics, was at a peak of creative flowering, when the humanities were in something of a decline and when philosophy at least in Germany 'enfeebled and slowly undermined the forces that could have resisted the modern political myths' (Cassirer was referring here to Heidegger's tacit endorsement of Nazism; Cassirer 1943). Whereas mathematics provided a meta-language for organizing the burgeoning knowledge of nature (O'Halloran 2006), philosophy, which had, since Descartes and Kant, played a similar organizing role also for the humanities, had begun to fragment, helped on in no small measure by the range of 'vitalisms' associated with the work of Bergson, Heidegger, Nietzsche and the pragmatists who we discussed earlier in this chapter. For the 'vitalists', as physics and the mathematical world had become severed from Life, and philosophy had been consumed by the arid abstractions of Logic (logical positivism), the consequent aridity was threatening Life itself.

Not only were the humanities internally fragmenting (proliferating parallel languages, in Bernstein's terms), unconstrained by a unifying philosophical meta-language, but they were decisively parting company with the natural sciences. Cassirer, like Hegel and Husserl before him, felt the need to return to first principles, to reassert the unity of man, as both a part of nature and separate from the rest of nature, and therefore the unity of all knowledge, while giving each branch of knowledge its distinctive due.

Cassirer's fundamental gesture was to assert, against the vitalists and the pragmatists, that knowledge, indeed all culture, was fundamentally formal in the sense of being necessarily symbolically mediated. In order to understand a knowledge form, one had to understand the logical structure of the symbols that constituted it. Cassirer distinguished, in his four-volume work *The Philosophy of Symbolic Forms* (Cassirer 1996), between three principal forms of knowledge, a three-fold division somewhat reminiscent of Bernstein's horizontal discourse, hierarchical and horizontal knowledge structures. But whereas Bernstein distinguished the internal structure of these forms principally in terms of their distributive potential, Cassirer discusses them more fundamentally in terms of their function, as to how each relates a symbol to its object. In the expressive function of symbols (paradigmatically found in mythic thought), the relation is mimetic; there is a unity of symbol and object, and the two are not distinguished. It follows that there can only be different myths, not better myths. In the representational function of symbols (paradigmatically, the case of language), the relation is analogical; there is an absolute disjunction between symbol and object, metaphorically distancing symbol-categories from the world of particulars. In the conceptual function of symbols (paradigmatically the case of science), the relation is properly symbolic (or conceptual); the object is viewed as a construction of the symbol. This frees the symbol category to be a general case, untied to any one particular or determinate context, and hence able to function as a signifier for the entire class of particulars (Verene 1969: 38). It is only with this disarticulation of symbol category and particulars that we are able to generate stable conceptual descriptions of the world that are not dependent on any one particular part of it, the condition for any objective description (Habermas 2001: 18). This progressive abstraction of the symbol system from particulars comes with a price, the loss of the 'living body' and an increasing dependence on 'a semanticised nature' (op. cit.: 24). Only the fourth symbolic form, art (the others being myth, language and science) for Cassirer successfully balances freedom and abstraction. The others all, to a greater or lesser extent, pay 'Descartes' price', the loss of immediacy for greater generalizing power (O'Halloran 2006).

We can see more clearly here than we can in the case of Bernstein how Cassirer extrapolates a set of distinctions drawn from a traditional evolutionary account of the history of consciousness to its 'systematic dimensions' (Verene 1969: 44), from an account of stages of development to differences of logical structure. To put this another way, Cassirer's theory of civilization presumes an increasingly sophisticated distancing of symbolic forms from their object domains, the costs mitigated by the reunifying power of the arts.[15] The conceptual extrapolation is identical in each case. We can also see an intriguingly parallel argument to that of Durkheim's, with both deriving the lineaments of scientific thought from that of mythic, or for Durkheim, religious thought. Yet Cassirer was acutely aware of the need to avoid the trap of setting up science (or at least physical science) as the prototype of all knowledge, and likewise of setting up strict logic as the prototype of intelligibility for all forms of the human spirit, as Hegel had done.

> Cassirer regards his philosophy of symbolic forms as an attempt to create a system that overcomes the tendency towards logic inherent in Hegel's system.
> *(Verene 1969: 35)*

In the terms developed in this chapter, Cassirer intended his system to provide an account of verticality (general/particular relations) that did not reduce all knowledge progression to the verticality requirements of physics. So where Durkheim had attempted to deal with the pragmatists' 'reduction to scepticism' with a purely conceptual attack on their principal premises, Cassirer attempted to avoid the cognate trap of the cultural pessimism of the vitalists by avoiding the subordination of spirit to logic in philosophy that culminated in the logical positivism that our contemporary vitalists (constructivists and pragmatists both) are trying to extricate themselves from. Cassirer's attempt is based on the differential internal structure of different knowledge forms, as it was for Bernstein and for Durkheim in his *Elementary Forms of Religious Life* (Durkheim 1995). Where Bernstein's account was based on the results of structural difference (pyramids and parallel languages), whose differential distribution he then set out to account for, Cassirer aimed for the principle that constructed the difference by theorizing the differential relation of concept to object in terms of differential objectification.

Cassirer starts by delineating two broad families of scientific concepts. The conceptually organized perception of things is organized into a set of organic forms, which constitute the sciences of nature and the conceptually organized perception of expressions is organized into a set of symbolic forms, or sciences of culture. Organic forms (or natural concepts) differ from symbolic forms in the form of objectification they effect. In organic forms the object is accounted for entirely – subsumed – by the natural concept via mathematicization; this is a subsumption that can be expressed in formal mathematical terms. The natural concept, expressed ideally as a law, allows for (in theory) the complete deduction of the object. In symbolic forms, or cultural concepts, by contrast, the concept and its properties characterizes but does not, (cannot precisely) determine the object.

What Cassirer is setting out here as the key logical distinction between the two families of concepts is the subsumptability of particulars by a structural law. As he puts it:

> We understand a science in its logical structure only once we have clarified the manner in which it achieves the subsumption of the particular and the universal.
>
> *(quoted in the translator's Introduction to Cassirer 2000: xxxv)*

Where the natural sciences aim for perfect subsumption, leading to a 'unity of being' (of a concept united with a particular), the cultural sciences aim for imperfect subsumption, leading to a 'unity of direction' whereby a concept indicates certain features of the particular but does not exhaust its semantic potential. The idea of 'imperfection' here should not be interpreted as some kind of deficit. Rather, the principal objects of the cultural sciences, expressions, exhibit a freedom that natural objects do not have because cultural objects are always mediated, in ways that natural objects are not, by a certain self-consciousness or reflexiveness. In other words, whereas the natural sciences generate concepts of things, the cultural sciences generate concepts of concepts. This places strict limits on the subsumptability of particulars by concepts claiming universality in the cultural sciences. The result is that descriptions in the cultural sciences can express regularities that have all the lineaments of truth but whose description may not be found in all details in any one particular case. The particular is classified by, but not subordinated to, the universal.

Cassirer's example is of Burkhardt's concept of the 'Renaissance man', which provides a generic description that will not be found in all aspects in any one particular renaissance man. Bernstein's vertical and horizontal discourses and knowledge structures are themselves examples of such concepts; there are others in sociology, although there are few in the sociology of education.

What we see Cassirer doing here is conceding the first part of the critique that Vico and the vitalists launched against scientific naturalism, namely, that the *mathesis universalis* (or mathematicization) is unable to explain cultural objects. In other words, for Cassirer, scientific naturalism is a special case, not the general case. But a special case of what? Cassirer provides the surprising answer: it is a special case of constituting objectivity. Perfect subsumption is one, but only one, form of constituting objectivity; imperfect subsumption is another. Both aim at the same end, namely, achieving the maximum absorption of the object by the concept, taking account of the particular form of resistance offered by the kind of object in question. Two conclusions follow; cultural objects are not analysable like natural objects; but that does not, in the least respect, absolve the cultural sciences from the obligation to truth, which is to aim for the maximum amount of abstraction or objectification possible under the circumstances consistent with the nature of the objects under study. Durkheim would not have conceded as much to the pragmatists, but curiously, the end result is the same: for both Durkheim and Cassirer, knowledge of the social must be objective in order to be knowledge.

The place of Cassirer in our account should be getting clearer. Whereas Durkheim asserts the objectivity of the social ('social facts'), he does so without showing in his methodological discussions in what way objectivity in 'social facts' might be differently constituted from the way it is in 'natural facts' – the primary and common feature of both for Durkheim is their externality. For this omission – since the discussion on pragmatism clearly shows it to be an omission – he is still in some ill-informed circles considered to have been a positivist. Bernstein, alternatively, displays what Cassirer might have called a 'conceptual formalism' which was not so much wrong as partial, a partiality that he only belatedly situated in a broader methodological framework with his discussion of internal and external languages of description. For his inadvertent imputed omissions he is still regarded, probably in the same ill-informed circles, as a 'structuralist'.

In his fourth study in *The Logic of the Cultural Sciences*, Cassirer (2000) makes perhaps his most daring move, which is to argue that formal and causal explanations are artificially separated, not only in the natural sciences since post-Newtonian science excised Aristotelian formalism,[16] but also in the cultural sciences. Both branches of science need reintegrating, but how could that be understood without a reversion to naturalism? It is this that Cassirer set out to do.

Cassirer distinguishes between four forms of analysis that together constitute a general approach to the sciences of culture. The first he calls the 'analysis of work' (as in the 'works of culture'), by which he means a general empirical classification of the object types to be studied in the cultural sciences. Having isolated the object types – the different material classes of culture such as art, religion, pedagogy etc. – a second analysis is called for that he refers to as the 'analysis of form' – that is, a morphology of the different forms in terms of structure and function.[17] Having established the essential formal properties of a cultural form, Cassirer argues that we need next to explore how the contents of these forms vary across social groups and temporal periods. This calls for what he refers to as an 'analysis of cause' a causal analysis of social and historical variation of formal configurations. Finally, and this mode of analysis can only come at the end, he suggests that we initiate an 'analysis of act', that is, an analysis of dispositions or habitus which constitute the subjective experiences of the cultural forms. What this betokens is a presumptive sequence of analyses that shows how descriptive, conceptual, causal and interpretive moments of analysis can be considered as parts of an overall analytical strategy. There are two points that deserve emphasis. The first is that each moment constitutes an 'objective' analytical move; the second is that 'causal' and 'formal' moments do not belong to organic and symbolic forms respectively. All scientific analysis in the cultural sciences can, in principle, embrace all of these analytical methods. With this, the unity of knowledge is once more preserved.

Crude as this may be, this approach displays Cassirer's cardinal virtue, which is to have demonstrated the essential unity of conceptual inquiry by showing the way out of the impasse that scientific naturalism, the dominant account of unity, had created. At the same time and in the most civil way possible he shows why the constructivist/vitalist alternative turns out to be the 'false sortie' that it is. The truth is that the failure of the natural sciences to deal adequately with cultural phenomena is no reason to reject a science of culture or a social science. In other words, Cassirer provides the outline of a philosophical justification for scientific objectivism in both the natural and social sciences.

The sociology of knowledge in educational studies: A way forward

Arising from the tension between being truthful and the idea of truth that was identified by the philosopher Bernard Williams, this chapter has taken four steps in the journey to find an adequate basis for the sociology of knowledge in educational studies (and more generally). First we set out to document the weaknesses of the social constructivist position as they emerged in the 1970s, and which, with few changes, are still with us today (and largely, but not entirely unchallenged) (Weiss, McCarthy and Dimitriadis 2006; Young 2006). To do this we drew on the remarkable parallels between Durkheim's diagnosis of the weaknesses of pragmatism and the problems that the 1970s social constructivism gave rise to. Our second step was to extend the discussion to Durkheim and establish his two fundamental insights for the sociology of knowledge. The first was that the sociality of knowledge does not undermine its objectivity and the possibility of truth, but is the condition for it. The second is the key role that he gives to differentiation (for him between the sacred and the profane) as the origins of speculative thought and the growth of knowledge. Despite these insights, Durkheim was more concerned with the conditions for the possibility of knowledge – the Kantian question expressed in sociological terms – than the development of knowledge itself. Furthermore, just as Kant's model of truth was Euclid's geometry, so for Durkheim it was the natural sciences. This limits the extent to which Durkheim's sociology of knowledge can, on its own, provide an adequate alternative to pragmatism and social constructivism.

Our third step was to turn to the work of the leading contemporary Durkheimian, Basil Bernstein, and his highly original analysis of knowledge structures and their variation. Bernstein takes Durkheim's insights further than anyone else. However, he is, like Durkheim, trapped in the assumption that physics represents the model for all knowledge growth. Ironically, this leads to his inability to provide the grounds for the progress that his own theory makes. Our fourth step is to turn to the German philosopher, little known among sociologists, Ernest Cassirer. Rather than classifying different knowledge structures, Cassirer classifies different types of objectivity, according to the relationship that the concepts of knowledge form have to their object. Crucially, this allows sociology to free itself from the trap of comparison with the mathematical sciences at the same time as not thereby renouncing the possibility of objective sociological knowledge; the natural sciences for Cassirer are a special case of objectification, not a model for objectivity itself.

We argue that Cassirer takes us further than Bernstein by theorizing the wellspring of knowledge progression – objectification – in terms of two different forms of subsumption. To put that in plainer terms: while Bernstein, despite his own best efforts, left us with an unsatisfactory account of knowledge progression for sociology, as a kind of lateral sprawl of new languages, Cassirer explains the differential prospects for knowledge growth in sociology in terms of the expressiveness of its object domain. Whereas it could be argued that Bernstein conceded too much to the sceptics in his account of sociological progress in terms solely of horizontal proliferation, not in terms of verticality, Cassirer allows us to reconsider sociology's prospects in terms of a different verticality. In addition, Cassirer's analysis suggests that sociology could be examined in terms of his four modes discussed in the previous section – 'work', 'form', 'cause' and 'act'. His argument is that these modes are equally applicable to all forms of knowledge. We have hardly begun to explore the implications of our journey for the sociology of education. Suffice to say, it would take us far from the well intentioned naiveties of social constructivism.

For sociology in general, it should be clear that it has an embarrassment of riches in terms of Cassirer's fourth mode (the interpretative, where the subjective outweighs the objective) and the first mode (where particularity is weakly subsumed into a generalizing conceptual framework, if at all). Where we remain weak is in the second and third modes, which refer to conceptual and causal analysis. This is manifestly where our best efforts should now be directed.

To return to Williams one last time: in his most artful way, Williams suggests that a commitment to truthfulness shorn from a commitment to truth ends up in a bogus valorization of sincerity, that principle most prized by the image industry. To imagine that sincerity, a commitment to knowing our inner selves, is sustainable without a commensurate commitment to knowing our external world, natural or social, is possibly the central illusion of our age. As Harry Frankfurt puts it in his unexpected and heartening little bestseller, *On Bullshit*:

> The contemporary proliferation of bullshit also has deeper sources, in various forms of scepticism which deny that we can have any reliable access to objective

reality ... [which leads to the] pursuit of an alternative ideal of sincerity ... Our natures are, indeed, elusively insubstantial – notoriously less stable than the natures of other things. And insofar as this is the case, sincerity itself is bullshit.

(Frankfurt 2005: 64–7)

It is the world beyond bullshit that is the one worth exploring. Further, it is (or should be) the world that education is about. The nature of that world, and the conditions under which it shapes the curriculum, defines the project of the sociology of educational knowledge.

Notes

1 See Nozaki (2006) and Moore and Muller (1999) for useful discussions of the problems that 'standpoint' theories give rise to.

2 It was of course over half a century since Durkheim made the theoretical case for the sociological study of education (Durkheim 1956). In the UK, Karl Mannheim had been appointed as the first Professor of Sociology of Education in 1946. However, he died within a year and, despite the efforts of those like Jean Floud and A. H. Halsey in the 1950s, it was not until the late 1960s that sociology of education in the UK became a distinct field of research and teaching within educational studies.

3 Perhaps the most sophisticated and influential example of this genre is the work of the American critical curriculum theorist, Michael Apple (1975).

4 One of the authors of this chapter was personally involved in these developments within the sociology of education (Whitty and Young 1976).

5 An example of the time is the Reader edited by John Beck *et al.* (1977) in which there were chapter headings such as education, rationality, ability and childhood as social constructs. We are not denying that such categories are, and can be usefully seen as, social constructs, but that social constructivism in the sociology of education set no limits on what could and could not be constructed in a particular context or over time. As Ian Hacking (1999) noted so perceptively, the idea of anything being a social construct is always true at a trivial level; the conceptual issue is in what circumstances is this of more than trivial significance.

6 The terms 'radical' and 'moderate' social constructivism are frequently found in the literature. However, from the point of view of our argument in this chapter, this differentiation misses the point that for even moderate forms of social constructivism, the limits on what can be 'constructed' are always only implicit.

7 Philosophers were easily seen as merely defending their professional interests; an example of what later became generalized as standpoint theorizing!

8 The idea of 'non-reformist reforms' was popular among left educationalists at the time, but never given much substance.

9 The idea of 'resistance' took on a life of its own far removed from Willis' original study and became elevated to the status of a 'theory (Giroux 1983).

10 Whereas in North America this 'theorizing' took the overtly political form of the 'critical pedagogy' associated with writers such as Peter McLaren and Henry Giroux, in England a less clearly defined body of 'educational theory' emerged that was exemplified in the work of academics such as Usher and Edwards (1994).

11 For a more measured commentary on these issues, see Haack (1998).

12 This of course is the premise of standpoint 'theory' referred to earlier. The kind of difficulties that such an approach to knowledge gets into, are well brought out, if unresolved, by Nozaki (2006).

13 This is not to say that such incorporation has not been attempted in a horizontal knowledge structure like sociology. From Max Weber and Talcott Parsons onwards, sociological

theory is strewn with largely unsuccessful attempts to integrate diverse sets of concepts into a single conceptual whole.

14 Or could they? Is not an epistemic community within sociology in which 'the past is in the present' assumed when we, in the first decade of the twenty-first century, engage with Durkheim's concept of anomie or Weber's concept of bureaucracy?

15 There are echoes here of Weber's far more pessimistic idea of disenchantment.

16 An excision that some argue is being rectified by 'modern' quantum physics.

17 An example of the kind of analysis that Cassirer is pointing to is Bernstein's famous morphologies of code orientation and pedagogy.

SECTION 2

Knowledge and curriculum futures

3

EDUCATION, GLOBALIZATION AND THE 'VOICE OF KNOWLEDGE'

Introduction

This chapter starts from a problem that is perhaps better expressed as a contradiction. On the one hand, 'knowledge' has undoubtedly become the major organizing category in the educational policies of international organizations and many national governments. Global similarities are increasingly apparent – whether they are expressed with reference to knowledge itself, to the knowledge society, to knowledge workers or *The Knowledge Promotion* (http://www.utdanningsdirektoratet.no/templates/udir/TM_Artikkel.aspx?id=2376) as the reforms of Norwegian secondary education are referred to. On the other hand, the category 'knowledge' appears to be used in an almost entirely rhetorical way; the meaning of knowledge is at best implicit[1] and at worst virtually empty of content. One consequence is that such policies deny or disregard the idea that access to knowledge in the strong sense that involves its claims to reliability is central to the whole purpose of education. Thus, what I shall refer to in this chapter as the 'voice of knowledge' (Moore 2007) as a distinctive factor shaping educational policy is lost. If I have accurately identified this trend and it continues, it is a highly problematic heritage that we leave to future generations – namely that there is no explicit knowledge that is important enough to be 'transmitted' to the next generation. It is a heritage that has none of the visibility of the environmental or sustainability crises, although arguably, addressing it is fundamental to whether we are able to deal with either.

The aim of this chapter is to explore this apparent contradiction and to begin to develop an alternative that takes the idea of the 'voice of knowledge' seriously. An issue that I touch on, but only by implication, is whether significant strands of the social sciences (and sociology in particular) may be part of the problem of denying a 'voice' for knowledge rather than being the basis for offering a viable alternative for the future (see Chapters 2 and 5).

The chapter contains five sections. The first section provides a number of examples of how knowledge is interpreted in international educational policies and raises the question 'why knowledge?' What purpose does such a focus on knowledge have in today's educational policies? My examples are drawn from the educational policies of international organizations such as the World Bank and new national curricula and national education policies (my illustrations are from Norway and England). I also refer briefly to the work of the Portuguese sociologist, de Sousa Santos, a leading critic of globalization, to indicate the terms within which the debate about education and the knowledge economy among globalizers and anti-globalizers has largely been set. My argument is that, despite treating knowledge as a main organizing category, international and national policy-makers *and their critics* in effect bypass what I (following Rob Moore) mean by the 'voice of knowledge'.

The second section begins to make explicit what the idea of the 'voice of knowledge' in educational policy might mean. It starts from a paper by Moore (2006), in which he draws on the critical realist tradition in the philosophy of science and establishes the epistemological basis for the idea of the 'voice of knowledge' in education. However, in my view, despite its strengths, critical realism does not move us very far towards conceptualizing a more adequate role for knowledge in educational policy.

The third section builds on Moore's ideas by arguing that the key idea implicit in a realist theory of knowledge is *knowledge differentiation*. This idea is elaborated through a brief account[2] of the ideas of the French philosopher, Gaston Bachelard.

The fourth section considers the educational implications of the idea of the social differentiation of knowledge with reference to the work of Durkheim, Vygotsky and Bernstein. The final section builds on the previous section to explore five forms of knowledge differentiation as they apply to the curriculum. The chapter concludes by returning to the idea of the 'voice of knowledge' as a potential shaper of educational policy.

Knowledge as the new global narrative

The striking thing about the many publications of international organizations and governments that refer to knowledge and the knowledge economy is that they don't feel the need to ask the question 'What is this knowledge that we are referring to?'; its meaning is simply taken for granted. As Susan Robertson (2007) puts it in a paper which started me thinking about this issue – 'Who can be against knowledge?' It is not therefore surprising, she writes, 'that the idea of knowledge articulates with the left as well as the right'. In UK terms, this use of 'knowledge' is an example of a characteristic New Labour or 'third way' doctrine – it includes everything, it sounds progressive (or at least modernizing) but it says nothing substantive.

It is the word knowledge, rather than the related term 'information' that has caught on as the key category in the new education policy literature. I suspect that the reason for this is that, despite its multiple meanings and absence of any referents, the word *knowledge* does retain a public association with ideas such as certainty, reliability and objectivity and even truth. Reference to knowledge therefore provides a kind of authority for policies that do not have to be justified in other ways. The authority of the term knowledge is taken over but not the basis of its claims.

A brief glance at documents produced by international organizations and governments indicates that the idea of knowledge acts as a license for a whole range of educational policies that have little directly to do with knowledge in the more specifically epistemological sense. Two examples of widely supported educational policies illustrate this point. The first is the emphasis on maximising learner choice and the associated tendency for learning to become little more than another form of consumption. In a world dominated by learner choice, knowledge loses all its authority. The second example is the popularity of the slogans 'personalized learning' and 'individual learning styles' and the gradual replacement of the terms education, school and college with their assumed elitism by learning and learning centres. This is not to underplay the importance of learners having an active role in any educational process as any level. It is rather to highlight the importance of distinguishing between the everyday or common sense knowledge that is acquired by individual learners in specific contexts and the idea that we acquire powerful knowledge (Chapter 8) to take us beyond our everyday experiences (Karpov and Heywood 1998). If this distinction is blurred or seen as unimportant, the role of teachers is reduced to little more than facilitation and support and we are not a million miles away from the idea of 'user-generated knowledge' that is associated with YouTube and Facebook (Keen 2007).

My argument is that an empty and rhetorical notion of knowledge and the increasing tendency to blur distinctions between the production of knowledge and its acquisition and between knowledge and skills – the latter unlike the former being something measurable and targetable – becomes a way of denying a distinct 'voice' for knowledge in education. Furthermore, excluding such a 'voice' from educational policy must disadvantage those learners (and whole societies, in the case of developing countries), who are already disadvantaged by circumstances beyond the school.

Illustrations of this 'emptying of content' can be found in the educational policies of many countries; I will mention two briefly – England and Norway. Since the end of the 1980s, but increasingly in the last decade the control of public education in England has been centralized under the Department of Education and Skills (DFES). Schools, local authorities, examination boards and research councils have increasingly taken on the role of agencies delivering government policy. The DFES, now two departments – the Department of Innovation, Universities and Skills (DIUS) and the Department for Children, Schools and Families (DCSF)[3], like all government departments, are now regulated under a Public Service Agreement (PSA) which governs the funds they receive from the Treasury.[4] The PSA for Education has five objectives broken up into 14 sub-objectives. All refer to generic targets and none make reference to any specific knowledge or curriculum content. Another illustration that is more obviously closer to what goes on in schools and colleges comes from the requirements laid down by the government for the new diplomas for 14 to 19 year olds (http://www.dcsf.gov.uk/1419/index.cfm?go=site.home&sid=52).

These requirements set out in considerable detail the packaging, module combinations, credit levels and pathways for the diplomas, but make only minimal reference to content. Targets which are based on a common set of levels, and common units for measuring volume of learning, have priority over reference to specific contents. The implications are that what might be assumed to be distinctive to formal education – the acquisition of specific knowledge – is treated as relatively unimportant. Institutions are held accountable and students assessed in terms of outcomes that are not content-specific.

The new Norwegian[5] curriculum reforms follow a similar trend. They are known, significantly, as *The Knowledge Promotion* (http://www.utdanningsdirektoratet.no/templates/udir/TM_Artikkel.aspx?id=2376). The new Norwegian curriculum is defined by five basic skills and a seven-part quality framework; each of the 12 criteria has to be reflected in the teaching of the different subjects; subject syllabuses no longer prescribe specific contents. It is this combination of basic (generic) skills and a quality framework, not the knowledge content of subjects which is built into the legislation, drives teaching, and defines what students have opportunities to learn, and how they are assessed.

A rather different example of the evacuation of knowledge is found in the publications of the well-known Portuguese sociologist, Buoventura de Sousa Santos, now largely based at Wisconsin, USA. It illustrates how the approach taken to knowledge by at least some of the left-wing critics of globalization and the role of international agencies leads to a similar evacuation of content. The works of de Sousa Santos are widely read in Brazil and he has played a key role in the Global Social Forum. In Brazil I have heard him spoken of as the new Paulo Freire. What he refers to as his 'epistemology of absent knowledges' claims to goes beyond what he sees as the 'blindness' of western science. He refers to it in a paper in the following terms:

> The epistemology of absent knowledges starts from the premise that *social practices* are *knowledge practices* ... non-science-based practices, rather than being ignorant practices, *are practices of alternative rival knowledges*. There is *no apriori reason to favour one form of knowledge against another*.
>
> *(de Sousa Santos 2001, emphasis added)*

Starting from a critique of mainstream economics, de Sousa Santos is trapped in a framework that associates epistemologies with particular social groups or world regions. The result is a concept of knowledge that equates it over-simplistically with power,[6] and is as empty, despite its radical rhetoric, as that of the World Bank.

The 'voice of knowledge'

What then might the idea of the 'voice of knowledge' that I have argued is increasingly absent in educational policies mean? I begin with what Moore (2007) identifies as its four elements. It must, he argues, be:

- *Critical* – be open to revision and embody a fallibilist notion of truth.
- *Emergentist* – in recognizing that knowledge is not reducible to the conditions of its production or the activities and interests of those involved.
- *Realist* – in recognizing that the objects of knowledge of both the natural and social worlds are realities that (a) are independent of our perception of the world and (b) provide limits to how we can know about the world.
- *Materialist* – in recognizing that knowledge is produced (and acquired) in specific historically created modes of production, or in Bourdieu's terms, intellectual fields.

Knowledge, it follows, from a realist perspective and in the sense that I as an educationalist use the word,[7] can be differentiated from the meanings we construct to make sense of the word in our everyday lives; it is not created by learners or even by learners with their teachers; it is acquired.

Although these propositions form a sound basis for any serious enquiry into the role of knowledge in education, the terms in which they are set are too general for them to be a basis on their own, for drawing any conclusions about educational and more specifically, curriculum policy. I will comment briefly on each proposition and suggest that the key underlying concept that can be derived from them and needs developing is the *differentiation of knowledge*.

Proposition 1: Fallibility

The idea of fallibility or 'openness to critique and revision' is usually associated with the natural sciences. However, it is no less important in the humanities and social sciences. Different concepts of fallibility arise from the ways in which different knowledge domains subsume the particular under the general (Joe Muller and I discuss this in an earlier paper, Young and Muller 2007). However, fallibility is always understood as being 'within a tradition or a discipline'. The dangers of breaking the link between 'openness to critique' and a tradition within which critique is located are well demonstrated by Anthony Kronman, the former Dean of Humanities at Yale. In his book, *Education's Ends: Why Our Colleges and Universities Have Given Up on the Meaning of Life*, Kronman describes how after the 1960s many humanities faculties in the USA rejected any notion of tradition and focused only on critique; this left them, he argues, open to the most extreme forms of relativism and political correctness (Kronman 2007).

Proposition 2: Emergence

This is the idea that powerful knowledge is the product of social conditions or contexts that do not wholly determine it. Examples might be the science laboratory or the classroom. Archives, libraries and the internet can also be conditions for the emergent properties of knowledge to be generated. However, this does not take place, as is sometimes assumed, in isolation from teachers or members of other 'communities of specialists'. These originating 'contexts' will leave their mark on the knowledge acquired and produced in them. However, what makes powerful knowledge powerful is its independence or autonomy from the specific contexts of its origin. Let's take an example, the English chemist Robert Boyle needed to be wealthy enough to build the laboratory on his estate in which he discovered what became known as Boyle's Law. However, today's aircraft designers do not need to read Steven Shapin's account of the gentry culture (Shapin 1995) of which Boyle was a part to understand and apply his law about how gas volumes change under pressure.

Emergence is a less straightforward idea in the social sciences. For example, Max Weber's concept of ideal types has emergent properties, which explains why it remains fruitful to this day. However, only a few sociologists will be familiar with the debates Weber had with the Marxists in the German Social Democratic Party which led him to formulate the idea. Contemporary sociologists could well gain additional sociological insights into Weber's ideas by reading Marianne Weber's account of his life in ways that would not be true for physicists reading Shapin's account of Boyle's life, however interesting they might find it.

Proposition 3: Real basis of knowledge

This is the idea that our claims to knowledge are not just claims; they say something about the world that is not dependent on how we conceive of it. If the sociology of knowledge is to say anything about the curriculum it must provide a theory that distinguishes between knowledge and non-knowledge – whether this is expressed as experience, opinion, belief or common sense. Likewise, if the nature of the objects of knowledge (our theories) limits what we can know about reality, we need to know how they are differentiated between different domains when we come to make decisions about the curriculum.

Proposition 4: Materiality of knowledge production and acquisition

These processes do not take place anywhere but in particular social contexts with specific rules and forms of organization. This idea of the materiality of knowledge production points to the importance of research into different forms of specialist knowledge communities and their role (and often their lack of role) in the design of curricula. In the UK, vocational education programmes preparing students for different occupational fields vary widely in how they interpret their knowledge base. Much of this variation can be explained in terms of the different roles that professional associations have in the design of programmes at pre- or non-professional levels.[8]

The conclusion that I draw from this brief discussion of Moore's four propositions about knowledge is that they have to be developed further. One way of doing this is through the idea, implicit in each proposition, that knowledge is socially differentiated. The next section draws on the French philosopher, Gaston Bachelard's historical epistemology to present a way of developing this idea.

The social differentiation of knowledge

The idea that there are real structured differences between types of knowledge that are not dependent on our perceptions – in particular between scientific and non-scientific knowledge – lies at the heart of the work of Gaston Bachelard, the French philosopher of science. In the UK, his work has been largely associated with Louis Althusser's flawed attempt to construct a 'scientific' Marxism. However, and here I draw largely on Christopher Norris' account, this is to miss the broader importance of Bachelard's work. Norris (2000) points out, rightly, I think, that Althusser, presumably for political reasons, misinterprets Bachelard and relied on a misplaced 'scientific' rigour that seeks to emulate the physical sciences in fields where different criteria apply. This habit, Norris argues, gives rise to 'various kinds of false analogy and wire-drawn metaphors' which find no justification in Bachelard's own work. Furthermore, Bachelard's epistemology is more historically grounded than that of critical realists such as Bhaskar; it focuses on distinct episodes in the history of the physical sciences. For this reason it is more useful for clarifying what the 'differentiation of knowledge' might mean in sociological terms. The following points are a necessarily over-simplified summary of the aspects of Bachelard's theory of knowledge which have particular relevance for the concerns of this chapter and are they are drawn largely from Norris' discussions.[9]

1   Bachelard established a basis for distinguishing science from pre- (or non-) science that has parallels with Lakatos' distinction between 'progressive' and 'degenerating' research programmes.
2   He develops a theory of how knowledge progresses from 'less efficient' to 'more efficient' concepts through the process of 'conceptual rectification and critique'.
3   He provides examples from the history of science of how knowledge 'progresses' by tracing the discontinuous development of ideas such as the 'atom' from the Greeks 'atomism' to modern atomic theory. In each case he shows how ideas are transformed from being largely metaphorical into increasingly precise and testable 'scientific' concepts.
4   He recognizes that a theory of knowledge must begin from 'the current best state of knowledge in the field concerned' – in other words, where a discipline is currently at.
5   He proposes a methodology for distinguishing between two kinds of historical enquiry which Norris argues are often confused in contemporary discussions – *histoire sanctionée* – the history of the growth of science (this focuses on those early steps, like Lavoisier's discovery of the role of oxygen in combustion, which led to further advances) and *histoire perimée* – the history of past scientific beliefs (those which were later rejected as leading nowhere). One of Bachelard's examples in this case was Priestley's attempt to explain combustion with the idea of phlogiston.
6   His historical epistemology is underpinned by a trans-historical set of principles associated with rigour, clarity, conceptual precision and logical consistency.

None of these proposals can be easily applied to the social sciences[10] and I am not aware of any attempt by Bachelard to extend his theory beyond the physical sciences.[11] However, his focus on the *historical* conditions for the growth of knowledge in any discipline does not imply that it must be restricted to the physical sciences or that the idea of a historical epistemology must take physics or any particular science as its model. Also for Bachelard, concepts are not just theoretical propositions, they are simultaneously embedded in technical and *pedagogic* activity – the material conditions for producing them. Thus he opens the possibility of a realist account of the differentiation and growth of knowledge and the role of educational institutions.

Approaches to the social differentiation of knowledge: Durkheim, Vygotsky and Bernstein

This section takes further the idea of knowledge differentiation by drawing briefly on the three theorists who focus specifically on the differentiation of educational knowledge – Durkheim, Vygotsky and Bernstein. Their analyses form the basis, I suggest, for a research programme into the differentiation of educational knowledge as the principles for a theory of the curriculum. The significance and range of work of the three theorists is only touched on briefly here. I have explored their ideas in more detail elsewhere (Young 2007c).

Durkheim

As a sociologist rather than a philosopher of science, Durkheim's theory of knowledge is broader than Bachelard's; he does not limit himself to the physical sciences and he does not differentiate between scientific knowledge and knowledge in any broader sense. The differences that he identifies between knowledge and experience can be traced back to his early rejection of Kant's transcendentalism and to the concepts – 'sacred' and 'profane' – that he developed in his studies of religion in primitive societies. Durkheim initially used the sacred/profane distinction to describe the separation of religion and everyday life that he found in primitive societies. However, the 'sacred' and the 'profane' became, for Durkheim, a basic distinction at the heart of all societies, even those that have become largely secularized. He saw the distinction as a form of social organization that was basic to science and intellectual thought; hence his reference to primitive religions as 'proto-sciences'. Without the conceptual and social moves from the everyday world of survival to the sacred world of totemic religion that those early societies made, Durkheim argued, no science and no knowledge, and indeed no society, would be possible.

Vygotsky

Entering adult life and beginning his short career at the start of the Soviet Revolution, Vygotsky inevitably focused on the immediate problems facing teachers in the new society. His primary concern was with how teachers could help students to develop the higher order concepts that they would not have access to in their everyday lives. Like Durkheim, his theory was about the differentiation of knowledge and he also relied on a binary distinction – between two kinds of concepts – the theoretical (or scientific) and the everyday. The task of the curriculum – and schooling more generally, for Vygotsky – was to provide students with access to theoretical concepts in all their different forms – from history and literature to the sciences and mathematics. Furthermore, he saw that access to higher order concepts was not a simple one-way process of transmission, but a complex pedagogic process in which a learner's everyday concepts are extended and transformed by theoretical concepts. From the point of the role of knowledge in education, the implications of Vygotsky's ideas are most clearly expressed in the work of the Russian Vasily Davidoff and his ideas of 'kernel knowledge' and learning as moving beyond the abstract and gaining a grasp of the concrete 'real' nature of things.

Bernstein

Bernstein (1971, 2000)[12] took Durkheim's ideas of knowledge differentiation further in a number of important ways. Here I will only refer to three brief points which focus on the issue of knowledge differentiation.

1   With his concepts of 'classification' and 'framing', Bernstein developed Durkheim's idea of boundaries as the key social category separating types of symbolic meanings. He used these concepts to show how boundaries in education play a major role in the development of learner and teacher identities.
2   Bernstein distinguished two types of educational boundary that are crucial for any curriculum theory – those between knowledge domains and those between school and everyday knowledge. He analysed the implications of both these types of boundary being blurred or dissolved.
3   Bernstein drew on Durkheim's concepts of the 'sacred' and the 'profane' and his argument that the 'sacred' represented a kind of 'proto-science' to develop a distinction between forms of the 'sacred' which he expressed as vertical and horizontal discourses. In his last work (Bernstein 2000), he began to analyse the curriculum implications of these distinctions.

Forms of knowledge differentiation and the curriculum

In this section, I want to comment briefly on *five* aspects of the social differentiation of knowledge that can be derived from the ideas of Durkheim, Vygotsky and Bernstein and to suggest that they could provide the basis for a theory of the curriculum that takes seriously the idea of the 'voice of knowledge'. Although each aspect has a distinct focus, there are overlaps between them and further conceptual clarification could no doubt reduce the number of types listed and define them more precisely.

The fundamental difference between knowledge and experience

Without this difference, which lies at the heart of Durkheim's social theory of knowledge, the idea of a curriculum is impossible. This has been demonstrated by the failed attempts of successive generations of progressive and radical educators to collapse the categories and construct an experience-based curriculum. The problems of the South African and Australian outcomes-based curricula, the English child-centred curriculum that followed Plowden and the more radical Queensland-based 'new basics curriculum' are among the many examples. Less publicized, but in social justice terms even more damaging, is the extent to which curricula based on the work experience of young people have been the basis of a wide range of vocational programmes which claim to offer educational possibilities to slow learners and those disaffected from schooling.

The conceptual separation of knowledge from experience was Durkheim's major point in his most explicitly philosophical book *Pragmatism and Sociology* (Durkheim 1983). In that book, he praised William James and the pragmatists for bringing philosophical questions about truth back to where he felt they should be located – in social life (or as he expressed it, in society) and not in academic philosophy. However, he criticized James and the pragmatists for having an undifferentiated concept of the social and society and therefore at least implicitly equating it with experience. For Durkheim experience is a powerful force but inadequate as an epistemological principle and no basis for reliable knowledge or for the curriculum.

The differences between theoretical and everyday knowledge

This is a narrower and more concrete expression of the first difference. If these differences are dismissed or blurred, it becomes increasingly difficult to make reliable decisions about what to include and exclude in the curriculum or indeed to say what formal education is for. There are two possible consequences of blurring the distinction between theoretical and everyday concepts. The first is that many kinds of knowledge are included in the curriculum, for broadly political reasons, which schools may not provide the conditions for acquiring – sex and moral education and employment-related skills are examples. The second consequence is that the contents that may be the condition for acquiring theoretical knowledge are excluded or replaced (as in the proposals for the secondary science curriculum in England). Thus on the grounds of popular relevance or pupil interest, the opportunities that students have for acquiring systematic theoretical knowledge that cannot be acquired elsewhere are restricted. Without a specification of the differences between theoretical and everyday concepts as well as a focus on the relationships between them that go beyond the moral or political standpoints of those involved, curriculum decisions are inevitably reduced to politics.

The differences between knowledge domains

These differences refer to horizontal aspects of the intellectual division of labour in Durkheim's terms and what Bernstein describes as the classification of educational knowledge. A theory of knowledge differentiation presupposes that domain differences are not arbitrary, but to some degree are the product of Bachelard's historical processes of 'rectification and critique'. An understanding of the extent to which domain differences such as those between disciplines and subjects have an epistemological as opposed to a merely conventional basis is crucial to the analysis of the links between domain boundaries, learner identities and learner progress and to addressing the debate around multi-, trans- and inter-disciplinarity and the limits of modularization and student choice.

The differences between school and non-school knowledge

These differences follow from Vygotsky's distinction between theoretical and everyday concepts and my interpretation of Bernstein's concept of the framing of educational knowledge. However, the differences between school and non-school knowledge have a specific importance in that they indicate why it is important to distinguish between the *curriculum* – as the conditions for acquiring new knowledge, and *pedagogy* – which refers to the activities of teaching and learning involved in the process of acquisition. This is a distinction that both Durkheim and Bernstein were somewhat ambiguous about. Both, but explicitly Durkheim, relied on an over-deterministic transmission model of education which played down the active role of the learner in transmission and the extent to which the *recontextualization* of school knowledge lies at the heart of pedagogy.[13] Vygotsky, on the other hand, was more sensitive to the complexity of pedagogic issues, but was less explicit about exactly what he meant by theoretical (or scientific) concepts. This may be why the socio-cultural and socio-historical activity theories of learning which locate their origins in Vygotsky's work have largely neglected the role of knowledge in formal education. From the perspective being developed in this chapter, while pedagogy necessarily involves the teacher in taking account of the non-school knowledge that his/her students bring to school, the curriculum explicitly does not.

Conclusions

This chapter began by noting the emptying of the concept of knowledge in the increasingly globalized debates about education and the knowledge economy and explored some of the implications of this trend in contemporary educational policy. In endeavouring to recapture knowledge as lying at the heart of the goals of all education, the idea of the 'voice of knowledge' does not divorce knowledge from knowers and hence from thinking and judgement. Rather it offers a counter to this divorce in much contemporary writing where thinking and learning are treated as if they were processes that can be conceptualized as educational goals independently of what the thinking and learning is about.

I have argued that the idea of the structured differentiation of knowledge is central to a more adequate conceptualization of its role in education. The chapter focused primarily on the differentiation of school and non-school knowledge and discussed some of the dimensions of this differentiation and their educational significance. The growth of knowledge, whether in a subject like physics or history, or in an occupational field like engineering or financial management, and hence the opportunities for acquisition open to new learners whatever their age, will depend on the continued process of 'rectification and critique', to return to Bachelard's apt phrase, by the various specialists involved. Making this process explicit is the task of a realist sociology of knowledge in relation to the curriculum, if the 'voice' of knowledge' is to shape educational policy and knowledge is not to continue to be an empty category. There is much to do.

Notes

1 As in the case of a lawyer whose new post was Head of Knowledge.
2 My account draws on Christopher Norris' excellent accounts of Bachelard's ideas (Norris 2000, 2005).
3 In 2010 the Coalition Government renamed the Department for Children, Schools and Familes (DCSF), the Department for Education (DFE).
4 I am grateful to Professor Alison Wolf (Kings College, University of London) for pointing out to me the important role of PSAs and their potential influence on what counts as successful learning in school.
5 I mention Norway for two reasons; one arises from a visit to two Norwegian universities, and the other because Norway has often been celebrated by English researchers as representing a model of strong educational policy-making (Payne 2002). My point is not to disagree with Payne, but to suggest that this 'emptying of knowledge content' under the guise of promoting knowledge can be found even in a country as little prone to 'marketising' and 'individualising' tendencies as Norway.
6 Of course, knowledge is about power and 'the powerful' will always try to define what counts as knowledge. However, it is not only about power; some types of knowledge *are* more reliable than others and we cannot afford to forget either aspect.
7 It is what I and I imagine most teachers (and parents) want their students/children to acquire at school that they will be unlikely to be able to acquire at home.
8 One of the most successful programmes of vocational education in England (in terms of progression both to employment and to higher education and professional level programmes) is that developed by the Association of Accountancy Technicians (AAT). A major reason for this is the key role played by the professional association of chartered accountants (the Institute of Chartered Accountants in England and Wales) with which the AAT is associated.
9 A much more detailed account of Bachelard's epistemological theory is given by Mary Tiles (1984), and by Christina Chimisso (2001) who locates her account in the context of Bachelard's work as a whole.
10 Althusser's failed attempt to apply Bachelard's proposals to Marxism as a theory of capitalism and his use of Bachelard's idea of an 'epistemological break' are an illustration of the difficulties.
11 George Canguilhem, who succeeded Bachelard at the Sorbonne, developed an influential historical epistemology with a focus on biology. However, I have not considered his work in this chapter.
12 I have only referred to two of Bernstein's many publications here.
13 Bernstein was the originator of the concept of 'recontextualization'; however, he was more concerned with its role in the structuring of pedagogic discourse than as a way of conceptualizing pedagogy.

4

ALTERNATIVE EDUCATIONAL FUTURES FOR A KNOWLEDGE SOCIETY

Introduction

Despite my choice of title, I do not claim to make any predictions in this chapter; my intention is to analyse some present trends in educational policy. My assumption is that such analyses provide us with the most reliable basis for shaping what is inevitably an uncertain future. I will focus on three trends in educational policy which are currently given a high profile by European agencies, international organizations and many national governments. I will argue that not only are the claims made for the policies difficult to justify, but that they are all too likely to lead to new inequalities. I shall be concerned more with the assumptions that the policies make and the alternatives that they neglect rather than the policies themselves.

The three policy trends are:

1   the introduction of national qualifications frameworks;
2   the shift to learning outcomes; and
3   the move from subject-specific to generic curriculum criteria.

Each trend will be familiar to anyone working in education, whether as an educational researcher, a policy maker or a teacher, especially in a country that is a member of the European Union (EU). However, they have not been widely debated up to now despite, as is certainly claimed by those emphasizing the shift to learning outcomes (CEDEFOP (European Centre for the Development of Vocational Training) 2008), being a radical new approach to educational reform and practice.[1] A possible reason for this lack of debate is that, while there have been critiques of each policy individually (Young 2007a, b, 2009a; Allais 2007; Young and Allais 2010), they have been treated as largely separate. Another possibility is that these policies appear to be being implemented through a process that researchers such as Ozga (2009), Lawn (2006), and Magalhães (2008) describe as 'soft power'. As Magalhães puts it in relation to the learning outcomes approach that underpins the Bologna process that is establishing the European Higher Education Area: 'it is being appropriated by the European Commission and implemented by means of "soft" law and "soft" instruments aiming at the fulfillment of political competitiveness' (Magalhães 2008). To the extent that these policies are associated with achieving such broad and taken-for-granted economic goals, it is perhaps unsurprising that they have not been subject to debate, either as means or ends in themselves.

Each of the three policy trends represents an attempt to 'open up' education systems, qualifications and educational institutions to a wider constituency, and all are identified with a broader set of progressive goals such as widening participation and social inclusion which few except those on the political right in England (Woodhead 2002, 2009) would disagree with. It may therefore be that critiques of these policies have been few because they can easily appear to oppose the widening of opportunities and to be justifying a return to elitism and social exclusivity.

Following a brief account of the three trends that I have referred to, I will consider some of the political issues that a critique of them raises, especially in relation to questions of overcoming elitism and promoting access. I will then explore the common assumptions of the three trends and the problems I see them leading to if they are not questioned. Finally, I will suggest an alternative approach to educational policy that focuses explicitly on the curriculum – or to put it more simply (although the argument is equally relevant to the education of adults), what do we want our young people to learn in school? Instead of starting with the reform of qualifications or the importance of specifying learning outcomes, however broadly defined, this approach starts with the question of knowledge and how the knowledge that we want learners to acquire needs to be distinguished from the everyday knowledge that they bring to school, college or university (Muller 2000; Young 2007a, 2009a, 2009b; Maton and Moore 2009).

Three policy trends

The introduction of national qualification frameworks

The emergence of national qualifications frameworks (NQFs), based on eight to ten educational levels that are expressed in terms of learning outcomes and are explicitly separated from any specific learning processes or programmes and cover all occupational and knowledge fields in 12–15 groupings, is a relatively new phenomenon and perhaps best seen as the latest global example of educational rationalization. Furthermore, not only does every country seem to want a NQF, but most of the leading international agencies are involved in persuading any countries that show reluctance that there is no other alternative if they want to be 'modern' and improve their economic competitiveness. By the end of the 1990s there were no more than five countries in the process of introducing a NQF – New Zealand, South Africa, Australia, and Scotland, and for vocational qualifications only, England, Wales and Northern Ireland. By 2009 this number had increased to 70 and is still growing.[2] Under the influence of the EU's own European Qualifications Framework, this number now includes most EU member countries and a much wider range of countries that have used it as a 'model', often supported by the European Training Foundation.

Enormous claims have been made on behalf of NQFs: that they will improve the curriculum, the delivery of education and the access and transferability of qualifications. Some of those promoting NQFs go even further; for example, the Commonwealth of Learning argues that qualifications frameworks represent 'new notions of knowledge', and a 'new hierarchy' in which education providers are no longer the leaders and standards-setters, and content (or inputs) is no longer the starting point for policies' (Commonwealth of Learning and South African Qualifications Authority 2008).

I and others have discussed the problems that NQFs lead to in some detail elsewhere (e.g. Young 2007b; Allais 2007). Here I will draw on some of this work to make two brief points. Firstly, NQFs are extremely diverse, so generalizations about the forms they are taking, let alone their impact, are difficult. However, the striking lack of evidence supporting the claims made for them has not hindered policy makers from treating them as some kind of 'magic bullet' for reforming education and training. In some countries, such as South Africa (and initially New Zealand), NQFs have been used to try to transform the whole education system, whereas in others, such as Scotland and Ireland (Raffe 2007) and France (Bouder 2003), the aims have been more modest and introducing a NQF is expected to do little more than provide a link between existing qualifications. The sad irony is that it is in developing countries, where the need to build an institutional infrastructure is greatest, that most is expected of an NQF and where it is likely that little, if anything, will be achieved. Those in Europe have some responsibility for this situation. Not only have a number of NQFs, such as that in South Africa, been largely funded by the EU, but many Europeans employed by international agencies as consultants (and here I include my own work in South Africa in the early 1990s) were carried away by the claims and radical rhetoric about what NQFs could do. Secondly, most NQFs have their roots in attempts to reform vocational education and in most countries the primary motivation for introducing a NQF has been economic. It is in making qualifications more portable and transferable with the hope that this will lead to the overcoming of skill shortages that most claims are made for NQFs.[3] This may account for the relative lack of interest in NQFs by educational researchers – at least those not concerned directly with vocational education and training. On the other hand, many NQFs are designed to include all levels and types of learning, even that which takes place in universities. It is not insignificant that many of the assumptions of NQFs about outcomes are found in the Bologna Accord that is establishing the European Higher Education Area that I referred to earlier (Magalhães 2008).

The shift to learning outcomes

The second trend – the shift to learning outcomes – subsumes NQFs and operates over a broader canvas. It is represented most clearly by the CEDEFOP report,

The Shift to Learning Outcomes (CEDEFOP 2008). This report argues that this shift applies to higher education, schools and vocational education and has implications not only for qualifications but for curricula, pedagogy and the role of educational institutions. In a sense the CEDEFOP report is arguing for and predicting the emergence of a completely new approach to educational policy that is underpinned by the split between outcomes and inputs that is found in virtually all NQFs. The Report draws on evidence from 32 countries and claims that there is a shift in educational policy from inputs – a focus on curricula, institutions and specialized pedagogies – to learning outcomes – a focus on what learners can do or know at the end of a learning process, which may or may not have involved study in a school, college or university. The term 'learning outcomes' is, however, almost useless as more than a policy slogan. It is not only ambiguous (Brockmann *et al.* 2008) but, as with any slogan, masks a set of political priorities more concerned with wrenching power from educational institutions than improving the quality of education and training (Young and Allais 2010). As with NQFs, enormous claims are made for this shift. For example, to again quote the Commonwealth of Learning, learning outcomes are a mechanism whereby: '*people outside of education institutions prescribe competences*, which are then used to determine the curriculum' (Commonwealth of Learning and South African Qualifications Authority 2008; emphasis added). It would be hard to find a clearer example of the reduced role of specialist educators that is expected in the future.

The move from subject-specific to generic skill criteria in national curricula

This trend focuses explicitly on the curriculum, not qualifications. So far I only have evidence from the UK (with separate examples from England and Wales, Northern Ireland and Scotland, all of which have new national curriculum proposals). However, there appear to be similar developments in Norway with its new Knowledge Promotion curriculum (Karseth and Sivesind 2010) and in New Zealand (Bolstad and Gilbert 2009). Here are some examples of this trend:

- Subject content of the curriculum is being reduced (for example, 16 year olds no longer have to know about the periodic table in science (Perks *et al.* 2006).
- Student choice is increased and they are allowed to choose what to study at an earlier age (they can now take a 'vocational' route from age 14 in England).
- Barriers between subjects are being weakened and cross-subject themes and generic criteria such as citizenship are increasingly emphasized (Whitty 2009).
- The curriculum and qualifications are broken up into small units and students are expected to put together their own curricula (Young 1998).
- Boundaries between school and non-school knowledge are blurred by introducing topical issues such as the environment and HIV/AIDS (Qualifications and Development Authority (QCDA) 2009; Royal Society for the encouragement of Arts, Manufactures and Commerce (RSA) 2006).

- Students are encouraged to draw more on their extra-school experience (QCDA 2009).
- Examination questions are expressed with less use of subject-specific concepts. One leading UK Conservative politician, Michael Gove (2009), gives examples of exam questions on nutrition in science for which it would be possible for a student to answer correctly even if they had not attended any science classes.

The common theme in these trends is the shift in responsibility for an individual's education from the teacher (and the curriculum) to the individual learner and his or her interests and choices. Individual choices by both student and teacher in the new modular curricula are constrained only by lists of generic learning outcomes, sometimes known as 'soft skills' such as 'thinking skills', 'learning to learn' and 'learning to work with others' (Muller 2009) which can be found in almost every new curriculum proposal.

However, these developments leave serious educational questions unanswered. For example, there is no evidence that such generic capabilities can be acquired, taught or assessed separately from specific domains with their specific contents and contexts. It is far from clear what educational purposes are achieved, beyond providing a general accounting mechanism, when generic criteria with no specific content replace subject-specific concepts such as 'valency' in chemistry which have a quite specific conceptual meaning. A similar point could be made about concepts in the humanities, social sciences and applied studies like finance or engineering or nursing.

Educational policy and the politics of the curriculum: A return to elitism?

Before addressing the problems that the three trends that I have outlined give rise to, and before I go on to suggest the basis for an alternative, I want to return briefly to the political charge that a critique of what I will call these 'opening' trends implies a conservative return to old forms of elitism. I will make four arguments.

Access to what?

Widening participation and improving access are aims closely associated with each of the trends I have referred to. However, as educational goals, they invariably fail to specify what the participation is to be in and what the access will be to. Educational access cannot, I would argue, unlike the right to vote or the right to a living wage, be an end in itself. The South African philosopher of education, the late Wally Morrow, sharpened the debate about access policies by introducing the useful concept of 'epistemological access' (Morrow 2009). This immediately raises the question of knowledge and 'access to what?' Unless questions about knowledge and curriculum content are raised, widening participation can lead to little more than the 'warehousing' of young people – a term used to describe how the majority of unemployed school leavers on training schemes in England in the 1980s left them with little, if any, more knowledge than they had when they began (Coffield *et al.* 1986). Morrow's concept of 'epistemological access' reminds us that the opportunities offered by educational institutions are not necessarily educational.

Education as an institution

My argument here is that education involves a pedagogic relationship between teachers and learners; it is therefore an institutional process, not an outcome or an output. Educational processes do have and indeed should have 'outcomes' for the learner and for society; however, evidence of learning outcomes that does not refer to the processes and programmes that lead to them captures only a very small element of their meaning.

People learn in a variety of different contexts; some are institutions and some are not. However, there is no such thing as non-institutional education. This is not to dismiss or undervalue informal, non-formal or experiential learning, or the learning that takes place in workplaces. What I want to emphasize is the importance of distinguishing between types of learning and between what can be learned under different conditions, and in particular the differences between the learning that is incidental to some other activity – as in homes, communities and workplaces – and the learning that is possible in specialized educational institutions such as schools, colleges and universities.

All institutions rely on traditions and past habits, and educational institutions are no exception. That is why we trust them, but that does not mean we should not criticize them or try to reform them. It does mean they have an inescapably *conservative* role which provides the basis for our trust. In the case of educational institutions such as schools, colleges and universities, part of their role is to conserve and transmit to new generations the 'powerful knowledge' (Young 2009b) that has been discovered by previous generations. Schools and other educational institutions are 'conservative' in the same sense that science and other disciplines are 'conservative'. This does not imply that the knowledge that they conserve and transmit is fixed or given – a point I will come back to. However, if educational institutions did not 'conserve' and transmit knowledge, each generation would have to reinvent it and there would be no social progress and no new knowledge would be produced. The crucial point is to distinguish between this conservative role of schools and their politically conservative role of preserving privileges and benefits for the few – a role that is a product of educational institutions being part of unequal societies; it is the latter form of conservatism that needs challenging, not the former. The relationship between these two types of conservativism – we might call them 'cultural' and 'political' – is a major but under-researched topic for the sociology of education. Few researchers up to now have clearly distinguished between them and most have concentrated almost entirely on the second or 'political' form.

The replacement of educational categories

This argument about the trend of educational policies draws on some ideas in a paper by my colleague, Stephanie Allais. She draws on the work of the economist Ben Fine and argues that the language of learning outcomes involves:

> A rewriting of education according to a very narrow economic script that is dominated by the idea of individuals (learners) making rational self-interested choices, supported by mechanisms such as quality assurance and outcomes-based qualifications which are designed to regulate the 'market in learning'.
>
> *(Allais 2009)*

Fine describes this as a form of 'economics imperialism' that is 'marked by the attempt to reduce as much as possible of non-economic activities (such as teaching and learning) to the optimizing (i.e. economic) behaviour of individuals' (Fine and Milonakis 2009). From this perspective, educational policy makers promoting the learning outcomes approach and learner choice as the 'drivers' of educational reform are in danger of replacing any specialized educational language and set of economics (for example, markets, choice and outcomes). This trend of replacing educational and political categories with those of market economics has a number of disturbing implications. For example, in the target-driven educational culture that has been introduced in the UK, students themselves are encouraged to forget that education has a distinct meaning that has little to do with ticking boxes and recording outcomes according to a prescribed list.[4] Another possibility is that, with learners having to choose between outcomes not subjects, and the disappearance of the idea that education is about promoting young people's (and adults') intellectual development, critiques illustrating how the market is encroaching on education will do little more than redescribe a world we know all too well. We are left, as it were, with having to accept, as Margaret Thatcher put it, in another context, that 'there is no other way'.

The real purpose of education

My final response to the charge that a critique of the three trends I outlined implies a conservative return to elitism is that these trends obscure the need for a debate about the purposes of education – whether school, vocational, professional or university. These purposes should be open to debate in every generation as they face new circumstances and new possibilities. Hence I restate my basis for engaging in such a debate in the following terms: 'The purpose of (formal) education is to ensure that as many as possible of each cohort or age group are able to acquire the knowledge that takes them beyond their experience and which they would be unlikely to have access to at home, at work or in the community' (slightly modified from Young 2009b). What this knowledge is and how it should be made available are, I suggest, the core questions for educational research and theory. The problem with each of the three trends which I have outlined – NQFs, learning outcomes, and the move from content-specific to generic curricular criteria – is that by reducing education to choices between outcomes, they neglect or disregard debates about the terms on which such choices are made.

Common assumptions in the three policy trends

In this section I want turn to two assumptions that the trends I have referred to have in common and explore their implications. They are:

- that a global process of *de-differentiation* of institutions, knowledge, and sites and types of learning is taking place; and
- that a language and set of concepts that are specific to education and its purposes are of decreasing importance.

The de-differentiation of institutions, knowledge and sites and types of learning

By de-differentiation I am referring to the idea that historically distinct institutions and activities are becoming more alike. It draws on a view about how modern economies are changing that can be traced back to debates in the 1980s about flexible specialization and the idea of a networked society.

One version of this argument is that industrialized countries are at a stage when they need to reverse the differentiation and specialization that was the basis for their industrial growth and development since the mid- or late nineteenth century. This change, it is argued, is partly, but not solely, a consequence of the emergence of standardizing technologies (particularly those based on electronics) that are transforming previously distinct sectors, occupations and knowledge fields.

This process of de-differentiation challenges most occupations. However, it goes right to the heart of education and the role of specialized educational institutions. Formal education as we know it is based on taken-for-granted but strongly held assumptions about the differences between types of knowledge and sites and types of learning. Most crucial is the assumption that those sites which specialize in the acquisition and production of certain types of knowledge need to be clearly distinguished from those which do not.

NQFs and learning outcome approaches exert a de-differentiating pressure that puts them at odds with this differentiation of knowledge, institutions and sites of learning. This is one of the reasons why in New Zealand, England and South Africa, universities, in particular, have resisted or found ways around such reforms. This resistance has no doubt partly been because such institutions have a long history of taking for granted their autonomy; however, it is also because the logic of an outcomes approach is to undervalue the specialized learning opportunities that they offer, and treat them as less and less distinguishable from learning outcomes that are available elsewhere. If education is defined by outcomes laid down within a national framework, why should they not be offered by any provider, as long as they sub-scribe to the quality assurance and assessment rules?

If the de-differentiation argument is accepted, then the grounds for claiming that learning opportunities must be linked to specialist teachers, programmes and institutions becomes weaker. Likewise the de-differentiation argument undermines the grounds for treating the curriculum as an opportunity to acquire specialized knowledge rather than just another response to individual or wider economic needs. The disciplines and subjects that have traditionally constituted the curricu-lum become little more than examples of how specialist teachers protect their priv-ileges. Furthermore, the logic of de-differentiation means it is no longer possible to claim objective grounds for a clear differentiation between school knowledge and the everyday or common-sense knowledge which people draw on in their lives and bring to school or college as pupils or as students.

It is these ideas, summarized by the concept de-differentiation, that I suggest underpin, albeit not explicitly, the logic of the shift to learning outcomes, the mar-ketability of outcomes and the claim that, for example, the level descriptors of a NQF can be the basis for equating aspects of someone's life experience with another person's doctoral thesis.

I am not suggesting that de-differentiation is more than a tendency. However, there are a number of problems with the claims that it makes as an account of social change. Firstly, of course, there are standardizing technologies. However, there is no evidence that developing fields of research or industry such as fuel cells, new materi-als, and bio- and nano-technologies, or new approaches to the care of those who are vulnerable or at risk, or to community banking and financial loans, are the product of standardization, or that specialization and differentiation will not continue to be the basis for the development of new knowledge. Invoking standardization is always attractive to those in power; it has brought obvious benefits in fields such as transport and it appears to increase the possibilities of making public services accountable in increasingly complex modern societies. However, the corollary is that standardization also inhibits progress and – as in extreme cases such as Stalinism – not only is it the basis of oppression but it always breaks down in the end. Knowledge progresses because it is open. The dilemma of standardization was the central problem that Weber and later Habermas addressed.

Standardizing has its place (industrial growth would have been impossible with-out it) and there is an assumption that it can be relatively seamlessly extended from industrial processes to an ever widening range of social processes. This takes new forms such as quality assurance, and the standardized sets of procedures for inform-ing appointments and bids for research funding. These processes mirror the develop-ments in the curriculum referred to earlier. Under the banner of fairness and objectivity, they represent a shift in power away from those with specialized knowl-edge to those with the procedural or generic knowledge of the rules which are embodied in standardization. Whether such developments can in practice lead either to innovation or to fairer decisions, as they claim to, rather than to more compliance and control, seems doubtful.

However, educational policy does not depend only on economic changes unless you accept the inevitability of Fine's 'economics imperialism' that I referred to earlier. As researchers, therefore, we have a responsibility to try to discover (or perhaps invent) a language and meaning for education for our time. The only alternative to current educational policies, with their focus on outcomes and learner choice, is in danger of being a conservative return to old traditions with all their elitist associations (Woodhead 2009).

Recovering the purpose of education for educational policies

Ben Fine's (2001) argument that the use of the language of economics is 'attempting to reduce education to the economic behaviour of individuals' has at least two implications. The first is that in dealing with the three educational trends that I referred to we are dealing with a form of economic ideology. Educational policy makers seem to be convinced that in introducing NQFs based on learning outcomes, they are responding to real economic changes rather than replacing educational concepts concerned with intellectual development by economic concepts concerned with optimizing choice behaviour. The challenge, then, is to take on this 'economization' of educational thinking without being idealist and neglecting the questions about market economics that were raised in different ways by Keynes and Marx. This leads me to make a sociological case for reasserting the positive educational purpose of differentiation and boundaries.

The second implication of Fine's argument is that if we reject the displacement of educational categories by economics that is expressed in the language of learning outcomes, we need to be explicit about what is distinctive about educational concepts and their logics. If we are able to do this, we have a chance of improving the intellectual capabilities of the whole population, and as the neo-institutionalists such as David Baker (2009) in the USA claim, making a real contribution to economic growth. I turn therefore, in the next section, to the origins of the three trends.

The three trends and their common origins[5]

I suggested that the trends I outlined at the beginning of this chapter can all be understood as attempts to open up the rigid, inflexible and elitist education systems that most European countries have inherited in one form or another from the nineteenth century and earlier. These systems were overwhelmingly static, because social and political imperatives were dominant and the inherent openness of knowledge was suppressed or denied. However, by the end of the nineteenth century (at least in Europe), two potentially democratizing social forces could not be avoided. They were the demand from below for the massification of schooling, and the explosion of knowledge about the social and natural worlds which challenged the traditional idea of knowledge and of the role of the curriculum as transmitting a fixed body of knowledge which students were expected to memorize. National systems dealt with these challenges in different ways and at different times. Some, like England, deferred any significant opening of access as long as possible – arguably until the second expansion of the universities in the 1990s. However, such marginal reforms could not deal with two basic problems that these societies generated:

- labour markets that could not absorb any more of the workers produced by such low performing systems of education and training; and
- mass schooling systems that were over-dependent on the culture of the middle class and a small section of the working class that was a condition for their relative success – Bourdieu's argument about the unequal distribution of cultural capital.

Mass schooling systems were divided along social class lines – to different degrees in different countries – with the curriculum as a major stratifying instrument. A key mechanism of this stratification was perceived, by those who opposed it, to be the form and content of the elite curriculum; it was overt, and strictly stipulated and paced. Its boundedness was seen to be the main problem, so it was the removal of the more overt of these boundaries that became a preferred solution for reformers. The 1990s phase of this process, which initiated the type of 'opening out' proposals I outlined, was probably led by the Delors report (1996), which introduced the idea of lifelong learning. It is the idea of a boundary-free, supposedly undifferentiated future, that underpins NQFs, and the shift to learning outcomes and the collapse of the school/non-school knowledge distinction as the basis for the curriculum.

It is impossible to deny that these trends are gaining ground in Europe and beyond, nor that they have powerful support from the characteristically unrealistic assumptions about the educational potential of digital technologies that are widely shared within the policy communities. The weakness that is common to all of them is that they misconceive and misrepresent educational boundaries as necessarily and only barriers to learning, access and participation. This misconception applies to boundaries between subjects; to those between the curriculum and the everyday experience of learners; between theory and practice; and, most fundamentally, between knowledge and experience. The counter-argument, traceable back to Emile Durkheim writing before World War I (Durkheim 1983), is that these boundaries are social, they have a history and were developed for particular purposes. However, they express real purposes and in that sense they are not arbitrary: they constrain what decisions we can make about the curriculum. This is not the place to go into the theoretical argument by the English sociologist Basil Bernstein which extended Durkheim's original ideas (Bernstein 2000; Young 2007a). Suffice to say, attempts to dissolve boundaries invariably create confusion for learners (witness the problems facing students on modular programmes). At the same time, the boundaries remain but become less visible in ways that are exaggerated for the most disadvantaged. In other words, against their best intents, the 'opening up' policies are likely to render the contours of knowledge less visible to the very learners that the more open curriculum hopes to favour – this is the argument made by Basil Bernstein with his concepts of visible and invisible pedagogies in the 1970s

(Bernstein 1975). Furthermore, these 'opening up' policies are unlikely to be taken up by the elite and private institutions, with greater inequality an almost inevitable consequence. In the English case, the elite fee-paying 'public' schools are already dropping public sector exams in favour of the 'more demanding' Cambridge Pre-U (for 18 year olds) and an examination based on the old, more subject-content-based Ordinary level certificate for 16 year olds that was abolished for state schools over 20 years ago. Different groups support the trends I have described, although they often have very little in common politically or educationally. As examples, there are the neo-liberals who are obsessed with promoting markets and individual choice, the radical social constructivists who hope that learning outcomes will free learners from authoritarian syllabuses and curricula, the supporters of generic criteria as the basis for a more unified system and a framework for integrating academic and voca-tional pathways (Yates and Collins 2010) and promoting equity; lastly, of course, there are the pragmatists who make the best, like most teachers, of what is current. However, they all share some underlying epistemological similarities. All end up with an instrumental and 'over-socialized' view of knowledge with its inevitable relativist consequences and a view of the curriculum as, at least to some degree, a tool for achieving particular political or economic purposes.

Towards a social realist alternative

The alternative I want to briefly outline arises from the previous analysis and draws on ideas in the sociology of knowledge that I have been working on with col-leagues, Johan Muller (Chapter 5) and Rob Moore (Moore 2004). The alternative is based on the assumption that there are specific kinds of social conditions under which powerful knowledge is acquired and produced and these are the conditions for real learning and, in the terms I used earlier, for 'epistemic access'. These condi-tions are not given; like the boundaries I referred to earlier, they are historical but they have a reality beyond individual perception and specific contexts. Their histo-ricity is denied by traditional elitist systems which are left with a false objectivity based on the givenness of knowledge. The 'opening out' trends for reducing cur-riculum content, basing the curriculum on learning outcomes, and giving priority to individual learners rather than the knowledge they are trying to acquire, deny both the historicity and objectivity of knowledge domains and specialist and increasingly global knowledge communities that are their social basis.

This alternative starting point for curriculum policy leaves us with a number of important questions which the trends I have discussed avoid. I will mention three:

1   How do we identify the most reliable criteria for making judgements about the selection, pacing and organization of knowledge in the curriculum? This takes us to two issues:

   (i)   How are links established (or in some cases re-established) between university-based disciplinary specialists and their school-based colleagues?

These links were crucial to the beginnings of the expansion of upper secondary education, but have been significantly weakened in the course of 'massification'.

(ii) How are subject-specific pedagogies developed in an era where generic concepts of pedagogy dominate educational studies?

2   Why do some forms of knowledge, most notably the natural sciences, tend towards specialization and others, characteristically the humanities, tend towards variation or diversification? And how do we conceptualize those forms of knowledge in the middle ground – the social sciences? Should the latter follow the sciences and economics in making their knowledge claims more robust and mathematically based or should they recognize that the phenomena they study require distinct forms of rigour which are not undermined by the reality that the potential for their knowledge to progress is limited? And what are the implications of these differences for the curriculum? Whereas the first tendency poses questions about sequencing, pacing and hierarchy, the latter poses questions of choice and its basis, of what to include in the curriculum, and when and on what basis.

3   Many programmes in upper secondary and higher education have a vocational or professional focus directed to different occupational sectors. This means that curricula inevitably point both to the demands of the occupational sector as well as the intellectual development of the learner. This raises the question hardly acknowledged by those involved in the design and development of professional and vocational programmes of how to balance and bring together the conceptual coherence which is the basis of intellectual development and the contextual coherence that relates to demands of any occupation or sector (Muller 2009).

The elite curriculum, developed at a time when knowledge changed very slowly, was content-driven and largely fixed. In its worst pedagogical forms, it was dominated by memorization and rote-learning. Consequently, the main alternative to the elite curriculum, as represented by the three 'opening' trends I outlined at the beginning of this chapter, was to take a stance against 'mere' content and 'mere' rote by stressing generic skills and the active role of the learner. In its most radical forms (Jessup 1991) such an 'over-socialized' view of knowledge opposes all stipulation of content and all forms of memorization as examples of pedagogic dictatorship. The logic of such a radicalism and its eschewal of content, either by reducing it or by leaving individual teachers free to decide and learners to choose, is to deny learners what I referred to earlier in this chapter as 'epistemic access'.

The eight generic competences agreed by the European Parliament[6] are an example of the swing away from content-based priorities, and the way in which concepts which depend on specific contents can get marginalized. Learner progression is a conceptual process and can only be stipulated in conceptual terms. It follows that concept-based stipulations cannot be generic; they necessarily involve content or what is being conceptualized.

Not surprisingly, defenders of learning outcomes and generic approaches to the curriculum would no doubt claim that this is no more than a new way of justifying the old content-based elite curriculum. However, the approach taken here makes a clear distinction between a content-based curriculum which treats knowledge as given and one which recognizes that knowledge changes and treats contents as carriers of concepts, not ends in themselves. Graduates may not remember or use much of their school or university curriculum in later life; however, it is through those contents they gain access to concepts and to ways of thinking that they are able to draw on as adults.

A reliable model for a curriculum and a pedagogy of the future has to embrace content, concepts and skills. Furthermore, it has to begin with the acquisition of specialized knowledge; generic competences can be no more than broad guidelines to teachers and curriculum developers. Such a model will apply in different ways to a general (or school) curriculum and to a vocational or professional curriculum and the different sectors, and in some cases the different ages of the learners they are concerned with. If the curriculum is too driven by content (as in the old elitist model), or skills and competences (as in the new generic models), some important educational goals (such as opportunities for progression) will get lost; in each case there will be implications for the distribution of educational opportunities and achievement.

Recognizing the differentiation of knowledge both between domains and between the curriculum and experience as a basic educational principle implies that concepts, skills and content are all important and must be stipulated in any curriculum. How this principle is applied will depend on the purposes of specific programmes and the prior experience of the learners. Failure to recognize this principle of differentiation will lead to a slowing down of any progress that has so far been made towards equalizing epistemological access. This has implications for both social justice and the possibility of a knowledge-based economy in the future.

Notes

1 As a European Commission document puts it, 'The concept of learning outcomes … is potentially revolutionary in its implications. It can help to define training standards and related curricula in a way that serves best the needs of both the learner and the labour market, provided that employers are involved in defining, designing, certifying and recognizing learning outcomes. It can help to develop a common language: instead of classifying jobs by occupational type and knowledge by education programme (as has been the case so far) we can now move toward describing both in terms of competence' (European Commission 2009).
2 In 2012 the figure was 130 (Young and Allais 2013).
3 The evidence, such as it stands, suggests that it is partnerships between educational institutions and between educational institutions and employers, not qualifications frameworks that are most crucial for achieving transferability and progression (Young 2009a).
4 Look at the CEDEFOP report, *The Shift to Learning Outcomes*, or look at an assessment portfolio for an outcomes-based qualification for work-based learning like the one of the UK's National Vocational Qualifications.
5 The final sections of this chapter draw on some ideas discussed in Chapter 5.

6 These are listed as the recommendations of the European Parliament on 18 December 2006 as follows:

- digital competence
- learning to learn
- social and civic competences
- communication in the mother tongue
- communication in foreign languages
- cultural awareness and expression
- mathematical competence and basic competences in science and technology
- social and civic competences.

(http://europa.eu/legislation_summaries/education_training_youth/lifelong_learning/c11090_en.htm)
Few would disagree with the list as a broad set of educational principles or priorities. The problem is that as curriculum principles, they do not specify the concepts that might give learners access to the concepts that the list implies.

5

THREE EDUCATIONAL SCENARIOS FOR THE FUTURE

Lessons from the sociology of knowledge

Introduction

This chapter is concerned with 'possible educational futures' not as a futuristic or predictive exercise but through an analysis of current trends in educational policy (Young 2009a). However 'futures thinking' has not been a major strand of research and theory in the sociology of education or in educational studies generally. As a result, it has been largely left to educationalists who give little explicit attention either to sociological debates about current social changes that are often masked by terms like globalization and knowledge societies, or with how the question of knowledge is understood in these debates (Young 2009b; Muller 2009). The typical approach of such thinking is to identify what is seen as the increasing mismatch between the schools and some of the global changes in the wider society. They tend to be concerned with how the formal education system and schools, in particular, almost systematically resist such changes. Furthermore, the assumptions of such 'future thinking' tend to be that certain wider social changes are not only inevitable but of positive benefit to humanity and that schooling in the future will have to follow them. This 'following' is invariably viewed as unproblematic.

The future of schooling in these scenarios is one of throwing off what is seen as its medieval past and adapting to global trends towards greater flexibility and openness to change from individuals; as a consequence it is predicted that schooling will become less and less differentiated from other social institutions. The following two not untypical, but in many ways very different examples of this kind of 'future thinking' will illustrate this point. The first is by Peter Mortimore, the former Director of the Institute of Education. In a *Guardian* column, he wrote:

> Many changes are affecting western societies. New citizens are importing different cultural and religious traditions, families are taking on different

configurations, work hours are becoming more varied and the internet is taking over our shopping, entertainment and information-gathering activities … People have become more conscious of individual rights, but are less deferential to those in authority.

Yet English schools … are slow to change … all but the most confident of head teachers are inhibited from experimenting with new approaches.

Many aspects of schooling have changed … the abolition of corporal punishment and the introduction of a national curriculum … But should there be more fundamental changes in how pupils are educated in order to *better match* [emphasis added] the way people live today? Should issues such as the sustainability of the environment and the dangers of obesity, drugs and Aids and, in the light of current events, financial education be given more prominence?

(Mortimore 2008)

Our second more overtly academic example is a paper by the distinguished sociolinguist, Gunther Kress (2008). Kress argues that global social changes are calling into question the appropriateness of:

- our dominant myths about education that are derived from an already quite distant past; and
- our assumptions about the homogeneity of the audience for education and about the ontological/epistemological security of 'knowledge'.

The school is increasingly left, Kress argues, 'without its legitimating purposes'. It is faced with:

an emblematic shift in the emphasis of educational rhetoric from teaching to learning … No institution [any longer] regulates *what is to be learned* … *no clear curriculum exists* … and knowledge is made by learners in relation to their needs, as tools to solve problems encountered by them in their lifeworlds.

(Kress 2008)

Kress goes on to claim that:

a significant proportion of the young are alienated from school – they no longer judge school to be of relevance to … the world as they experience it. … What the school actually offers is … no longer of interest to these young people. … the responsibility (for the transition from school to work) now falls on the young themselves.

(Kress 2008)

Mortimore is pointing to a greater emphasis, in a possible 'curriculum of the future' on 'relevant' and contemporary themes. His argument is not unlike that of the Qualifications and Curriculum Authority (QCA) in its new curriculum proposals which shift the balance in school science from subject content to what might be relevant and have personal meaning for pupils. However, neither the QCA nor Mortimore tell us how such themes might be addressed by teachers in ways that go beyond a sharing of opinions on issues such as the HIV/AIDS epidemic that involve complex bodies of specialist knowledge in fields such as micro-biology.

Kress tells us that the future is here today and that it is largely educationalists, unlike young people, who are too blinded by tradition to see it. Whether his future in which schools adapt and respond to the 'demands' of the next generation will really empower and enthuse them is another question.

In this chapter we will draw on some ideas in the sociology of knowledge to tell a rather different story about schooling and its possible futures in an increasingly global society. We shall argue that a focus on the conservative nature of educational institutions, their resistance to change, and their perpetuation of anachronistic forms of authority and archaic curriculum priorities that bear little relation to the demands of the contemporary world, is very limited as a basis for 'future thinking'. First, it fails to distinguish between the inherently 'conservative' role of schools as institutions involved in the 'transmission of knowledge' from one generation to another and 'conservatism' as a tendency of all institutions to resist change and preserve the privileges of more powerful groups. We need to distinguish between these two forms of conservatism if we are to envisage how schools will continue to transmit knowledge (and values) from one generation to another in the fast changing societies of today. Second, a focus on changes in the wider society, and how schools should adapt to them plays down the extent to which, if schools are agencies of cultural transmission, they will have a logic of their own which may go against the immediate demands of young people even it is in their long-term interests.

Education and the sociology of knowledge

Research in the sociology of knowledge has had a significant if controversial influence on debates about education in the UK and elsewhere, at least since the early 1970s. Although this influence can be traced back to the appointment of Karl Mannheim to the Chair in Sociology of Education at the Institute of Education in 1946, it was not until the 1970s that sociological ideas about knowledge began to be taken seriously within educational studies. Furthermore, it has only been in the last decades that a distinctive social realist research tradition — the theme of this review — began to emerge in the UK (Moore 2004; Young 2007a), in South Africa (Muller 2000; Gamble 2006), in Australia (Wheelahan 2007), and in a number of Latin American and other European countries such as Portugal and Greece. The major resource for this work has been the ideas/theories of the English sociologist, Basil Bernstein, who died in 2001, and the inspiration that he found in the ideas of the French sociologist Émile Durkheim writing a century ago. However, this emerging tradition in the sociology of education has also drawn on a number of wider developments in (i) sociological theory (Collins 2000; Bourdieu 2004), (ii) the sociology of science (Collins and Evans 2007), (iii) philosophy (Norris 2006;

Bachelard (see Tiles 1984)) and (iv) linguistics (the Sydney Systemic Functional Linguistics Group who explicitly tie the notion of knowledge to the wellsprings of language (Christie and Martin 2007)).

This chapter begins by locating the intellectual origins of a specifically *realist* sociology of knowledge in the early twentieth-century work of Émile Durkheim (1983). However we will suggest that its emergence as a strand of research within the sociology of education in the last decades has been as much a critical response to other developments in the broad field of educational research and in educational policy as a rediscovery of a social realist tradition in mainstream sociology. These developments in social and educational research include:

- social constructivist/post-modernist views of knowledge and truth that are found in much sociology of education as well as more broadly across the humanities and social sciences (Kronman 2007); and
- socio-cultural theories of learning that have, implicitly and sometimes explicitly, dominated educational research in a range of fields such as science education, work-based learning and diversity studies.

These theoretical developments have been paralleled by a number of policy developments that have their roots in the new neo-liberal politics and its celebration of markets. Examples include:

- the increasingly 'instrumental' focus of educational policy which conceptually, albeit not politically, has many affinities with the list above. For example, it is increasingly difficult to make a public case for education for its own sake, i.e. 'to promote young people's intellectual development'; and
- the uncritical enthusiasm of research funders and policy makers for the educational potential of digital technologies and the challenge that this poses for the role of specialist educational institutions and the role of teachers (Keen 2007; Sharples *et al.* 2007).

The distinctive implications of the ideas discussed in this chapter follow from their recognition of (a) the *necessary objectivity* of knowledge as a condition for any kind of enquiry or reliable prediction about the future and (b) that knowledge is *emergent from* and *not reducible* to the contexts in which it is produced and acquired. At the same time a social realist approach implies an explicitly historical approach to thinking about future trends. Without such a historical approach to knowledge, predictions are likely to be little more than extrapolations from the present as if the present itself had no history.

The dilemma posed by a recognition that knowledge is both 'objective' and historical is not new and takes us back at least to Hegel. It is a dilemma that lay at the heart of the sociology of knowledge that was established a century ago by Durkheim, Weber and Mannheim and has been continued more recently by Habermas, Randall Collins and others.

We argue that it is important to distinguish what we refer to as 'social realist' theories of knowledge from the two approaches that have set the terms for most debates about knowledge in the social sciences and in philosophy. The first of these approaches – symbolized perhaps by logical positivism and its empiricist parallels in the social sciences – can be described as invoking an asocial or *'under-socialized'* epistemology that defines knowledge as sets of verifiable propositions and the methods for testing them. It treats their *social* production in particular historical contexts and within the boundaries of particular disciplines as implicit or taken for granted. The second approach, which arose in direct response to the first – what we here refer to as *'over-socialized'* – plays down the propositional character of knowledge and reduces questions of epistemology to 'who knows?' and to the identification of knowers and their practices. In contrast, a *social realist* theory sees knowledge as involving sets of systematically related concepts and methods for their empirical exploration *and* the increasingly specialized and historically located 'communities of enquirers' (an idea first expressed by the American philosopher Charles S. Peirce) with their distinctive commitment to the search for truth and the social institutions in which they are located.

A social realist approach to knowledge and its educational implications

The emergent, non-reducible and socially differentiated character of knowledge has, we suggest, potentially profound educational implications. Examples of such implications, which deserve a paper in themselves, and which we can only list here, include the importance of:

- the distinction between curricula and pedagogy;
- the 'non-arbitrariness' of boundaries between knowledge domains and between school and non-school knowledge;
- the 'objective' basis of the authority and professionalism of teachers and other experts;
- the inescapably hierarchical nature of pedagogy;
- the conditions for and definitions of creativity and innovation;
- the epistemological constraints on the scope of policies for widening participation and promoting social inclusion;
- the limitations of 'generic skills' as a model for 'general education'; and
- the crucial importance of 'subject-specific content' and the importance of distinguishing between 'subject content' – as the relatively stable component of subject knowledge – and 'information' (such as what is available on the internet) which is never stable and always changing.

Running through all these themes is an emphasis on the irreducible *differentiatedness* of knowledge. Knowledge is structured, in part independently of how we acquire it, and knowledge fields differ in their internal coherence, their principles of cohesion, and their procedures for producing new knowledge. These internal differences are mirrored in the different forms of social relation between the actors that practise in the institutions of those fields: knowledge relations and social relations vary in tandem.

The distinction between the 'structural' and 'social' conservatism of education institutions referred to earlier is important in identifying the epistemological 'constraints' on curriculum design. Social realism views the former as a condition for progress and innovation and the acquisition of knowledge. However, it is easily confused, especially by those seeing themselves as educational radicals, with the 'social conservatism' of educational institutions which preserves the power and privileges of particular groups. Gramsci's well-known critique of the Gentile reforms of Italian education in the 1920s makes this distinction clearly. He defended the structural conservatism of the old curriculum against the 'progressive' changes proposed by Gentile which would exclude subordinate classes from access to knowledge via spurious forms of 'vocationalism' (Entwhistle 1979).

The second distinction that we want to make is between the two meanings of the idea of education as 'cultural transmission'. In everyday language, transmission refers to 'passing on' – of a signal, a message or a disease. Education also involves a 'passing on', of knowledge, or more broadly, a culture. However, whereas the everyday meaning of the transmission of a signal is a one-way movement in which the receiver is the passive recipient, the cultural or knowledge transmission that is associated with education is a much more complex process that involves the active role of the 'recipient' in making the knowledge his/her own. The research literature mistakenly polarizes these two meanings of transmission. An example is Anna Sfard's well-known and in many ways perceptive essay on theories of learning (1998). Her analysis leaves the polarity unresolved because she treats learning as a generic process separable from 'what is learned'. In contrast, we would argue that 'learning' always implies 'learning something'; there is a parallel here with Alastair MacIntyre's (2002) argument that teaching as a generic concept is empty – we always 'teach something'. It follows that learning necessarily involves cultural transmission or the transmission of knowledge. The transmission of culture, increasingly but not exclusively through educational institutions, from generation to generation, is what distinguishes human from animal 'societies', and enables them to reproduce and progress. Cultural transmission is always reproductive but potentially, although not necessarily, progressive.

We argue that a social realist approach which gives priority to the knowledge that is (or is not) being transmitted, while at odds with much contemporary educational thinking which focuses largely on the learner and his/her experience, provides a more reliable basis for identifying underlying trends and imagining possible futures or, in Eric Olin Wright's evocative phrase, 'real utopias'.

By emphasizing the *social differentiation* of both knowledge and institutions, social realist approaches challenge the widely shared assumption that boundaries are always barriers to be overcome rather than also conditions for innovation and the production and acquisition of new knowledge. As Bernstein (2000) argues, boundaries play an important role in creating learner identities and are thus the conditions for acquiring 'powerful knowledge' as well as barriers to learning. It follows that:

- the global future of education is not necessarily one of greater flexibility, portability, and transparency;
- it will continue to be important to *differentiate* learning in schools, colleges and universities from learning in homes, workplaces and communities; experience itself cannot be the sole or primary basis for the curriculum; and
- as learners cannot actually 'construct' their own learning (because, in Foucault's pithy phrase, they can't know what they don't know), the role of teachers cannot be reduced to that of guide and facilitator rather than as a source of strategies and expertise.

Three scenarios for the future

The role of boundaries and the social differentiation of knowledge are the key principles which we draw from the sociology of knowledge in identifying possible future scenarios. Bearing these assumptions in mind the next section explores three possible future scenarios for the next 20 to 30 years.

The three futures (or scenarios for the future)

Future 1 – Boundaries are given and fixed – the 'Future' is associated with a naturalized or 'under-socialized' concept of knowledge;

Future 2 – The end of boundaries – the 'Future' is associated with an 'over-socialized' concept of knowledge;

Future 3 – Boundary maintenance as prior to boundary crossing. It follows that it is the variable relation between the two that is the condition for the creation and acquisition of new knowledge.

Future 1 – Boundaries as given and fixed – a naturalized or under-socialized concept of knowledge

Every mass education system has its primary but not its only origins in an elite system;[1] that is, a system for transmitting elite cultural knowledge to the 'select few', sometimes the 'elect', who are most usually the offspring of the dominant classes. Such systems involve induction into the dominant knowledge traditions that keep them dominant. These traditions are overwhelmingly static, because their boundaries are fixed by social imperatives that override the conditions for knowledge and its innate dynamism, fecundity and openness to change. They are socially conservative in this dual static sense. By the end of the nineteenth century (at least in Europe), three democratizing social forces bore down on this elite template. The first was the generalized demand from below for access to schooling – the demand for it to massify. The second was the explosion of knowledge about the social and natural worlds. This explosion of 'powerful knowledge' challenged the traditional idea of the curriculum as 'knowledge of the powerful', and gradually but steadily eclipsed the outmoded canons of the old elite system. Much later the knowledge priorities of social movements, both feminist and post-colonial were incorporated. Elite educational systems found in every country had to deal with this triple challenge. Future 1 represents attempts to continue the elite system whilst opening access to broader social forces as marginally as possible.

At some point, expanding elite systems meet a number of inbuilt limits with which they have to contend. These limits include:

- the inability of labour markets to absorb any more workers trained in the same conservative mould; and
- the limits of a mass schooling system to induct all children with equal success into elite knowledge traditions that require the middle-class home as a critical adjunct and condition for that success.

To widely varying degrees all mass schooling systems have failed to overcome these limits and failed to 'compensate' for the unequal distribution of conditions for success that they give rise to.

The default position to deal with this ongoing scandal has been one or other type of tracked or streamed system which preserves the elite track for the elite and a trickle for the mass. For the rest, one or more kinds of vocational track is provided, that in their worst forms represent 'dumbed down' versions of elite knowledge – mathematical literacy, communications or 'popular science' for example (Young 2007a; Wheelahan 2007). This so-called 'vocational' curriculum becomes proceduralized, increasingly so with technology. Lauder's (2008) 'digital Fordism' shows that this proceduralism is not limited to the disadvantaged – and access to 'powerful knowledge' is blocked for the mass. The result is a system overtly stratified along social class lines, with schooling as its principal instrument. Its destiny is to be perpetually seen as unfair, and hence resisted. In this sense, Future 1 is a recipe for social divisiveness, inequality, unhappiness, and conflict. The mechanism producing the injustice is perceived, by those who oppose it, to be the form of the elite curriculum – overt, strictly stipulated and paced. Its boundedness is seen to be the main problem and the condition for greater social justice and less inequality, at least as far as the Future 2-ists are concerned, is the removal of these boundaries.

In the Future 1 scenario there are few new sources of innovation within the education system. Education and the wider context will continue to exist as two parallel worlds. We can however predict increased differentiation based on locality and the conservatism of traditional cultures, increasing divisions between north and south, and, for example, between different fundamentalist traditions. Treating boundaries as given, not social, becomes in this scenario a basis for maintaining and legitimizing existing power relations and restricting sources of debate. There are of course no pure forms of Future 1 even in autocracies; however it would be a mistake to think that Future 1 has no future. Many elements of Future 1 linger in the English system, for example (Fitz, Davies and Evans 2006) and it is probable that they will linger on well into the future. The worst case consequence of this scenario is expressed most stridently and evocatively in Samuel Huntington's *Clash of Civilizations* (1998) and more colloquially in George Bush's 'War on Terror'.

Future 2 – the end of boundaries – an 'over-socialized' concept of knowledge

As we have already indicated, Future 2 is born in 'progressive' opposition to Future 1. It envisages a steady weakening of boundaries, a de-differentiation of knowledge and institutions, a blurring of labour market sectors, and a greater emphasis on generic outcomes rather than inputs as instruments of equalization and accountability. Elements of the ideals of Future 2 can be seen in the scenarios suggested by Mortimore and Kress which we referred to at the beginning of this review.[2]

To the extent to which such learner-directed trends, coupled with the wider introduction of digital technologies, are endorsed, we shall see a de-professionalization of teaching at all levels and the de-specialization of research. It is a trend that will meet resistance from the forces underpinning Future 1, but it is a trend everywhere gaining ground in Europe and beyond.

The curricular 'instrument of choice' for those seeking to pursue boundary weakening and de-differentiation is, using the term in its broadest sense, modularization. Among the expressions of this boundary weakening, various combinations of the following are likely to be found:

- *the 'integration' of school subjects* – as boundaries between subjects and between school knowledge and everyday knowledge are weakened;
- *the stipulation of curricular content in generic, usually skill or outcome terms* – also as a consequence of boundaries between subjects and knowledge fields being weakened;
- *the promotion of formative over summative assessment* – as boundaries between the achievement scores of different learners are weakened;
- *the introduction of unified national qualification frameworks* – as the boundaries between different (especially academic and vocational) qualifications are weakened; and
- the promotion of facilitative rather than directive teaching – as the boundaries between experts and neophyte learners are weakened.

Our position, as we stated above, is that educational boundaries are social but also *real*; that is, they cannot be dissolved, at least in the short term, without serious consequences for most if not all learners. What such de-differentiating mechanisms are most likely to achieve is not to dissolve the boundaries, but to render them invisible – an invisibility that is exaggerated for the more disadvantaged. That is to say, against their best intents, the main effects of Future 2-ists – those endorsing progressive pedagogy and its variants – is to render the contours of knowledge and learning invisible to the very learners that the pedagogy was designed to favour – namely the learners, invariably but not always those from low income homes, who fall behind their peers. Where Future 1 produces stratification and resistance, Future 2 also produces stratification; however, this time it is of a covert kind, because the overt targets associated with Future 1 are now submerged, and the unfortunate learners who stumble – for stumble they do – cannot see what it is, this time, that causes them to stumble. This too causes disaffection, a disaffection that, together with more specifically material factors, lies at the root of much of the youth apathy described so well by Gunther Kress, as well as its more destructive cultural forms, such as self and other-directed violence. In other words, whereas the overt stratification of Future 1 leads, at least optimally, to opposition and the 'voice' of the excluded, the covert stratification of Future 2 leads increasingly to a variety of individualized 'exit' strategies that feed a disintegrating public culture. The proponents of Future 2 find themselves unwittingly becoming the legitimizers of this trend in their denial of the special worth of expert knowledge, in their at least implied validation of all cultural forms as equal[3] and in their uncritical celebration of experiential forms of knowing.

The 'end of boundaries' scenario of Future 2 is unlikely to lead to access to specialist knowledge disappearing in the elite and private sectors and institutions. What is more likely is that that public education will replace unequal access to knowledge by increasing access to qualifications leading to credential inflation as qualifications are competed for but have less and less worth – either as use value or exchange value.

A critical exploration of the role of boundaries in the production and acquisition of new knowledge enables us to argue that, despite clear political differences between neo-liberals, who are obsessed with promoting markets and individual choice at any price, and the radical social constructivists, who want to free learners from what they see as the authoritarianism of expertise, they share an underlying epistemological similarity. Both end up with an instrumental view of knowledge with its inevitable relativist consequences. Future 1 and Future 2 are in this sense epistemological mirror twins: they may differ in their proclaimed rhetorics, their means and desired goals, but their end result is, uncannily, the same.

Future 3 – Boundary maintaining and boundary crossing as conditions for the creation and acquisition of new knowledge in the emerging global context

Future 3 arises out of the critique and analysis we have made of Futures 1 and 2. It will in a sense be a demonstration of what a social realist theory of knowledge can offer and why it is needed if our alternatives for the future are to have any degree of reliability. Future 3 is based on the assumption that there are specific kinds of social conditions under which powerful knowledge is acquired and produced. These conditions are not given; they are historical but also objective. Whereas their historicity is denied in Future 1 – boundaries are given and taken for granted, the historicity and objectivity that is embodied in the critical role of specialist communities is denied in Future 2. At best Future 2 offers an increasingly boundary-less and fragmented global de-differentiation, together with a naïve optimism about the potential of new 'bottom up' social movements and epistemologies located in a metaphorical 'South' (Hardt and Negri 2000; de Sousa Santos 2001, 2008). In contrast, Future 3 emphasizes the continuing role of boundaries, not as given entities, whether in the brain (neuro-science), in the mind (ahistorical rationalism) or in the world of human practice (pragmatism and dialectical materialism), but in defining domain-specific as increasingly global specialist communities as a basis both for the acquisition and production of new knowledge and human progress more generally. The contemporary British philosopher Christopher Norris expresses this scenario, following Habermas, as the 'unfinished project of modernity'. We find it, albeit expressed in different ways, in the theories of both Max Weber and Émile Durkheim writing over a century ago.

The last section of this chapter explores a number of the features of Future 3, their implications and how they may change. We shall consider, although our list makes no claim to be comprehensive, the following:

- boundaries and their types – in relation to both knowledge and institutions and their interdependence with particular reference to the case of disciplines and their future;
- knowledge as real (powerful knowledge) and the social as real (knowledge of the powerful) and how the two ideas might be held together;
- preferred curriculum and pedagogic models; and
- implications for educational inequalities.

Boundaries and their types – the future of disciplines

The most critical point about knowledge in the next 50 years is to understand why some forms of knowledge tend towards specialization and others towards variation or diversification. These different tendencies in the development of knowledge have critical implications for the curriculum and education more generally. The first tendency poses questions about sequence, pace, and hierarchical organization, whereas the latter poses questions predominantly of choice, of what to include in the curriculum and, at its extremes, of the absence of any objective criteria at all. The intimate link between knowledge form and curriculum organization is what a social realist approach to the curriculum seeks to elucidate.

It has become fashionable to proclaim the end of disciplinarity (Gibbons *et al.* 1994; Nowotny *et al.* 2001), but disciplines seem almost obstinately to linger on. They do, it is true, morph and adapt, as do all robust social forms, but reports of their end are much exaggerated. This does not mean that new disciplinary formations do not periodically appear. They do. However new formations invariably arise from existing disciplines, first in the form of 'regions'(Bernstein 2000) or groupings of existing disciplines around new problems; only later do they form into discrete identifiable formations, with their own stable communities. The reason for this is that, as we said earlier, knowledge boundaries are not arbitrary, and the internal forms they foster and the social relations that sustain them shake down over time into stable socio-epistemic forms. These forms are determined by the strength of the boundary appropriate to each form, and consequently, by how each form of knowledge develops or grows.

Disciplines differ, first, by their form of conceptual advance; and second, by their form of objectivity. As to the first, some disciplines tend towards robust, conceptually justifiable advances. Their knowledge structure is determined by their ever-advancing conceptual spine which tends towards unity (which does not mean that there is only one conceptual spine in the discipline). The curriculum implications of this type of conceptual advance is that these disciplines in their mature form develop long 'hierarchies of abstraction' which are best learnt in sequence under the guidance of specialists (mathematics and science are the most obvious examples). We may say that these disciplines are, in a specific sense, concept-rich. It is not that they necessarily involve large numbers of concepts (the number of concepts does not distinguish them from a wide range of disciplines). It is that that they have long sequences of hierarchically-related concepts. Getting stuck at any rung of the hierarchy usually means that conceptual learning stops. Other disciplines tend towards advance through variation or diversification of concepts; this, however, is less about concepts than it is about different contents or content-clusters, although there is usually a macro-conceptual organizing principle (the 'past' (or more abstractly time) for history and 'space' for geography, for example) involved. Still others develop practically, by developing new skills and ways of doing things. Practical development may refer to new practices within traditional manual crafts like cabinet making or to new forms of conceptual practice such as software development or website design. Concepts, content, and skills are embedded in each discipline, but their relative salience is what differentiates them.

All disciplines, in order to be disciplines, have objects of study, and in order to be robust and stable, display objectivity – that is to say, they possess legitimate, shared and stably reliable means for generating truth (Chapter 2). Truth is, by this account, a stable partnership between the objects of study and an informed community of practitioners. Disciplines, however, display differing albeit equivalent kinds of objectivity, depending on whether their object is natural or social.[4] The more social the object, the greater is the limit on the object being subsumed by the concepts of the discipline. Each form of objectivity nevertheless has to meet the same criteria of analytical adequacy – the simplest, maximum degree of subsumption by the disciplinary concept without distortion of the particular object.

The reason for rescuing a strong notion of objectivity from the Future 2-ists is so as to re-instate a strong and trustworthy notion of expertise (Collins and Evans 2007). The erosion of expertise and the loss of trust in specialist knowledge has been an inadvertent consequence of the relativism of boundary-less thinking (Muller 2000). Trust in strong knowledge and in the judgements of specialist knowers has been hollowed out by common sense scepticism. Amongst adults in Europe, at least those born post World War II, this has led to a peculiar form of self-deception – we deride specialized knowledge and knowers even as our lives are ever more dependent upon them. For example, we live in ever-more medicalized worlds even as medical litigation rates grow exponentially.

The youth of our society have not yet evolved the protective strategies of self-deception; many inherit a social derision towards strong knowledge from their parents and the media; as a consequence they fail at school for lack of trying hard enough to master something they perceive as meriting such widespread diminishment (Menand 1995). Even as specialist knowledge grows apace at the cutting edge borders, the English education system may finally be failing to produce enough highly specialized practitioners of the future because the young have inherited the popular wisdom that the prize is not worth the effort. This underwrites too the swing to instrumentalism. If knowledge is not valued in its own right, then its social worth can only be measured by its usefulness. It is sobering to reflect that this corrosive popular wisdom is wholly absent in the emerging economies of South Korea, China and India. Silicon Valley in California could not have happened without a majority of engineers recruited from the East. Another such leap forward will almost certainly emerge in the East rather than the West if Future 2 prevails. Thus decisions about the 'curriculum of the future' will have lasting long-term effects.

Preferred forms of curriculum and pedagogy

To say that we live in a knowledge economy has two principal implications for schooling: the first is that the economy and the society that supports it places a premium on advances in knowledge, though paradoxically not necessarily on its reproduction, as we have shown above. This means that in a time of accelerated knowledge development, specialization and variation (or diversification) become the dominant social codes, and the curriculum comes under increasingly frequent pressure to constantly adapt. This is less apparent in the university curriculum because their communities of practitioners live close to the nexuses of advances in knowledge – indeed, they are driving them. What it does mean, and where this becomes visible, is that this marks a new distinction between those higher institutions that are driving advances in knowledge and those that are not. This hierarchy is currently very crudely marked by global rankings, and far more sophisticated examples are certain to be developed in due course. There is no doubt that the economies and societies of the future will continue to require robust signalling mechanisms for ranking the productivity of knowledge producers. The second implication is that, even in those disciplines where concepts have traditionally taken a back seat – like history, for example – advances will increasingly be conceptually driven. This does not mean that new historiographical approaches will be plucked from the air, rather that new digital technologies will allow forms of investigation that produce facts not previously able to be brought to light and require new conceptual advances. The MRI scans that are driving new advances in neurology are an example. There are parallels in demography, the Large Hadron Collider in physics and in nano-technology across a range of biological sciences.

These developments have some specific implications for the curriculum and for pedagogy. The elite curriculum, developed at a time when knowledge changed very slowly, was content-driven, and in its worst pedagogical form, was memorization and rote-learning driven. Consequently, the main alternative to the elite curriculum, which finds its most sophisticated expression in Future 2 thinking, has taken a stance against 'mere' content and 'mere' rote – and in its radical forms against all stipulation of content and all forms of rote learning or memorization. This opposition finds expression in the emergent Future 2 consensus around generic skills and outcomes-based curricula (Mangez 2008; Lundahl *et al.* 2008). In other words, in articulating an alternative to the rigidities of Future 1, Future 2 has swung from content-based to skills-based priorities. In both of these formats, especially in the latter, concepts get short shrift. This is because conceptual progression can only be signalled or stipulated in conceptual not skill-based terms. Because concept-based stipulations necessarily involve content (what is being conceptualized), this looks, at least to Future 2 sensibilities, far too like the old content-based priorities of Future 1. The result is that even in concept-rich subjects like science, the curriculum becomes under-stipulated in a Future 2 world as is indicated by the latest curriculum proposals for school science from the QCA (Perks *et al.* 2006).

These tendencies are not insurmountable obstacles for well-resourced schools able to recruit teachers with strong subject qualifications, who can fill in the gaps. It is however, inevitably a problem for schools servicing poor communities that cannot attract such teachers. What happens in such schools is that teachers lack clear markers in the curriculum and fall behind without knowing it, or miss out conceptual steps that may be vital later on (Reeves and Muller 2005; Smith, Smith and Bryk 1998). At the same time, students fall behind until a conceptual terminus is reached and they lack the resources or motivation to progress. This tendency is exacerbated by the favoured non-directive (facilitative) pedagogy of Future 2 that eschews strong signals from the teachers, especially regarding evaluation and assessment. Contemporary research shows unequivocally that in the concept-rich subjects, strong signalling in assessment is critical for improving the performance of pupils from both poor as well as well-off homes (Morais, Neves and Pires 2004; Hoadley 2007; Bourne 2004; Muller and Gamble 2010).

Implications for educational inequalities

Future 3 argues for the importance of recognizing the 'differentiatedness' of knowledge. Two implications follow. First, curricular formats that are too ideologically fixed on only content (Future 1) or skills (Future 2), give some subjects short shrift, as well as having implications for the distribution of educational opportunities and achievement. Second, recognizing the differentiation of knowledge makes explicit that concepts, skills and content are all important and must be stipulated in the curriculum. Failure to do so means a slowing down of any progress that has so far been made towards equalizing epistemological access. This has implications for both social justice and the viability of a knowledge-based economy in the future.

Concluding note

We have framed our predictions for the future of education in terms of three scenarios and on the basis of a social realist theory of knowledge. We have indicated our preference for the Future 3 scenario on both social justice and epistemological grounds and pointed to the negative outcomes that are likely to follow if Future 1 or Future 2 continues to remain dominant. As we have implied, these Futures are ideal types rather than predictive descriptions and must be judged as Max Weber pointed out long ago, in terms of how useful they are in identifying the tendencies and possible unintended consequences of current policies.

On the other hand, we have said little about which Future is most likely to dominate in the next 30 years. This is both a political and an educational or cultural question. It is political because it relates to questions of power and the reality that the curriculum inevitably expresses 'knowledge of the powerful'. Insofar as the neo-liberal combination of markets and accountability and institutional ranking continue to dominate educational policy, Future 2 is likely to dominate. Neo-liberalism, however, is under challenge, at least in the field of economics and financial management. It is difficult to predict the impact of such changes on educational policy. One possibility is that a greater scepticism about the growth possibilities of service occupations may lead to a resurgence of manufacturing and a greater valuing of science-based knowledge.

Predicting likely futures is also a cultural question because, for better or worse, epistemological constraints will shape what curriculum policy can do, whoever has power and whatever the economic constraints. In a sense we might rephrase Marx's famous but ambiguous aphorism about 'men making history' in recognizing that epistemological constraints, like historical circumstances for Marx, are not 'of our own choosing'. This chapter (and the research tradition that it is part of) is an attempt to re-assert the long-term educational importance of these constraints. Our purpose is not to defend a conservative position or to look back to a 'golden past'; far from it. It is to confront the view (which we share) that access to powerful knowledge is a right for all not just the few, with a theory of 'powerful knowledge' and how it is acquired and the crucial role of formal education in that process. Not surprisingly, this leads us, at least in the short term, to a pessimistic view, one presciently expressed by Gramsci 80 years ago:

> We are still in the romantic phase of the active school, in which aspects of the struggle against mechanical and Jesuitical education have been unhealthily emphasized for reasons of polemical contrast; we must now enter the 'classical', rational phase, and discover in the ends to be attained the natural source of new methods and forms.
>
> *(Gramsci 1965)*

The short-term possibilities of Future 2, Gramsci's 'active school' present a seductive scenario for governments and international organizations as well as appearing to offer short cuts to some learners – perhaps real learning is easy and fun and more

like a game. This, we are convinced is a false dawn and likely to punish the disadvantaged most. There is no sign of it catching on in our elite schools – quite the
opposite.

Futurology is in its nature a highly inexact science, because we never have all the
facts at hand. That being said, two things do not necessarily follow: because we do
not have all the facts at our disposal does not mean the trends we discern are not
probable; more pertinently, because the scenarios we sketch and their projected
consequences have a certain apocalyptic ring to them does not mean they are necessarily exaggerated or wrong. As the novelist Philip Roth once said:

> Any satirist writing a futuristic novel who had imagined a President Reagan
> during the Eisenhower years would have been accused of perpetrating a piece
> of crude, contemptible, adolescent, anti-American wickedness, when, in fact,
> he would have succeeded, as prophetic sentry.
>
> *(Roth 1984)*

That prophetic sentries are still welcome is certainly an encouraging sign.

Notes

1 They are never immune from the influences of working class and other movements.
2 This does not mean that we imply that either Mortimore or Kress would endorse our
characterization of Future 2.
3 An example is the influential Portuguese sociologist Bouoventura de Sousa Santos in his
'epistemology of absent knowledges' which he claims goes beyond what he sees as the
'blindness' of western science. Here is how he refers to it in a paper in the *European Journal
of Social Theory*:

> the epistemology of absent knowledges starts from the premise that social practices are
> knowledge practices … (and that) non-science-based practices, rather than being ignorant
> practices, are practices of alternative rival knowledges. There is no apriori reason to favour
> one form of knowledge against another.
>
> *(de Sousa Santos 2001)*

4 This does not deny, of course, that in a deep sense, even the concepts of the natural sciences
are social.

6

CURRICULUM AND THE QUESTION OF KNOWLEDGE

The legacy of Michael Gove

Introduction

The earlier chapters in this section have emphasized the neglect of the question of knowledge both in current educational policies and in much curriculum theory. In 2010, the Conservative-led coalition government in the UK with Michael Gove as Secretary of State for Education introduced its policy for schools that gave a central role to knowledge in the form of a curriculum based on academic subjects for all pupils up to the age of 16. The question that this chapter addresses is: Was this the knowledge-led curriculum that we have argued for and refer to in Chapter 5 as Future 3, and if not, how did the Coalition Government's proposals differ from ours? The chapter begins by examining Gove's legacy,[1] and in particular his critique of the policies of his Labour predecessors as Secretary of State, in light of our analysis of curriculum futures in Chapter 5. It goes on to raise some questions about their different concepts of knowledge and concludes by considering some of the questions that need to be asked, if a Future 3 approach to the curriculum that one goes beyond the Future1/Future 2 debate – is to be developed.

The Govean legacy and its contradictions

On 15 July 2014, Michael Gove was replaced as the UK's (excluding Scotland) Secretary of State for Education by Nicky Hunter, a little-known junior minister. Normally such a reshuffle of ministers would be of little significance outside Parliamentary circles. However, in this case it was a major political issue for the national and specialist education media. Unlike the vast majority of those who came before him (with the exception of Kenneth Baker in the late 1980s), Michael Gove had a clear educational vision and he used his four years as Secretary of State to implement it. The curriculum part of his vision was, at least superficially, simple.

An academic subject-based curriculum was the right of every child, regardless of his or her background or ability. His distinctive emphasis, at least as an ideal, was that such a curriculum should be the right of *every* child, at least up to the age of 16.

Although Gove was in many ways a typical Conservative in his politics (pro-market, anti-large state and anti-EU), his belief that a common subject-based curriculum should be the right of *all* pupils up to the age of 16 represented an ideal which is open to interpretations that are far from conservative (at least politically) and even challenges the well-established traditions of some on the left. In articulating the idea that there is knowledge – for him it was existing academic subject knowledge – that all students have a right to, Gove is expressing his politically 'Conservative' position, as is indicated by his frequent use of the English public schools and grammar schools as his model. However, such a principle was, for Gove, a starting point for a curriculum for *all* children. Gove's linking of the curriculum and the idea of social justice, however rhetorical, is an issue that all previous governments of both political parties had studiously avoided. It may be that in articulating this link between curriculum and social justice, he was 'touching a nerve' for the educational community. Both the left and the right identify with the idea of a common education for all, but even the left tend to see this in organizational not curriculum terms (Benn 2012).

Despite the contradictions in supporting a curriculum that historically had been restricted almost entirely to elite schools, Gove's reforms of the National Curriculum, public examinations, and the ranking of schools on their performance were geared to making this vision a reality. He assumed that acquiring this 'subject knowledge' was like 'cars stopping at red lights'. In other words, it was what every sensible parent wanted for their children, and it was the responsibility of teachers, supported by government, to make this a reality for as many pupils as possible. It was this conviction that led him to minimize consultation on his reforms and to be accused by some of implementing a solely personal agenda. It is hard to judge how far he was right in relation to parents. However, what soon became clear was that his vision was vehemently opposed by most of those in the schools who were responsible for delivering government policies. His reforms were at odds not only with virtually every curriculum change of the preceding decades, but with the views of the majority of the wider education community (at least its more vocal members) including the teacher unions, local education authorities, and the university faculties responsible for teacher education (*The Independent*, 13 March 2013).

Gove asserted not only the value of an academic curriculum, but that it should be the bench mark for assessing *all* students up to the age of 16. In contrast, his opponents in the education community and many on the left such as the former Secretary of State and *Guardian* columnist, Estelle Morris, argued that such a curriculum would discriminate against 'non-academic' students, who should have a curriculum adapted to their interests, aptitudes and experience. Examples of curricula representing such a view can be traced back to the 1970s programmes of the then Schools Council with its euphemistic titles such as 'mathematics for the majority' and science, history and geography 'for the young school leaver'. More recently, the differentiation of the curriculum for pupils over the age of 14 led to the massive

expansion of pre-vocational and personal development courses that were introduced by successive Labour governments between 1997 and 2010, and the popular
Opening Minds initiative of the Royal Society of Arts. What these programmes
had in common was that access to subject-based concepts was not treated as a priority; all started with what the designers hoped were topics and themes that would
interest the group of students who chose not to continue with academic subjects.
The rationale for such curricula varied in emphasis from a pragmatic response to the
disaffection from the academic curriculum of many pupils, especially those from
disadvantaged homes, to a combination of scepticism about the objective value of
academic subject-based knowledge and the importance of respecting cultural diversity. In practical terms the consequences of these different rationales differed little.

It was his opponents' defence of such curricula that led Michael Gove to characterize them as both 'enemies of promise' – for having low expectations of students from poor homes, and 'crypto-Marxists' – for laying the blame for the failure
of students from disadvantaged homes on the 'evils of capitalism'. Gove's conviction about what schools are for placed their failure for a significant proportion of
pupils firmly in the hands of four groups: the *teachers*, and especially head teachers,
who he thought had lost confidence in the true purpose of schools; *the academic
educational community*, whose criticisms of 'the system' did little more than lend support to the disillusionment of many teachers; *the parents* who had either been misled
by teachers or were even too frightened to express their real views about what they
wanted for their children; and *the students*, who had not learned (or perhaps had not
been taught) that acquiring knowledge, like anything worthwhile, requires persistent and disciplined hard work. It is hardly surprising that the few attempts to argue
for a subject-based curriculum by opponents of Gove within the education community were treated as little more than an endorsement of his policies (White and
Young 2012).

There were two sides to Gove's policies which it is useful to distinguish. One is
his critique of much dominant educational thinking and its commitment placing
the child rather than knowledge and the teacher as the starting point of the curriculum and pedagogy. The second is his positive vision of education, its respect for
knowledge and its version of a subject-based curriculum. As a politician and a
conservative first and a liberal educationalist second, it was his critique that dominated his thinking. His typically Conservative assumption, no doubt, was that as a
subject-based curriculum was 'in the order of things', and would inevitably re-assert
itself among parents, once its critics had been exposed. In the remaining sections of
this chapter, I want to examine both his critique and his policies in light of the arguments we developed in Chapter 5 which we wrote in 2009, a year before the
Coalition Government was elected and Gove took up his post.

Gove's policies through the lens of the 'three futures' analysis

Our starting point in Chapter 5 was to analyse changes in the curriculum since the
beginning of mass education in terms of their changing assumptions about knowledge.

We distinguished two curriculum models – Future 1 and Future 2. Future 1 viewed knowledge as part of tradition, handed down from generation to generation, and largely static and given. In other words, it saw the future as always in continuity with the past. We described the Future 1 curriculum as having, at least implicitly, an asocial concept of knowledge; it evolved like any tradition but not as a consequence of either the development of new knowledge or of changes in the wider world. Bearing in mind the country's educational history, Future 1 was inevitably for the few, associated with elite schools and concentrating only on those likely to be in positions of power in the country or the empire when they became adults. Future 1 saw the goal of the curriculum as transmitting a sense of the past as a model for the future; in the nineteenth and early parts of the twentieth century, this was achieved largely through the study of the classic texts of Rome and Ancient Greece.

Opposition to Future 1 in the nineteenth century, with notable exceptions, focused on its restricted access to a minority, and not to the tradition itself. Opportunities at school level were gradually expanded within the Future 1 framework with the establishment of local grammar schools and new universities from the late 1880s and the broadening of the curriculum to include the sciences.

In Chapter 5 we argued that two changes began to undermine the rigidity and exclusiveness of Future 1 at least as the country emerged from its pre-industrial past. The first was the growth of knowledge, especially in the sciences, and its associated differentiation and specialization; the second was the combination of democratic pressures for access and the demand for skills and knowledge by the growing industrial, extracting, manufacturing and later, service sectors of the economy. These changes were followed, in the mid-twentieth century, by the collapse of the youth labour market which left large sections of 15 and 16 year olds with no option but to stay on at school. The Future 2 response to this situation is important because it was the primary focus of Gove's critique and, to a lesser extent, his alternative policies; a point I will return to.

The English version of Future 1 was sufficiently flexible, at least in the short term, to be able to incorporate many of the pressures for change. The concept of being initiated into a tradition associated with studying the classics was broadened to include modern literature, and the emerging scientific disciplines, and later the applied sciences, especially engineering and medicine, and more recently, the growth of the social sciences. Each development contributed to the growing importance of the natural sciences and their claims for equal status with the humanities – a development evocatively dramatized by the famous debate between C.P. Snow and F.R. Leavis (Muller 2011b). However, Future 1 left its mark on the English tradition by continuing to privilege the superiority of the intrinsic – as opposed to the extrinsic – value of studying the natural sciences and the lack of recognition and status of their industrial applications. The continuation of the Future 1 view of knowledge as part of a tradition – a kind of secularized theology – had contrasting consequences. On the one hand, it was celebrated in the country's success (at least until recent decades) in winning Nobel Prizes. On the negative side, its view of knowledge, even in the sciences, as 'what we know' may account at least in part, for the slow growth and low status of the applied sciences, and the steady de-industrialization of what had been, in the early nineteenth century, the first industrial economy.

It was the successive phases of a largely consumer-oriented expansion of higher education from the 1980s together with the further collapse of the youth labour market which resulted in whole new sections of each cohort staying on at school that made the assumptions of a Future 1 curriculum untenable as a model for the future. Without major improvements in the quality and standards reached by all secondary school students – an issue that was not on anyone's agenda until the late 1970s – Future 1 was no basis for a substantial expansion of post compulsory or higher education. In the case of higher education, expansion was increasingly led by student choice, less and less guided by the traditional links and assumptions about knowledge shared between the staff of the upper forms of secondary schools and their university colleagues. What began to give way, because it did not appear to be associated with any significant group's interests, was, from the 1980s, the exclusive role of the upper secondary (sixth form) curriculum and its A-level examinations as the main entry route to universities. A gradual process of curricular diversification took place that included a broader range of A-level subjects, the expansion of non-academic (pre-vocational) courses offering routes to an increasingly diversified and more vocational higher education sector and a range of post-16 programmes with the goal of employability rather than employment or university entry. In Chapter 5 we referred to these developments as Future 2. What they had in common, in England at least, was an implicitly social constructivist view of knowledge as an object of social interests that could be manipulated for different purposes and not limited by epistemic rules. It followed that there was no limit to the diversification of a post compulsory curriculum that no longer relied on an assumption that it was (a) inflexibly selective or (b) based on the same epistemological assumptions as university degrees. Gove's critique of these developments was backward – looking in the sense of being from the perspective of Future 1; however, it was also essentially ahistorical. It failed to engage with how these Future 2 developments, whatever their limitations as new pathways of opportunity, represented a real response to the backwardness and elitism of what came before (Future 1). It is perhaps worth noting that although our Future 1/Future 2 analysis was premised on an epistemological argument in the sociology of knowledge, the policy debates it was analysing were based on much more traditional assumptions surrounding the justification of selection in terms of the distribution of abilities. The clash between Future 1 and Future 2 that was played out in post compulsory and higher education from the 1970s is a more recent example of an old debate about selection and access which, as so often in the country's educational history, avoided questions of purpose and whether the options posed were the only alternatives. At the end of this chapter I will return to this issue and the possibility that once a curriculum is understood in terms of the knowledge it gives access to rather than in terms of selection and the assumed distribution of abilities, a much more extensive range of alternatives can be envisaged and explored.

By the first decade of the third millennium, Future 2 expansion had lost any sense of overall strategy, and relied increasingly on current fashions in cultural studies and the largely rhetorical claims for a knowledge economy (Guile 2010) with little consideration of what this 'knowledge' might mean (see Chapter 3). Future 2 thus laid itself open to Gove's critique that expansion had dispensed with any concept of knowledge and standards. However, while valuable in bringing the question of 'knowledge' to the centre of debates about the curriculum, Gove relied on a marginally modernized version of Future 1 and led to largely circular debates between the rigidity and exclusiveness of Future 1 and the relativism of Future 2. Furthermore, his subject-based curriculum was limited by its concept of knowledge that failed to distinguish between a Future 1 knowledge tradition which treats it as primarily a resource for maintaining a privileged social order and the broader role of tradition as a necessary basis for acquiring and creating new knowledge. I will use this distinction to extract the 'rational kernel' of both Future 2 and Gove's version of Future 1, not in order to replace them with a third supposedly better model, but as a step in developing the tools for thinking about what a modern knowledge-based curriculum might involve.

The Future is backwards; Gove's alternative

In Chapter 5, we traced Future 1 back to the beginnings of mass education in the nineteenth century. In its dominant form, Future 1 viewed the school curriculum as a given and only appropriate for a small (albeit slowly growing) elite. It was symbolized by the study of the classics of Ancient Greece and Rome, which was gradually extended to Anglo Saxon and early English writers such as Chaucer. It was predominantly literary and humanistic. As a curriculum for setting standards of moral character for an elite, its idea of leadership involved being subservient to traditions established in the past rather than being prepared to understand a world that was changing and so could no longer be taken as given. It had its less conservative and less elitist forms in the writings of Matthew Arnold and, much later, Richard Tawney, both of whom believed that such a curriculum could be extended to all. However, both still retained its backward-looking and largely literary view of culture.

While endorsing many of the features of the Arnoldian curriculum, as in his list of favoured writers which ended with Thomas Hardy, Gove realized that such an exclusive and fixed curriculum had emerged in a past which no longer existed. His endorsement of STEM; subjects and his recasting of computing studies as a fourth science of coding, are examples of how he distanced himself from the assumptions of Future 1. However, these were add-ons to a view of knowledge as a tradition to be complied with. They did not involve a new concept of knowledge.

There were other ways in which the curriculum Gove endorsed looked backwards. His admiration for the English public schools gave him a view of successful teaching as a 'craft for graduates' who would pass on what a society already knew in any subject to the next generation. Like other crafts which change little, teaching, he thought, could be learned 'on the job' as many teachers in those schools still do. Teaching for Gove was still 'passing on the knowledge one had acquired'. It did not involve, as in other professions such as medicine, the acquisition of a body of developing specialized knowledge. In the case of teachers this specialized knowledge – poorly developed and even less respected in England – would need to be focused round subject-based didactics (Taylor 2014; Shalem 2014); professional education in schools and universities would involve the integration of this 'theory' and practice in the schools. It was his view of teaching as a 'craft for graduates' as well as what he disliked in what he thought teachers learned on courses in University Faculties of Education that no doubt led Gove to remove the requirement that academies and free schools, unlike other schools funded by the government, could only employ qualified teachers.

The second and related way in which his concept of education retained elements of Future 1 was that it did not distinguish between knowledge as 'something produced by research' within certain specialist communities (usually universities) from knowledge as 'what was valued and trusted' and 'what was already known'. However, Gove was far more of a politician and a reformer than an educationalist and his positive alternatives for a future curriculum were less important to him than exposing the flaws in how he thought educationists had responded to the weaknesses, backwardness and elitism of Future 1.

Future 2 reforms – political and academic critiques

It was the education community's response to the elitism of Future 1 which Gove's criticism focused on and that we described in Chapter 5 as Future 2. This is important for this book, not because we intend to rehearse his criticisms, but because they make explicit the way in which the question of knowledge has been systematically neglected in the educational reforms of the last 40 years and the extent to which the consequences of policies, which have their roots in progressive and often left-wing politics, can undermine opportunities for those they are designed to benefit. It is an irony that it has taken a Conservative politician to highlight this fundamental contradiction at the heart of our education system. It is unlikely that such a contradiction would ever have been raised by Labour politicians but, regardless of our political loyalties, as researchers we have to take up opportunities, wherever they come from. One of the lessons from Gove's period of office, disturbing though it is, is that there is no straightforward correspondence between political and educational judgements. Furthermore, by emphasizing the long history of educational ideologies that treat knowledge as if it is inescapably part of how inequalities are maintained, we may go some way to explaining the difficulties facing those who want to stress the link between knowledge, freedom and social justice.

As we argued in Chapter 5, Future 2 had its origins in the period of political optimism that followed World War II and the awareness that a future democratic education system could not be built on the taken-for-granted elitism of Future 1. We contrasted what we describe as the 'under-socialized' or asocial view of knowledge of Future 1 with the emerging social constructivist view of knowledge of Future 2. This was articulated in its academic form by the so-called 'new sociology of education' of the 1970s that we discuss in Chapter 1, although its curriculum implications had their beginnings a decade earlier.

Future 2 and its 'over-socialized' view of knowledge was how we have depicted the emerging consensus within the educational community since the 1970s and earlier. This chapter has focused largely on how this view was expressed in secondary schools, particularly in their response to low achieving pupils staying on at school. However, its expression, as in the child-centred approach to the early years' curriculum, which came to be symbolized by the Plowden Report as long ago as 1967, has probably been even more significant. What is striking but little commented on is the curricular division between early years' education in the state and private sectors (Menter 2013). The persistent differences between the child-centred curriculum of state-funded primary schools and the subject-led curriculum of schools for the same age group in the private sector – known significantly as 'preparatory schools' – is a strangely unresearched topic. These 'preparatory' schools saw and still see themselves as preparing pupils for entry into fee-paying 'public' schools and the 'common entrance examination' that their pupils take on leaving. They provide a kind of early induction into 'public school life' within a subject-based curriculum and as a consequence, their pupils have, since the earliest 'prep schools' were founded towards the end of the nineteenth century, been taught largely by subject specialists, often from the age of seven and eight.

Future 2 and its social constructivist assumptions

While the relativist implications of the social constructivist view of knowledge are invariably denied both by curriculum designers and teachers involved, they leave implicit how such curricula are designed and implemented. Curricula developed according to competence criteria are an extreme example (Young 2011). An 'over socialized' view of knowledge denies any external reality. As a consequence it cannot distinguish knowledge from experience and is sceptical of any curriculum that goes beyond what teachers and pupils co-construct together in the classroom (Yandell 2014). Somehow, the interests of the teachers are treated as having a degree of objectivity or at least validity of their own; a strange idea for an occupation that claims to be a profession. It is almost as if teachers are members of a kind of proletariat and the agents of their own and their pupil's history.

For secondary schools it was the Newsom Report in the 1960s (Central Advisory Council for Education (England) 1963) and the curriculum reforms that followed that first exemplified the practical consequences of social constructivism. If there is no objectively 'better' knowledge, there is no knowledge that needs be treated as an entitlement for all pupils. The idea of a 'right to knowledge' had its English origins in the nineteenth century in the struggle to extend access to education led by the nascent trade union movement and associated with the Chartist slogan of 'really useful knowledge' (Johnson 1979). However, later reformers such as Newsom reversed such ideas; the idea of 'better' knowledge as the basis of a curriculum for all became seen as an imposition by a minority elite on the majority. This attitude is reflected in the recent comment in the press of one head teacher. In welcoming Gove's dismissal as Secretary of State, he was quoted as saying that that such subjects as 'economics, and physics … are not suitable for many of our children' – a curious inversion of the argument that academically selective secondary schools denied access to knowledge to the majority of students who were not selected. In the mind of head teachers such as the one quoted, this becomes the assertion that a subject-based curriculum discriminates against disadvantaged pupils, or in the sociologist Pierre Bourdieu's words is 'an arbitrary culture imposed by arbitrary powers' (Bourdieu 2011).

There was an attack on knowledge in the Newsom Report, Half our Future, although it was not seen in those terms at the time. For Newsom, the 'right to knowledge' was interpreted somewhat paternalistically for those pupils described as 'non-academic' as 'the right to a curriculum best suited to their needs and abilities'; the Newsom Report took for granted that these needs were not academic but practical or vocational.

Mainstream educational thinking accepted the idea of a curriculum divided on its principles of knowledge. On the other hand, Future 2 radicals, of which I was one in the 1970s, assumed that the divisions between subjects and disciplines that they saw as the hegemonic, oppressive and archaic forms of 'official knowledge' (a term introduced later in a book by Michael Apple (1993)) and common experience would wither away. In an increasingly democratic society everyone's 'knowledge' would 'count'. These were the promises of slogans like 'popular education' and more recently, 'critical pedagogy' that became popular in the USA from the 1980s and came to dominate much curriculum studies. Debate about such ideas was at best muted, and critical pedagogues like Peter Mclaren were feted across the world. At the same time the numbers of students getting good grades increased year by year. No one, neither academics nor politicians, wanted to risk being seen to criticize pupils or teachers by suggesting that this might be an indicator of a growing credentialism or even a 'dumbing down' of the curriculum rather than of more informed students emerging from a fairer system.

With a few exceptions among academics, the only critiques of Future 2 throughout the 1980s and 1990s came with the brief re-emergence of the Black Papers of the 1970s which were easily dismissed as right-wing propaganda. However, similar critiques were to emerge in more subtle and influential forms in the first decade of the twentieth century in the publications of right-wing think tanks such as Politiea, Policy Exchange, Reform and Civitas. It was these publications which provided much of the research and polemics that Gove was to draw on when he became Secretary of State. By then Future 2 ideas were firmly established in the publications of the Qualifications and Curriculum Development Agency (QCDA), and of left of centre think tanks, like DEMOS, which echoed the Newsom Report's 1960s arguments discussed earlier.

The development of an increasing differentiation of the curriculum for post-14 students, initiated by Conservative governments in the 1980s and 1990s, was taken much further by successive Labour governments in the period 1997–2010; it was justified by the steadily rising numbers of pupils gaining some form of qualification. An 'over-socialized' sociology of knowledge was drawn on, at least implicitly, to justify treating practical and academic subject-oriented courses as equivalent with the result that there was a massive expansion of the former, as schools tried to improve their ranking on performance tables.

This process might have continued unchallenged if it had not been for the election of the Coalition government in 2010, the appointment of Michael Gove as Secretary of State and the report he commissioned by Alison Wolf (Wolf 2014). Wolf's Report argued that the certificates acquired through the accreditation of learning outcomes rather than written examinations were in effect worthless, except in improving the performance of schools; they did not lead to employment, were not respected by employers and few of those with these certificates progressed to higher level courses which might have led them to future employment.

It was these attempts to develop more inclusive alternatives to the assumptions of Future 1, its elitism, its backward-facing focus and its sheer irrelevance to twenty-first century circumstances that we characterized as Future 2 in Chapter 5. It was this Future 2 curriculum with its emphasis on learner choice; the 'natural' development of children (especially in their primary school years); its relativist view of knowledge; its blurring of boundaries both between different knowledge domains and between school and non-school knowledge; and its denial of the authority relations at the heart of all pedagogy, that was challenged head on by Michael Gove and his policies and which, not surprisingly, generated so much antagonism from the educational community. It was his attempt to force the teachers to face the reality that their role was to provide access to knowledge which most children would not have access to at home that antagonised the education community. He was in effect accusing them of denying access to knowledge to disadvantaged children. It was hardly surprising that this led to such vitriolic opposition to everything that he stood for. In political terms it was this antagonism initially from the education community, but later more broadly, that led to his downfall. From a political perspective, it was not the policies themselves that were the problem but divisions within a party that was already wracked by divisions over Europe. A party preparing to fight a General Election could not afford to lose such a key constituency as parents and teachers. Some had started to be worried by Gove's policies on examinations and the admission problems that the expansion of academies and free schools was bound to lead to. As a political decision Gove's removal as Secretary of State was undoubtedly a success. A notable feature of the political debates and campaigns leading up to the General Election on 7 May 2015 which the Conservative Party won, was that education was hardly mentioned.

The limitations of critiques

My concern in this chapter has not been with politics but with the nature of Gove's educational attack on Future 2 and its possible consequences. His view of the curriculum was based on a return to a subject-based curriculum, established a century ago for an elite but now to be applied to all students. It was hardly surprising that his curriculum policies and any defence of a subject-based curriculum were interpreted as calling for a return to Future 1 with its backward-looking elitism, its taken-for-granted view of knowledge as 'what some of us already know', and its 'transmission' model of pedagogy.

The debate, such as it was, became between a Gradgrind vision of the past (how Gove's policies were seen by the education community) and a curriculum shaped by learner choices and disregarding access to the knowledge that going to school was about, as seen by Gove. It is hard to see how such a debate could lead to a new vision of schooling appropriate for the twenty-first century. Both Future 2 as a response to the weaknesses of Future 1 and Gove's response to the excesses of Future 2 have a common weakness; neither recognize the growth of knowledge as the central issue both for the curriculum and for a more just society. The fashionable emphasis on twenty-first century skills such as 'learning to learn', 'problem solving', and 'working with others' (although not to be dismissed in themselves), denies any distinctiveness to the substantive knowledge that today's students need access to. In contrast, while Gove's emphasis on 'subjects for all' can be welcomed, his reliance on a backward-facing Arnoldian view of subjects as 'the best that has been thought and said' is more an assertion of control and accountability than an entitlement of all students to the foundation of new knowledge. Without a more adequate concept of the knowledge that all students are entitled to, Gove's subject-based curriculum lays itself open to Bourdieu's charge quoted earlier that subjects represent a 'cultural arbitrary imposed by arbitrary powers' (2011). With the loss of Gove's drive and vision as Secretary of State, it is difficult to predict the future of the school curriculum. A most likely future is a drift into a less antagonistic debate between versions of Future 2 and a more traditional Conservative defence of subjects.

The final section of this chapter outlines an alternative approach to the curriculum based on the view of the purpose of schooling as extending access to 'powerful knowledge' to a progressively widening proportion of each cohort. It is not a set of principles for a new curriculum, but a research agenda for discovering the knowledge 'about the specialization of knowledge' that would be the basis for such a curriculum.

Beyond Future 1 and Future 2 and the Govean critique

The importance of the Govean legacy is that it has brought subjects and knowledge back into curriculum debates. While in their existing form subjects need to be criticized, the form they take is in significant ways, shaped by their role in a curriculum that can be described as 'knowledge of the powerful' (see Chapter 9). However, they can no longer be dismissed as just 'official knowledge'. The weakness of the legacy that Gove leaves us with is that subjects, treated as an inherited tradition, could somehow define the purposes of schools in the twenty-first century. This is not so different from the curriculum that emerged before the production of new knowledge moved from the fringe to the centre of a country's concerns. When the Future 1 model of knowledge was being established in the grammar and public schools of England in the mid-nineteenth century, physics was still part of natural philosophy, medical research barely existed, neither Oxford nor Cambridge had Professors of Engineering and no undergraduates studied the social sciences. Much has changed since then in education. However, these examples tell a story. Although no more than the surface expressions of a view of knowledge located deeply in the past, they are not so far removed from Gove's subject-based curriculum.

The questions Gove did not ask

Gove attempted to re-invent a model of an academic subject-based curriculum as a counter to what he saw as the denial of knowledge by Future 2. That diagnosis is one we can go along with at least in part. However, his basis for an alternative was an unrealistic return to the past. It emphasized the taken for granted role of boundaries in supporting the acquisition of knowledge, both those between subjects and those between the curriculum and the experience of pupils and both of which had been de-emphasized by Future 2. However, he assumed he was returning schools to something natural – expressed in the joint enthusiasm by teachers and pupils for subjects and the openings to the world that they give. No such time ever existed, or if it did, it was for a tiny minority. As such his model of a curriculum fails to address the two most basic problems of our time – how to inspire the pupils of all ages to grasp the curriculum sufficiently to think beyond what the curriculum provides and how to create a curriculum that engages that large section of each cohort in the early years of secondary school if not before that have lost interest in acquiring new knowledge.

Gove emphasized knowledge in the form of subjects but it was as if this knowledge was there waiting to be acquired by pupils who would be inspired by teachers with a passion for their subjects; that will always be a small minority. What he did not address, and as a politician we should not expect him to, is that we also need 'knowledge about subjects – the forms that knowledge should take in curricula' – what it is, if it is really to be a basis for creating new knowledge and for enabling beginning learners to acquire that knowledge. My criticism, and he is only partly to blame, is that like all political leaders, in a complex society, they cannot rule by charisma – they need expertise – in this case the expertise of curriculum theorists, those he ignorantly grouped together as 'crypto-marxists' or, 'the blob'. If he had had a different educational vision he would have searched, in this country and beyond, for curriculum specialists who he might have turned to. Regrettably, as I argue in chapter, curriculum theory is in a sorry state and at best a promise. It would have required remarkable foresight for him to have seen what was necessary and it is up to us as curriculum theorists to show the way. In the last few paragraphs of this chapter we can do no more than begin the journey and hope that another visionary politician picks it up.

If schools are institutions which specialize in the acquisition of knowledge, what has educational research, especially curriculum theory, got to offer politicians and policy makers about this knowledge? Very little is the answer at present. A knowledge-based curriculum is fine as a slogan, it tells us something about what to avoid but very little about this knowledge and how it might be paced, selected and sequenced if it is to really extend access. We cannot assume that knowledge reveals itself. Any worthwhile body of knowledge like a curriculum or a subject is specialized to its purposes. In our current traditions of subjects and curricula we have some resources, but if we are not to fall back on Future 1 and its elitism, we need research which questions that and extends these traditions and goes beyond them. Here we do no more than point to some of the questions neglected by the Gove legacy which saw knowledge only as a tradition and not as a source of going beyond it; some of the questions are touched on elsewhere in this book.

- What is a subject, how do new subjects emerge and what is subject knowledge and how do they change? What are their permanent features and how do subjects differ in the ways their concepts are related to each other and methods of enquiry?
- How do the different subjects relate to their originating disciplines and how useful in posing this question are the tools for enquiry we already have like Bernstein's 'recontextualization' and his 'pacing, sequencing and selecting'?
- Do all subjects have to rely on disciplines as their epistemic resources or are there other ways of designing systematic and coherent curricula that do not collapse into lists of 'generic skills'?
- How do subjects vary in providing teachers with the basis for making judgments about pupils across the sciences, social sciences, humanities and arts?
- How do different subjects support students' year-on-year progression and what Chris Winch refers to as the possibilities of 'epistemic ascent' (Winch 2012)?
- What practical skills or 'how to' knowledge is involved in learning different subjects?
- If subjects and their boundaries are a source of learner and teacher identity, in what contexts should teachers encourage students to cross boundaries?

This is only a beginning. The difference between the Govean subject-based curriculum and the Future 3 curriculum that we referred to in Chapter 5 is that in the former, these and other questions are taken for granted as already answered within the traditions of the different subject communities, each with their different concepts of subject knowledge, their different curriculum purposes, their different relationships to other subjects, and to disciplinary specialists in the universities. Nothing could be further from the truth. If we are serious about extending access we need to know its real limits; for example, there are limits to the extent to which you can learn about Tolstoy if you do not learn Russian; likewise the extent of one's mathematics sets limits on how far you can go in understanding aspects of physics.

Subjects as associations of specialists are a rich source of answers to these questions. On the other hand, there is much they take for granted. And much that they and we do not know, especially about progression is stipulated in different specialist subjects. Much that is in subject traditions is positive in being a basis for acquiring new knowledge, but some is negative; some traditions and methods may just never have been questioned. For Future 3, these are research questions both within the subject communities and beyond. They are questions that arise if progression or epistemic ascent are priorities for a wide range of learners.

Conclusions

Three arguments have been made in this chapter that are likely to be contrary to those of many educational commentators and researchers. The first is that the questions about knowledge in education that Gove's reforms raised should have been raised by educational researchers or even politicians on the left; however they were not. They were raised by a Conservative politician and even if we disagree with his answers, we cannot deny the importance of his questions. The second argument is that his legacy leaves us much more to do than he ever envisaged. We have very little knowledge about knowledge – especially in how it is structured in curricula to promote acquisition.

Third, despite being critical of Gove's backward-looking approach to the curriculum, I have dwelt on two positive outcomes of his period of office. The first is his opposition to a trend in curriculum policy that relativizes knowledge and blurs the distinction between knowledge and experience. While appearing to be progressive, this trend has in practice masked the denial of knowledge to many, especially the most disadvantaged.

A further positive outcome has been that his policies opened up a long overdue debate about the purposes of schools, what should constitute the school curriculum and what it should be aiming to achieve? I have concentrated here on the English context. However, I would argue that the questions they have given rise to in England, and even the antagonism that Gove's policies has generated and the opposition within the educational community, are issues that, to different degrees, all countries will have to address.

Gove's conservative and backward-looking concept of a subject-based curriculum is no basis for achieving its own goals of making an entitlement to knowledge a possibility for all pupils; if anything, it could lead to the opposite. There are already warning signs as schools advertise themselves as offering a knowledge-led curriculum which has become a slogan, whereas it should be a set of questions. Finally, and consistent, hopefully, with the overall aims of this book, this chapter has argued that 'knowledge about knowledge' is a specialist form of enquiry that is the responsibility of curriculum theorists and subject specialists together. We have much taken-for-granted knowledge of subjects, but this has only got us so far; actually we know rather little about subject knowledge especially if we are serious about the claim that it is, at least potentially, 'knowledge for all'.

Note

1 It is significant that the Labour opposition has almost systematically avoided this debate and concentrated as has in the past on organizational issues – in this case the chaos and confusion that the expansion of academies and 'free' schools has led to.

7

THE FUTURE OF KNOWLEDGE AND SKILLS IN SCIENCE AND TECHNOLOGY HIGHER EDUCATION

There is an undercurrent of confident futuristic prognostication in much contemporary popular writing about education, and in the projections of some scholars too. Education, it seems, is 'out of step' with the times in general, and the labour market in particular. Universities are regularly lambasted for not providing the skills future workers in the 'knowledge economy' will need (see Case 2011 for a discussion regarding engineering), skills which, ironically, are often at the same time said to be changing rapidly. Solutions appear to many soothsayers to be blindingly obvious. 'Lifelong' learning is for some the remedy (see, for example, Knapper and Cropley 2000), although the prospect of a society of Sysiphyan learners comes close to Orwell's dystopia. For others, the newer technologies provide the answer (Bates and Poole 2003). Others believe that learning must be liberated from the dead hand of outmoded disciplines and those that profess them. More audaciously, we are told that traditional forms of research no longer produce what we need, and we are ushering in a new era of transdisciplinary, trans-institutional research called 'mode 2', to distance it from its discredited 'mode 1' forebear (Gibbons *et al.* 1994).

Some years ago, in response to a commission from the Beyond Current Horizon Programme headed by Carey Jewitt, Michael Young and I resolved to venture into the cauldron of futurology, to give our account of what was happening from a sociology of knowledge perspective (Chapter 5). The result was an exercise in 'futures thinking' of a special kind. We tried to project a developmental trajectory from the past into the future, from an ideal type we called 'Future 1' to another called 'Future 3'. The aim of this present chapter is to elaborate the argument of that chapter in the context of science, technology, engineering and maths (STEM) in higher education, in so doing examining their implications for STEM education now and in the near future.

There are two *basic departure points* in the original account of significance for the present one:

First, there is no doubt we are living in a time of increasing *specialization* of knowledge in the STEM domain, driven equally by new discoveries and inventions, new technological challenges, and new elaborations in the division of labour – that is, new kinds of jobs and the obsolescence of older ones (Brown and Lauder 1996). In our educational lifetimes, the increasing specialization of knowledge is a defining condition that educators especially in concept-rich domains like STEM simply have to adapt to. Increasing specialization entails an ever-increasing addition of new knowledge and with it, an ever-increasing rise of the cognitive demand bar at each level of the educational ladder. All STEM teachers know this means having to deal with a curriculum that is already bursting at the seams, and they have to avoid solving the problem the 'easy way'. This 'easy way' is to increase the pacing (compressing and speeding up) of curriculum material, which in turn favours students from privileged backgrounds because they are better equipped by virtue of being educated in cognitively rich environments by better qualified teachers to respond to the increased volume of novel material. The position taken here is that we are ethically bound to search for formats of learning that help us to expand opportunities for students from less privileged educational backgrounds, not shut them down. In educational terms, however, this is only where the debate begins, and doesn't yet indicate how this should be done.

The second departure point is the ineluctability of the *differentiatedness* of knowledge. Different knowledges (disciplines and their curricular carriers) have different epistemic and social properties. This has entailments for differential arrangements for doing research; for differential forms of collegiality; differential forms of curriculum coherence; and so on (Muller 2009). Complex high-specialization professional faculties like health sciences, engineering and architecture are a dynamic conglomeration of different socio-epistemic communities each with their distinct cognitive and cultural styles (Becher 1994; Becher and Trowler 2001), whose differences have to be managed if they are not to bump ceaselessly into one another.

What the scenarios paper does in addition is sketch three notional scenarios or 'futures', based on fundamentally different ways of dealing with these above two departure points. Scenarios 1 and 2 are plain enough. The first is what I will call *traditionalism*, a position based on what we (Chapter 5) called an 'under-socialized' concept of knowledge; the second is *progressivism*, a reaction to traditionalism, which ends up, we argue, with an 'over-socialized' concept of knowledge. These scenarios clearly display similarities as well as differences across the terrains of schooling and higher education.

Scenario-sketching of this kind can easily lead to envisaging a straightforward progression path from scenario 1 moving on to scenario 2, and eventually to scenario 3. Such an impression of inevitability would be illusory. Scenario 1 was designed as a civilizing device for the youth of the elite, where the content of the curriculum was regarded as relatively fixed and of primary importance. It fell victim to its own internal shortcomings, principally, for the purposes of this chapter, that it could cope neither with a massifying, diversifying system nor with the exponential growth of new knowledge after the 1950s. Scenario 2 emerged as a liberatory alternative emphasizing the creative activity of teachers and learners and, in trying to deal with the rapid growth of innovation and diversity, foregrounded activity and backgrounded what was to be learnt – the increasingly specializing knowledge base. STEM higher education followed an analogous pattern.

Scenario 2 is the one that is in place today, increasingly put under pressure by blind spots of its own, and will form the main focus of this chapter. Nevertheless it must be stressed that each scenario has, or had, a rational kernel to it. Traditionalism was lost sight of in the enthusiasms of scenario 2, and we must take care that we don't do likewise with scenario 2 at the same time as we retrieve what is good in scenario 1, casting them both in new terms under changing conditions in what we call scenario 3, our social realist alternative.

The argument to be made in this chapter is that it is important to take each of these scenarios seriously. Traditionalism in the sphere of STEM has meant an approach to knowledge as either a form of rationalism which elevates theory and hence the theoretical disciplines; or a form of empiricism which elevates propositional knowledge ('facts'), usually both (see Chapter 14). This is no accident. Both Descartes (rationalism) and Bacon (empiricism) were necessary for scientific and technological take-off in the seventeenth century (Gaukroger 2008). They ground the very idea of knowledge progress and hence of the roots of specialization. They are consequently the bedrock of science and technology's self-image. In this sense, in science and engineering faculties, they will always be with us, at least in the research domain. Pedagogically, though, they can lead to a curiously undynamic view of the curriculum and of teaching and learning.

Traditionalism fosters elitism because, as it expands to accommodate growing demand without fundamental attention to its form and changing social base, it replicates enduring patterns of social privilege. This is so for the reason already alluded to: as the curriculum copes with specialization pressures by upping the pace of transmission and increasing demand levels, it is the already-prepared learners who cope best. The enduring symptom of traditionalism's blind spot is high levels of student drop out and repetition. This had led to successive models of scenario 2 'first aid' which have had some effect but have not solved the problem. There have been a series of technological/technocratic means for addressing the problem, massive open online courses (MOOCs) being just the most recent, but these often just displace the problem, by laying it at the door of students; after all, one does not 'drop out' of an online course so much as de-register for lack of interest. What they share with traditionalism is that they all take for granted the fixity of the knowledge horizon and locate the problem 'out there' with the educational participants, or the technologies that mediate them.

It is largely to tackle traditionalism's creaking view of learning and teaching that led Academic Development[1], at least in South Africa, to embrace the second scenario during the period of its growth and expansion in the 1960s, 1970s and 1980s (see Scott 2009 for an historical account), often as an article of faith or badge of professional identity, and, until recently, rather uncritically. This has begun to change (see Case 2011; Shay 2012; Luckett 2009).

Progressivism has a number of things going for it. Its founding insight, rooted in a constructivism which opposes rationalism and empiricism equally, is that however apparently fixed the knowledge horizon might appear, it is always the product of human activity and its history. This shift of view, to the *activity*, was initially dramatically liberating, both politically and epistemically (and see also Chapter 2 above). Because of its refusal to take social and educational hierarchies as given and unchangeable, progressivism in South Africa was initially aligned with the democratic movements of the 1960s and 1970s, and continues to be claimed for progressivism today.

Constructivism as a theoretical movement underlying pedagogic progressivism (Moore 2012) was a serious attempt to establish a sociological basis to debates about the curriculum. It has shed considerable light on the processes of pedagogy and learning (see, for example, Biggs and Tang 2007) just as its counterparts in the sociology of science have shed light on the processes of scientific discovery (see, for example, Pickering 1992). However, in its attempt to socialize knowledge, the curriculum and pedagogy, it tended to slip into a relativism that threw the baby (knowledge, truth, objectivity) out with the bathwater (a static and ahistorical view of knowledge). Because knowledge is originally constructed is no reason to doubt that some of it, at least, is worthwhile, true and objective, or that a spirit of truthfulness is something to be prized (Williams 2010).

In STEM, the case for the constructedness of reality and truth must have been hard to maintain in the face of hard-nosed scepticism from the scientists, and an equally hard-nosed pragmatism from the engineers. But its corollary, that things of the world could be changed by righteous human endeavour, stuck, probably striking some kind of chord with the 'can do' engineers. If the verities of education were constructed, then they could be changed. The teacher and the learner, the two founts of activity, became the focus of the scholarly academic development gaze, still overwhelmingly the case today (Case 2013). If the attempt to make a difference failed, then it must have been for want of epistemic fortitude and sociopolitical will. Consequently, there is all too often more than a whiff of moralism in some contemporary academic development writing.

This focus on the activity (or on 'practice') has, probably inadvertently, tended to draw a veil over the knowledge base on which successful action depends, and hence most crucially, over the differential curriculum requirements of specialized knowledge. In other words, the focus on the activity of teaching (and learning) mostly leaves out of view the different kinds of knowledgeability on which that teaching rests, which is sometimes even seen as a virtue (Dall'Alba and Barnacle 2007). Hence, almost against its initial liberating intents, progressivism (scenario 2) has tended to get stuck with an over-socialized and undifferentiated conception of knowledge as activity. To put that another way: scenario 2, especially in the Anglo-American tradition, has ended up with a notion of 'practice' as skill, competence, or punctual performance, a 'thin' version rather than the more capacious sense of educational 'practice' signalled by the German term 'kompetenz', which is a 'thick' notion incorporating formal knowledge, past abilities, and moral character (Winch 2010; Bohlinger 2007).

Scenario 1 and scenario 2 are each movements of their time. Because they each describe a partial truth of the STEM educational situation, they each display a certain incorrigibility. This means that, amongst their core constituencies, they continue to function as the 'one and only' account, the 'one best system' (Tyack 1974), in opposition to others which then become false pretenders. As a consequence, they have become embroiled in a polarized debate between their respective positions. We had the Culture Wars of the 1970s, the Science Wars of the 1980s, each describing a certain fierce engagement at the buffer zone between them. A low intensity Pedagogical War has flared up intermittently, for example, in engineering and medicine, between the proponents and opponents of 'problem-based learning' (Case 2011; Hartman 2014). Since the position of each suppresses important aspects of the other, this has led in education to a fruitless oscillation from one to the other and back again. In the universities and in Academic Development in particular, this has led to the educational progressives hunkering down and chipping away at the perceived certainties of their academic colleagues in the science and technology departments and faculties, without much signal success except in the small-scale research and intervention studies that fill the research publications.

Scenario 3 is the name Michael Young and I have given to the space that explores what it means to move the debate forward by combining the positive features of each and trying to avoid their worst features. However, we are not presuming that one can simply survey strengths and weaknesses and make a judicious selection. As indicated above, the two scenarios are thoroughly socio-historical phenomena and they leave behind specific historical sediments and path dependencies. In the case of STEM education, this has meant a residual scenario 1 orientation in the mainstream STEM departments and a spirited scenario 2 orientation in response, or opposition, amongst the Academic Development practitioners, with many variants in between. Academic Development generally, and in STEM, leans thus to a basic scenario 2 orientation. One way to move forward, the analysis above suggests, is to confront the tendencies towards de-specialization and de-differentiation inherent in the scenario, and thereby to at least foreground the tendential limitations of the position.

I will list some potential de-differentiating features of scenario 2, but will explore only one briefly in the remainder of this chapter. Most if not all of them arise as over-extensions of the basic postulate of scenario 2, namely, its fundamental activity or *practice orientation*. As I said above, this orientation has had positive effects because it socializes the basically ahistorical orientation of scenario 1, and it liberates by emphasizing the moment of dynamism and transformation immanent in the very notion of action. At the same time, the practice orientation has all too often led to a valorization of:

- agent-centred experience at the expense of specialized kinds of knowledge;
- learner differences at the expense of knowledge differences;
- a generic pedagogy, say outcomes-based or problem-based learning, instead of considering pedagogies as specific to kinds of knowledge; and

- skills at the expense of knowledge. I will explore this further (see also Chapter 13 below).

There is something powerfully intuitive about the notion of skills in science and engineering education. It points directly to competencies that successful students must be able to display, and to what unsuccessful students can't do. Yet how are these to be stipulated in non-circular terms? How do we say what the student must be able to do without stating the obvious – 'the student must be able to do a successful design project'? Yet what this seemingly 'obvious' point hides from view is the fact that 'doing a design project' entails a dramatically different curriculum and pedagogical arrangement, an 'integrated' code rather than the traditional 'collection' code they will have been accustomed to in their courses up to that point and which requires quite different 'recognition rules' in order to meet the new evaluation expectations (Kotta 2011).

The problem of skills-stipulation in STEM as elsewhere in education is that it is very hard to describe skills (or 'techniques', or 'outcomes' and other 'can do' surrogates) in other than general or generic terms, which right at the outset obscures the speciality and differentiation of the knowledgeable practice in question (Winch 2014). In things like the fourth year design project in engineering, for example, it is manifestly a 'can do' kind of thing we are talking about. But it is a different 'can do' than the one expected and required by the traditional courses – or by the 'design project' in architecture, for example (Carter 2014). Which 'can do' or 'know-how' employers are referring to when they say that students 'can't do' stuff is thus far from obvious. What kind of knowledge is 'know-how', and how might it vary?

Winch (2013) has suggested that every area to be educationally mastered in the curriculum can be described in terms of:

- *know that*, or propositional knowledge; and
- *know-how*, or procedural knowledge.

More to the point here, there are three different kinds of 'know-how' knowledge. The first kind is what is called *inferential know-how* – knowing how the conceptual knowledge (the 'know that') learnt in the regular courses of chemistry and chemical engineering, for example, hangs together, and how to negotiate the epistemic joints that link the various knowledge 'bits' together. Already between these two subjects – chemistry and chemical engineering – the internal inferential relations, the internal conceptual logic, will differ, because of their different epistemic purposes, a potentially confusing difference which must be mastered via their respective recognition rules (Smit 2012).

The second kind is *procedural know-how*,[2] which is not really a satisfactory name because it sounds of somehow lesser status ('that's just procedural knowledge') than its epistemic twin. In fact it points to a more risky and uncertain kind of knowledge where the neophyte learns how to find out new things, find out what warrants and tests work under what circumstances, what the tolerances and limits are in real situations, forming new judgements that lead to solutions that work in the world.

The third kind of know-how Winch discusses is *personal know-how*, which is the idiosyncratic knowledge accumulated through diverse experiences in the process of actually 'doing it'. Most of this won't be codified, unless the practitioner takes the trouble to publish it in a trade or academic journal, or in more important cases, via a patent or registered software (Foray and Steinmueller 2002).

Added to this, Winch distinguishes also a range of different more practical 'know-hows' that are usually conflated when educators loosely talk about 'skills' or 'practical expertise'. As Winch says:

> Within the Anglo Saxon countries it is almost a reflex to talk about occupational know-how in terms of skill, as if there were no other kind of practical ability worthy of consideration. This tendency has had deeply damaging effects on the ways in which professional and vocational curricula are thought about.
>
> *(Winch 2014)*

These practical 'know-hows' include techniques, skills, transversal abilities, 'project management' (what Winch means here is something like the multi-level, multi-'skill' demands of a design project), and occupational capacity. These are all different and failure to grasp one or more could jeopardize competence in the whole.

The first point about these different knowledges is that they are *cumulative*, in three senses. First, the learner must have reasonable mastery of the *know that* (the conceptual content) before she can begin to grasp how the *know-how* works (Bengson and Moffett 2007). Second, the learner must be taught to grasp the inferences and the inferential relations before she will be able to venture out into uncertain territory with the *procedural know-how* with any confidence. Third, the various know-hows are themselves nested – they also ascend epistemically (Winch 2013), which is to say, they also have features of greater or lesser complexity which must be correctly sequenced in a coherent curriculum.

The second point, already stressed above, is that these various parts of the curriculum are *epistemically different*: they require different kinds of stipulation, they entail different recognition and realization rules, they have different evaluation criteria, and they entail different pedagogic relations, as Kotta (2011) showed. The main point is that simply calling them 'skills' doesn't help us describe what they are, or understand what goes wrong when students don't 'get' them, or can't 'do' them (see also Allais 2014).

This chapter advances the following tentative predictions for the future of STEM education. The first is that, unless matters change drastically – which they show no sign of doing at present – the diverse knowledges of the STEM disciplines will continue to advance and specialize apace. Demands for access to, and demands for, STEM knowledges and practical know-how will also escalate, bringing larger and more diverse constituencies into the universities. This will soon make the viability of a scenario 1 pedagogic arrangement, however patched and propped up by scenario 2 efforts, unworkable, if it has not done so already. The spotlight will thus come to focus more and more on scenario 2 efforts, which will probably become bolder and more ambitious. In order for these to achieve their aims of a fairer and more just access to knowledge, scenario 2 will have to make more visible the epistemic obstacle course that is the evolving STEM curriculum. To do so will require illuminating the differential *internal epistemic and pedagogic architecture* that we require students to negotiate. Which parts do they get with ease? Which parts seem difficult to which kinds of students? Are we making it more difficult for them by arranging things in this way rather than that? Can we illuminate the recognition and realization rules more clearly? In this way what Young and I (Chapter 5) called scenario 2 will begin to make way for an emergent alternative scenario, for a more robust scenario 3, that is better equipped to negotiate the specializing future.

Notes

1 Academic Development, also referred to in the literature as Education Development, is concerned with staff development, and in South Africa, student development.
2 Confusingly, 'procedural knowledge' is usually the name given to inferential knowledge that is coded into an algorithm, a piece of software, a routine. What it means in this sense is a set of relations that have been tested so often in so many situations that they can be taken as a reliable shortcut – until they no longer work. Following Winch, I am using it in a broader sense here.

SECTION 3

The idea of powerful knowledge

8

WHAT ARE SCHOOLS FOR?

Introduction

Every parent and teacher needs to ask the question 'what are schools for?' They are not, of course, the only institutions with purposes that we should question, but they are a special case. Like families they have a unique role in reproducing human societies and in providing the conditions which enable them to innovate and change. Without schools each generation would have to begin from scratch or – like societies which existed before there were schools – remain largely unchanged for centuries. There are, however, more specific reasons why it is important to ask the question 'what are schools for?' today. Since the 1970s, radical educators and many critical sociologists have questioned the role of schools and have seen them in largely negative terms. I shall argue that despite having an element of truth which we should do well not to forget, these critiques are fundamentally misconceived. John White, the philosopher of education, has offered a critical but explicitly positive answer to the question (White 2007). However, like the negative critiques, by failing to specify what is distinctive about the role of schools, he does not take us very far. I begin this chapter therefore by reviewing these two kinds of answer. I then go on to explore the implications of an alternative approach that locates schools as institutions with the very specific purpose of promoting the acquisition of knowledge.

For rather different reasons, the question of knowledge and the role of schools in its acquisition has been neglected by both policy makers and by educational researchers, especially sociologists of education. For the former, a focus on the acquisition of knowledge is at odds with the more instrumental purposes that are increasingly supported by governments.

For many educational researchers a focus on knowledge masks the extent to which those with power define what counts as knowledge. However, there is no contradiction, I shall argue, between ideas of democracy and social justice and the idea that schools should promote the acquisition of knowledge.

The 1970s and 1980s critics of schools

In the 1970s, negative views of views of schooling came largely from the left and were given considerable support by researchers in my own field – the sociology of education. The idea that the primary role of schools in capitalist societies was to teach the working class their place was widely accepted within the sociology of education (Althusser 1971; Bowles and Gintis 1976; and Willis 1977). The few working-class students that did progress to university were seen as legitimating the fundamental inequalities of the education system as a whole.

In the 1980s and 1990s, this analysis was extended to refer to the subordination of women and ethnic and other minorities. However, these analyses rarely went beyond critiques and presented little idea of what schools might be like in socialist, non-patriarchal, non-racist societies. Radical critics such as such as Ivan Illich (1971) went even further and claimed that real learning would only be possible if schools were abolished altogether.

The post-structuralist turn in the social sciences

In the late 1980s and the 1990s, under the influence of post-modernist and post-structuralist ideas and the collapse of the communist system in Eastern Europe, Marxism and other grand narratives foretelling the end of capitalism (and even of schooling) lost their credibility. As a consequence, the critiques of schooling changed, but more in style than substance. They drew much on the work of the French philosopher Michel Foucault, who grouped schools with hospitals, prisons and asylums as institutions of surveillance and control; they disciplined pupils and normalized knowledge as subjects. The difference between thinkers such as Foucault and the left-wing ideas of earlier decades was that the 'post-Marxist' theorists dispensed with the idea of progress and any idea of a specific agency of change such as the working class. For Foucault there was no alternative to schooling as surveillance – all social scientists and educational researchers could do was to offer critiques. He expressed this point in the following terms:

> I absolutely will not play the part of one who prescribes solutions. I hold that the role of the intellectual today ... is not to prophesy or propose solutions since by doing so one can only contribute to the determinate situation of power that must be critiqued.
>
> *(Foucault 1991, quoted in Muller 2000)*

It is not surprising, therefore, that these critiques were not listened to by policy makers – they really had little to say about schools, except to other social scientists.

Governments' responses

At the same time as the emergence of post-structuralist ideas, another set of ideas – neo-liberalism – came to dominate economics and government and, indirectly, education. Neo-liberals argued that the economy should be left to the market and governments should give up trying to have economic or industrial policies. The logic of this position was followed through with enthusiasm by governments of both main parties in the UK, with profound implications for schools. While ceding to the free market any role in the economy (with the exception of the control of interest rates), governments devoted their efforts to reforming the school system or improving 'human capital'. New Labour went even further than the Tories; they argued that the market offered the best solution for improving the public as well as the private sector – and education in particular. This had two consequences that are relevant to the question 'what are schools for?' One has been the attempt to gear the outcomes of schools to what are seen to be the 'needs of the economy' – a kind of mass vocationalism. The control of much post-compulsory education and even some schools and local education authorities has been put in the hands of sometimes willing but often reluctant private employers. The other consequence has been to turn education itself into a market (or at least quasi-market), in which schools are forced to compete for students and funds. I call this the de-differentiation of schooling. Schools are treated as a type of delivery agency, required to concentrate on outcomes and pay little attention to the process or content of delivery. As a result, the purposes of schooling are defined in increasingly instrumental terms – as a means to other ends. With schools driven by targets, assignments and league tables, it is no wonder that pupils become bored and teachers experience 'burn out'.

New goals for old?

In seeking to reassert the distinctive purposes of schools, I want to consider two alternative answers to my starting question. The first can be found in John White's paper for the Philosophy of Education Society of Great Britain called 'What Are Schools for and Why?' (White 2007). No one could take issue with his claim that schools should promote human happiness and well-being. The problem is that such goals apply equally to all institutions (except perhaps prisons) and they say nothing specific about what schools are for and what distinguishes their role from that of other institutions. In his paper White is dismissive of the idea that subjects or disciplines might define the purposes of schools. He makes the curious argument that the subject-based curriculum was a middle-class device designed in the eighteenth century to promote the interests of the rising bourgeoisie of the time. It is inconceivable, he argues, that a curriculum with such origins could be the basis for schools for all in the twenty-first century. In my view his argument is deeply flawed for two reasons.

First, as Baker and LeTendre (2005) have shown, the contemporary curriculum in the UK is remarkably similar to that found in most developed countries, despite their very different histories. Furthermore, the historical fact that this curriculum was developed by a particular fraction of the middle class in the late eighteenth/early nineteenth century is no grounds for describing it as a middle-class curriculum. It would be equally flawed to describe Boyle's law as a middle-class law on the grounds that Boyle was an eighteenth-century upper middle-class gentleman! The particular historical origins of scientific discoveries are interesting, as are the historical origins of scientific laws; however, these origins have nothing to say about the truth of a scientific law or about the merits of a particular curriculum.

My second reason for rejecting White's argument is that it does not address the question why parents, sometimes at great sacrifice, especially in developing countries, have historically tried to keep their children at school for longer and longer periods. Nor does it tell us what parents expect as a result of these sacrifices. Despite asking the question 'what are schools for?' White also ends up, like the government and the post-structuralists, in de-differentiating the goals of schools. As a result we have surveillance for Foucault, employability for New Labour and happiness and well-being for John White. I certainly prefer the latter but it is hardly a guide for those responsible for the curriculum.

Let us go back to Foucault for a moment. When he puts schools in the same category as prisons, asylums and hospitals, he misses both the history of the political struggle over mass schooling and what is distinctive about schools. I want to focus briefly on the first of these points and develop an argument about the implications of the distinctive purposes of schools.

Struggles over the purposes of schools

The historical struggle over the purposes of schooling can be seen in terms of two tensions. The first is between the goals of *emancipation* and *domination*. Since the Chartists in this country in the nineteenth century and more recently in the case of Bantu education in South Africa, dominant and subordinate classes have attempted to use schools to realise their widely different purposes. One only has to remember that Nelson Mandela was a product of the schools for Africans that predated Bantu education to be reminded that even the most oppressive school systems can be used by some as instruments of emancipation. The second tension is between the question 'who gets schooling?' and the question 'what do they get?'

The struggle over schools in this country has, with a few exceptions, taken the second question as given and focused on the first. The terms in which each of these questions has been debated have of course changed. The 'access' question began with the campaign for free elementary schooling in the nineteenth century, led to struggles over the 11-plus and selection and now is expressed in terms of the goals of promoting social inclusion and widening participation. Interestingly the idea of a struggle over access has been replaced by a largely top-down approach associated with government policies for 'widening participation'. Debates over the question 'what do they get?' also go back to the Chartists in the nineteenth century and their famous slogan 'really useful knowledge'. This was an attack on the domination of the curriculum by Scripture. The Chartists' idea was revived on the left in the 1970s but such questions are far less widely debated today.

The legacy of earlier debates can be seen in two contrasting concepts of education that underlie present-day government policies. One might be called 'education as outcomes'. In this approach to education policy, teaching and learning become dominated by the setting, assessing and attaining of targets and the preparing of students for tests and examinations. Less visible is a very different idea of education that still finds expression in the idea of subject syllabuses. It is the idea that the primary purpose of education is for students to gain access to different specialist fields of knowledge. The idea of education as the transmission of knowledge has, with some justification, been heavily criticized by educational researchers. However, my argument is that these criticisms miss a crucial point. They focus on the mechanical one-way and passive model of learning implied by the 'transmission 'metaphor and its association with a very conservative view of education and the purposes of schools. At the same time, they forget that the idea of schooling as the 'transmission of knowledge' gives transmission a quite different meaning and explicitly presupposes the active involvement of the learner in the process of acquiring knowledge. The idea that the school is primarily an agency of cultural or knowledge transmission raises the question 'what knowledge?' and in particular what is the knowledge that it is the schools' responsibility to transmit? If it is accepted that schools have this role, then it implies that types of knowledge are differentiated. In other words, for educational purposes, some types of knowledge are more worthwhile than others, and their differences form the basis for the difference between school or curriculum knowledge and non-school knowledge. What is it about school knowledge or the curriculum that makes the acquisition of some types of knowledge possible? My answer to the question 'what are schools for?' is, therefore, that schools enable or can enable young people to acquire the knowledge that for most of them cannot be acquired at home or in the community, or, for adults, in workplaces. The rest of this chapter is concerned with exploring the implications of this assertion.

What knowledge?

In using the very general word 'knowledge' I find it useful to distinguish between two ideas – 'knowledge of the powerful' and 'powerful knowledge'. 'Knowledge of the powerful' refers to who defines 'what counts as knowledge' and has access to it. Historically and even today when we look at the distribution of access to university, it is those with more power in society who have access to certain kinds of knowledge. It is this that I refer to as 'knowledge of the powerful'. It is understandable that many sociological critiques of school knowledge have equated school knowledge and the curriculum with 'knowledge of the powerful'. It was, after all the upper classes in the early nineteenth century who gave up their private tutors and sent their children to the public schools to acquire powerful knowledge (as well, of course, to acquire powerful friends). However, the fact that some knowledge is 'knowledge of the powerful', or high-status knowledge as I once expressed it (Young 1971, 1998), tells us nothing about the knowledge itself. We therefore need another concept in conceptualising the curriculum that I want to refer to as 'powerful knowledge'. This refers not to who has most access to the knowledge or who gives it legitimacy, although both are important issues; it refers to what the knowledge can do – for example, whether it provides reliable explanations or new ways of thinking about the world. This was what the Chartists were calling for with their slogan 'really useful knowledge'. It is also, if not always consciously, what parents hope for in making sacrifices to keep their children at school; that they will acquire powerful knowledge that is not available to them at home.

Powerful knowledge in modern societies in the sense that I have used the term is, increasingly, specialist knowledge. It follows therefore that schools need teachers with that specialist knowledge. Furthermore, if the goal for schools is to 'transmit powerful knowledge', it follows that teacher–pupil relations will have certain distinctive features that arise from that goal. For example:

- they will be different from relations between peers and will inevitably be hierarchical; and
- they will not be based, as some government policies imply, on learner choice, because in most cases, learners will lack the prior knowledge to make such choices.

This does not mean that schools should not take the knowledge that pupils bring to school seriously or that pedagogic authority does not need to be challenged. It does mean that some form of authority relations are intrinsic to pedagogy and to schools. The questions of pedagogic authority and responsibility raise important issues, especially for teacher educators, which are beyond the scope of this chapter. The next section turns to the issue of knowledge differentiation.

Knowledge differentiation and school knowledge

The key issues about knowledge, for both teachers and educational researchers, are not primarily the philosophical questions such as 'what is knowledge?' or 'how do we know it all?' The educational issues about knowledge concern how school knowledge is and should be different from non-school knowledge and the basis on which this differentiation is made. Although the philosophical issues are involved, school/non-school knowledge differences raise primarily sociological and pedagogic questions. Schooling is about providing access to the specialized knowledge that is embodied in different domains. The key curriculum questions will be concerned with:

- the differences between different forms of specialist knowledge and the relations between them;
- how this specialist knowledge differs from the knowledge people acquire in everyday life;
- how specialist and everyday knowledge relate to each other; and
- how specialist knowledge is pedagogized.

In other words, how it is paced, selected and sequenced for different groups of learners.

Differentiation, therefore, in the sense I am using it here, refers to:

- the differences between school and everyday knowledge;
- the differences between and relations between knowledge domains;
- the differences between specialist knowledge (e.g. physics or history) and pedagogized knowledge (school physics or school history for different groups of learners).

Underlying these differences is a more basic difference between two types of knowledge. One is the *context-dependent* knowledge that is developed in the course of solving specific problems in everyday life. It can be practical – like knowing how to repair a mechanical or electrical fault or how to find a route on a map. It can also be *procedural*, like a handbook or set of regulations for health and safety. Context-dependent knowledge tells the individual how to do specific things. It does not explain or generalize; it deals with particulars. The second type of knowledge is *context-independent* or *theoretical knowledge*. This is knowledge that is developed to provide generalizations and makes claims to universality; it provides a basis for making judgements and is usually, but not solely, associated with the sciences. It is context-independent knowledge that is at least potentially acquired in school, and is what I referred to earlier as *powerful knowledge*.

Inevitably schools are not always successful in enabling pupils to acquire powerful knowledge. It is also true that schools are more successful with some pupils than others. The success of pupils is highly dependent on the culture that they bring to school. Elite cultures that are less constrained by the material exigencies of life, are, not surprisingly, far more congruent with acquiring context-independent knowledge than disadvantaged and subordinate cultures. This means that if schools are to play a major role in promoting social equality, they have to take the knowledge base of the curriculum very seriously – even when this appears to go against the immediate demands of pupils (and sometimes their parents). They have to ask the question 'is this curriculum a means by which pupils can acquire powerful knowledge?' For children from disadvantaged homes, active participation in school may be the only opportunity that they have to acquire powerful knowledge and be able to move, intellectually at least, beyond their local and particular circumstances. It does them no service to construct a curriculum around their experience on the grounds that it needs to be validated, and as a result leave them there.

Conceptualizing school knowledge

The most sustained and original attempt to conceptualize school knowledge is that developed by the English sociologist Basil Bernstein (Bernstein 1971, 2000). His distinctive insight was to emphasize the key role of knowledge boundaries, both as a condition for the acquisition of knowledge and as embodying the power relations that are necessarily involved in pedagogy. Bernstein begins by conceptualising boundaries in terms of two dimensions. First, he distinguished between the classification of knowledge – or the degree of insulation between knowledge domains – and the framing of knowledge – the degree of insulation between school knowledge or the curriculum and the everyday knowledge that pupils bring to school. Second, he proposed that classification of knowledge can be *strong* – when domains are highly insulated from each other (as in the case of physics and history) – or *weak* – when there are low levels of insulation between domains (as in humanities or science curricula). Likewise, framing can be *strong* – when school and non-school knowledge are insulated from each other, or *weak* – when the boundaries between school and non-school knowledge are blurred (as in the case of many programmes in adult education and some curricula designed for less able pupils). In his later work, Bernstein (2000) moves from a focus on relations between domains to the *structure of the domains* themselves by introducing a distinction between vertical and horizontal knowledge structures. This distinction refers to the way that different domains of knowledge embody different ideas of how knowledge progresses. Whereas in vertical knowledge structures (typically the natural sciences) knowledge progresses towards higher levels of abstraction (for example, from Newton's laws of gravity to Einstein's theory of relativity), in horizontal (or as Bernstein expresses it, segmental) knowledge structures like the social sciences and humanities, knowledge progresses by developing new languages which pose new problems. Examples are innovations in literary theory or approaches to the relationship between mind and brain. Bernstein's primary interest was in developing a language for thinking about different curriculum possibilities and their implications. His second crucial argument was to make the link between knowledge structures, boundaries and learner identities. His hypothesis was that strong boundaries between knowledge domains and between school and non-school knowledge play a critical role in supporting learner identities and therefore are a condition for learners to progress. There are, however, a number of distinctive aspects to how Bernstein uses the idea of boundary, all of which can be traced back to Durkheim (Moore 2004). First, boundaries refer to *relations between contents* not the knowledge contents themselves. Second, although strong boundaries have traditionally been expressed in disciplines and subjects, from Bernstein's perspective, this is a historical fact, and the disciplines and subjects that we know are not the only form that strong boundaries can take. Third, strong boundaries between contents will have distributional consequences; in other words, they will be associated with certain inequalities of outcomes. Fourth, whether it is associated with creating new knowledge (in the university) or extending the acquisition of powerful knowledge to new groups of learners, innovation will involve crossing boundaries and calling identities into question. That is to say, school improvement from this perspective will involve both stability and change, or, in the terms set out in this chapter, the inter-relation between boundary maintenance and boundary crossing.

Conclusions

This chapter has argued that whatever their specific theoretical priorities, their policy concerns or their practical educational problems, educational researchers, policy makers and teachers must address the question 'what are schools for?' This means asking how and why schools have emerged historically, at different times and in very different societies, as distinctive institutions with the specific purpose of enabling pupils to acquire knowledge not available to them at home or in their everyday life.[1] It follows, I have argued, that the key concept for the sociology of education (and for educators more generally) is *knowledge differentiation*.[2]

The concept of *knowledge differentiation* implies that much knowledge that it is important for pupils to acquire will be non-local and counter to their experience. Hence pedagogy will always involve an element of what the French sociologist Pierre Bourdieu refers to, over-evocatively and I think misleadingly, as symbolic violence. The curriculum has to take account of the everyday local knowledge that pupils bring to school, but such knowledge can never be a basis for the curriculum. The structure of local knowledge is designed to relate to the particular; it cannot provide the basis for any generalizable principles. To provide access to such principles is a major reason why all countries have schools.

The concept of knowledge differentiation sets a three-fold agenda for schools and teachers, for educational policy makers and for educational researchers. First, each group (separately and together) must explore the relationship between the purpose of schools[3] to create the conditions for learners to acquire powerful knowledge and both their *internal structures* – such as subject divisions – and their *external structures* – such as the boundaries between schools and professional and academic 'knowledge producing communities' and between schools and the everyday knowledge of local communities.

Second, if schools are to help learners to acquire powerful knowledge, local, national and international groups of specialist teachers will need to be involved with university-based and other specialists in the ongoing selection, sequencing and inter-relating of knowledge in different domains. Schools therefore will need the autonomy to develop this professional knowledge; it is the basis of their authority as teachers and the trust that society places in them as professionals. This trust may at times be abused; however, any form of accountability must support that trust rather than try to be a substitute for it.

Third, educational researchers will need to address the tension in the essentially *conservative* role of schools as institutions with responsibility for knowledge transmission in society – especially as this aspect of their role is highlighted in a world increasingly driven by the instabilities of the market. However, 'conservative' has two very different meanings in relation to schools. It can mean preserving the stable conditions for acquiring 'powerful knowledge' and resisting the political or economic pressures for flexibility. A good example is how curricular continuity and coherence can be undermined by modularization and the breaking up of the curriculum into so-called 'bite-sized chunks'. The 'conservatism' of educational institutions can also mean giving priority to the preservation of particular privileges and interests, such as those of students of a particular social class or of teachers as a professional group. Radicals and some sociologists of education have in the past tended to focus on this form of conservatism in schools and assume that if schools are to improve they have to become more like the on-school world – or more specifically the market. This takes us back to the tension between differentiation and de-differentiation of institutions that I referred to earlier in this chapter.

This chapter has made three related arguments. The first is that although answers to the question 'what are schools for?' will inevitably express tensions and conflicts of interests within the wider society, nevertheless educational policy makers, practising teachers and educational researchers need to address the distinctive purposes of schools. My second argument has been that there is a link between the emancipatory hopes associated with the expansion of schooling and the opportunity that schools provide for learners to acquire 'powerful knowledge' that they rarely have access to at home. Third, I introduce the concept of knowledge differentiation as a principled way of distinguishing between school and non-school knowledge. Contemporary forms of accountability are tending to weaken the boundaries between school and non-school knowledge on the grounds that they inhibit a more accessible and more economically relevant curriculum. I have drawn on Basil Bernstein's analysis to suggest that to follow this path may be to deny the conditions for acquiring powerful knowledge to the very pupils who are already disadvantaged by their social circumstances. Resolving this tension between political demands and educational realities is, I would argue, one of the major educational questions of our time.

Notes

1 If set in a broader theoretical context, this chapter can be seen as locating the role of schools in the links between modernization and social justice.
2 In beginning with a *theory of knowledge differences* and not just the fact of differences, the concept of *knowledge differentiation* is quite distinct from (and a critique of) the superficially similar idea that there are different types of knowledge.
3 Here, 'schools' is shorthand for all formal educational institutions.

9

ON THE POWERS OF
POWERFUL KNOWLEDGE

Introduction: Knowledge in question

The primary aim of this chapter is to make a positive case for the idea of 'powerful knowledge' as a sociological concept and as a curriculum principle. We seek to clarify its conceptual bases and to make its meaning, and the arguments it implies, less ambiguous and less open to misunderstanding. This will enable us to suggest some of the research and policy options that it opens up.

It is an appropriate time for such a task as the concept has been called on in a growing number of academic, practitioner and policy contexts in England and elsewhere. In academic contexts it has become the subject of sometimes-acrimonious debate. Among philosophers, it has been discussed unfavourably by some (White 2012b) and though less directly, favourably by others (Cigman 2012). In recent papers John Beck (Beck 2012), so far the only sociologist who has commented directly on the concept, raises a number of related issues that we only touch on in this chapter. The concept has been favourably drawn on by researchers in the teaching of history and geography (Counsell 2011; Firth 2011), among teachers in a number of broader-based fora[1] and in academic contexts in a number of countries outside the UK – in particular New Zealand, Australia, South Africa, and Portugal. In policy contexts, it has been acknowledged as influential by the Expert Panel of the English *National Curriculum Review* (2011) and by the South African Review Task Team of the *National Curriculum Statement* (2009).

In this chapter we begin by making some brief comments about the specific origins of the contemporary usage of the concept from our perspective. We make this proviso because the two words 'power' and 'knowledge' are too general, too evocative, and open to too many diverse meanings for them not to have been used together in other ways and at other times. The concept, as recently used, has its origins in the history of our discipline – the sociology of education – and in changes in the way some of those in the discipline have approached the curriculum and the question of knowledge. However, it is not, we shall argue, a narrowly discipline-specific concept. It is best understood as derived from what, despite its older roots, is a relatively new way of thinking sociologically about knowledge (Collins 1998) and stands in contrast to more traditional sociologies of knowledge which have tended to associate the sociality of knowledge with bias. More specifically, it has focused on the social basis of academic disciplines, subjects and the curriculum itself, that are found in schools, vocational and technical colleges, as well as universities and programmes of professional education (see, for example, Muller 2009; Moore 2007; Young 2008a, 2008b; Wheelahan 2007, 2010; Beck 2012; Case 2011; Rata 2012). It emphasizes how the sociality of knowledge underpins its emergent 'objective' character and thus avoids slipping into the relativism that had plagued many other sociological approaches to knowledge.

The idea of 'powerful knowledge' owes a primary debt to the French sociologist Émile Durkheim, probably the first sociologist of education, and his assumption that we are not only 'social' beings but also – and which is for Durkheim the same thing – 'differentiating' and 'classifying' beings. In particular, we not only differentiate our knowledge from the world of which we have experience, but we differentiate within knowledge as well. That knowledge is social for Durkheim means that it takes its meanings from us as social beings in identifiable and challengeable ways, but in ways that are quite unlike those associated with our everyday experience and opinions.

We also differentiate knowledge from our opinions and experience because it explicitly recognizes, even if we do not always know how or why, a relationship to a reality that is independent of us. Quantum theory is the most reliable theory of the physical world there has ever been and in that sense it is as near as we have got to physical reality. At the same time physicists do not know quite why it gives us such reliable predictions. Physics, like any powerful knowledge, pre-supposes that the natural world is real and that current knowledge is the nearest we get to what that reality is. At the same time, quantum theory is probably the knowledge most at odds with our everyday understanding: it tells us that that the particles that constitute matter are in many places at the same time and that matter takes the form of both a particle and a wave.

We differentiate knowledge because in important ways not all knowledge is the same. We differentiate knowledge according to the best way we have to date of representing the differentiation of reality. We intuitively feel that some knowledges are 'better' – epistemically, morally or aesthetically – than others, and that they represent criteria about what is true, what is beautiful and how we should treat our fellow human beings and the non-human world that are more universal than others. If we accept the fundamental human rights principle that human beings should be treated equally, it follows that any curriculum should be based on an entitlement to this knowledge.

The second lesson we derive from Durkheim is that like all human progress, better ways of knowing are always associated with specialization, with the intellectual division of labour, and its relationship with the social division of work and occupations. Powerful knowledge therefore is specialized knowledge, whether it is quantum theory or Tolstoy's novels, although not all specialized knowledge is powerful knowledge in the sense we are using power, as examples like scientology indicate. But such examples are easy, and it is to deal with more difficult cases that we need as clear and rigorous a set of criteria as possible with which to decide which knowledge deserves a place in the curriculum on the basis of this argument.[2]

Our argument is not that specialized knowledge has a higher cultural value than non-specialized knowledge. Specialization is not a basis for denying respect or value to non-specialist common sense knowledge that people draw on in their daily lives. Specialist knowledge is 'powerless' in enabling someone to find their way about a house or city with which they are unfamiliar or helping a friend who has lost a child. The difference between specialized and non-specialized knowledge is a difference of purpose and, as we will argue, a difference of structure; it is not a difference of value, except in relation to those purposes. A community healer's 'knowledge' has human value as part of its wider culture, but for the purpose of treating HIV/AIDS, it is hardly dependable.

Third, to produce new specialized knowledge requires specialist institutions like universities and research institutes. To transmit such knowledge to the next generation also requires specialist institutions. These may be universities, colleges or schools. Specialized knowledge is not acquired or produced informally as part of people's everyday lives. Hence the crucial link between the entitlement to 'powerful knowledge', the curriculum and the universal right to schooling. Only if you do not think there is 'better knowledge' that all have a right to, would the principle of social justice reject the entitlement to specialized powerful knowledge through the curriculum.

Why then is there opposition to the idea of powerful knowledge as a curriculum principle? Let us start with the word 'powerful' and its strong association with the idea of 'power of someone over something or someone'. This takes us directly to one objection to powerful knowledge; it can be seen as fundamentally undemocratic, in two senses. In the first sense, powerful knowledge as we have described it is never distributed to all in an egalitarian manner. This is itself a consequence of specialization; not everyone can be equally specialized in all things, even though everyone can, at least in principle, be offered access to the basic powerful knowledge deemed critical for responsible citizenship in a society. Powerful knowledge is not only distributed unequally, but those who tend to get it are generally those already privileged – 'in power' in this sense. This has led in turn to a conflation of the two senses of power, a conflation that is not only a category mistake but also one that has had tragic consequences. The 'Lysenko affair' in the Soviet Union, when Stalin ordered the yield of crops to be improved, is one such (Lecourt 1980; Young 2008b). Another is the 'Mbeki affair', which refers to the South African state's refusal to distribute antiretroviral medication to AIDS sufferers on the grounds that the then President Mbeki had decided that it was 'poison' (Weinel 2007).

This argument is supported by the specific way in which science, technology, engineering and mathematics (STEM) subjects have come to be seen by governments as compulsory for a curriculum based on powerful knowledge, even though they may not refer to the concept itself. There is no question that STEM subjects provide the most successful ways of transforming, predicting and controlling aspects of the material world, even if they do not always predict the unintended consequences of such transformations. This explains the increasing emphasis put on STEM subjects by governments at the expense of subjects that do not seem to offer as much in terms of control over either the physical or the human environment.

Are STEM subjects then the only exemplars of powerful knowledge? Perhaps to avoid this conclusion, some philosophers argue that schools should not make knowledge acquisition their primary goal but should treat schools more as families, cities or communities – that is, with the goal of maximizing human well-being (White 2011, 2012). Only if knowledge, whether from the sciences or humanities, contributes to human well-being, they argue, should it be included in the curriculum. Plausible as this seem, the supporters of well-being or happiness rather than knowledge as a curriculum goal end up with an instrumental view which polarizes knowledge and well-being and denies the idea that knowledge may have intrinsic worth; it assumes that somehow well-being can be separated from the mastery of knowledge (Cigman 2012).

Is there a broader definition of power than that associated with STEM subjects? A historical viewpoint is instructive. The STEM subjects are relative newcomers to the canon and the curriculum in universities and schools. After the theological domination of the universities began to wane from the late Middle Ages in Europe, it was the humanities as expressions of elite culture that dominated the school and university curriculum, culminating in the Arnoldian definition of liberal education as involving 'the best which has been thought and said'. This expressed the humanitarian ideal of the cultivated citizen in the nineteenth century and was followed by similar ideas expressed by T.S. Eliot and F.R. Leavis. However, the balance had already begun to shift away from the humanities to the sciences after the beginning of the Scientific Revolution in the eighteenth century when the maturing sciences broke free from speculative (Aristotelian) philosophy and 'trial and error tinkering' as the main way to establish bodies of knowledge with conceptual and theoretical depth and empirical warrant (Collins 1998; Chapter 11).

There are two ways of seeing this shift towards STEM-based powerful knowledge from the 'worthwhile' knowledge of the humanists – a contemporary parallel of the earlier shift from Trivium to that of the Quadrivium (Durkheim 1977; Bernstein 2000; Muller 2009). One is as a form of democratization of the curriculum. If STEM subjects are the nearest we can get to universal knowledge (for example, physics is the same everywhere), it could be argued that they are in principle 'democratic' in that they do not rest on the cultural assumptions of any particular group but only the reliability and objectivity of their concepts and methods. By contrast, the humanities rely largely on traditions. To put it another way, the humanities represent the cultural 'knowledge of the powerful' (Young 2008a) in a world where such knowledge compares less and less favourably, on universal criteria, with STEM subjects. It is easy to see how, by raising the very question of specialization and powerful knowledge, one can end up with a view of non-STEM subjects as less than powerful, and hence less and less deserving of space in the contemporary curriculum and less worthy of support from public funds.

We will counter this view later in this chapter. In this introduction, we have set out to argue that there are three distinctions essential to an understanding of what we have referred to as 'powerful knowledge'; and why it might be a useful concept for the purposes we set out at the beginning. The three distinctions are cumulative; that is, each depends on the one(s) prior to it. They are:

- the distinction between 'knowledge of the powerful', and 'powerful knowledge';
- the distinction between non-specialized knowledge and specialized knowledge; and
- the distinction between specialized powerful knowledge and specialized less powerful knowledge.

We have touched on all three in this introduction. The first distinction reminds us of the difference between two questions we might ask about knowledge and the curriculum; who decides what counts as knowledge and why? And what can any form of knowledge do for those who have access to it (Chapter 8)? Although, in its initial formulation, and as Beck (2012) makes clear, 'powerful knowledge' and 'knowledge of the powerful' were presented as a dyad, it is the former concept that has raised the ire of the philosopher, John White (2012),[3] and been picked up in curriculum as well as sociological debates. In what follows, therefore, we will concentrate on the latter two distinctions, examining more closely the possible sociological grounds for distinguishing first between knowledge proper and other forms of belief; and second, between possible grounds for distinguishing between the degrees and types of power associated with different forms of specialized knowledge. In this way we hope to focus more and more directly on the title of our chapter – the power (and powers) of powerful knowledge.

Two exemplary theorists of specialized knowledge: Durkheim and Vygotsky

There are two exemplary accounts of why it is important, especially for those directly involved in education, to draw a distinction between kinds of knowledge, and why this distinction is crucial to distinguishing between specialized forms of knowledge and the other kind of knowledge that we all make use of in our daily lives. They approach the problem in different ways, but each succeeds in establishing a socio-epistemic rationale for specialized knowledge.

Émile Durkheim (1858–1917)[4]

The importance that Durkheim gave to differentiating between knowledge and experience, can be traced back to his criticisms of Kant in his doctoral thesis, which later became his first book *The Division of Labour in Society* (Durkheim 1993). He developed his alternative to what he saw as Kant's 'transcendentalism' with his concepts 'sacred' and 'profane' that arose from his research into the religions of primitive societies in his book *The Elementary Forms of Religious Life* (Durkheim 1995) that was published towards the end of his life. Durkheim initially used the sacred/profane distinction to describe the separation of religion and everyday life that he found in the societies he studied. He noticed these two quite distinct ways of thinking and forms of social organization discussed in the ethnographies of the time. Furthermore, as he was looking for the most general characteristics of all societies, the distinction became, for him, a basic social and conceptual form of differentiation at the heart of all societies, even those like the France of his time that had become largely secularized. He saw the difference as referring to two systems of symbolic meaning and argued that in their initial attention to the 'after life' and the 'problems of survival in everyday life' they were the precursor of the later differentiation between 'theory' and 'practice' that became the basis for the development of science and all forms of intellectual speculation in modern societies. For this reason he referred to the examples of the sacred that he found in the religions of primitive societies as 'proto-sciences'.

Thus, Durkheim argued that the conceptual and social differentiation of the everyday world of survival (the profane) from the totemic systems which allowed people in primitive societies to speculate about the afterlife (the sacred) became the social basis of science and other forms of knowledge that could be developed free from the exigencies of everyday contexts and problems. Without this separation, he argued, no society as we know it, and no social progress, would have been possible. In contemporary terms, his 'profane' and 'sacred' categories provided the social basis for separating practical and everyday problems from the theoretical/intellectual/conceptual problems that historically became secularized to include science and other forms of intellectual activity. Hence Durkheim offers an account of the specialization not only of occupations but also of knowledge itself. It is of course very different from that offered by Marx. Whereas for Marx philosophy should become a philosophy of praxis or action, for Durkheim the knowledge that we need as a basis for understanding the world and therefore the possibility of changing it, is separate from and prior to the practical activities people are involved in every day. Given that Marx relied on the practical business activities of his friend Engels to give him time for his theoretical activities in writing *Capital*, it could be argued, that in this respect at least, Durkheim had the better theory!

What Durkheim offers us is a sociological account of the development of knowledge and how it progresses. The conditions for knowledge to be reliable have to be a priori not a posteriori to its development. For Durkheim, to rely on usage or, in modern terms 'whether something works', opens the door to relativism. After all, what happens if an idea turns out 'not to work'? We don't know why and we have no principles for envisaging alternatives. In *Pragmatism and Sociology* (1983), that we referred to earlier, Durkheim's target was the American pragmatist William James (1970) and to a lesser extent the young John Dewey (1908) who much influenced the leading French philosopher of the time, Henri Bergson.

In some ways the early pragmatists were not so different from today's constructivists; their claim was that something was true 'if it fitted with experience' or 'was useful'. He saw these ideas as undermining the conditions for the trust in, and the growth of, science and consequently the possibilities of a fairer society.[5]

There are two strands of Durkheim's work that are important for our argument about 'powerful knowledge'. The first arises from his criticism of Kant's idea that we rely on knowledge that is a priori. This meant for Kant that the foundation of knowledge was either 'in the mind' or in some transcendental realm. For Durkheim the only solid foundations for knowledge were those rooted in reality and for him reality was social. The second issue that Durkheim focused on was specialization both in the occupational structure and in the growth of knowledge – both as aspects of changes in the division of labour. This raised the question that was at the heart of his sociology and beyond the scope of this chapter: how do societies based on specialization hold together and not fragment? In his later works he began to explore possible solutions through the role of education and the growth of professions as 'mediators' of specialized knowledge.

Lev Vygotsky (1896–1934)

Vygotsky's short career began shortly after Durkheim died, in 1917 (at the beginning of the Soviet Revolution) with the publication of his essay on Shakespeare's Hamlet and his critique of the dominance of behaviourism in the psychology of his time. However, he soon began to focus on the problems facing teachers in the new society in which the autocratic culture of Tsarism was still dominant, where few teachers were trained, and when schools for all were only just being established. The idea of specialization or the differentiation of knowledge from experience arose from his theory of human development as a cultural process and his belief that all people had a right to, and a potential for, developing higher order thinking that they would not have access to except through attending school.

Like Durkheim, Vygotsky relied on a binary distinction although not in the way it has often been used by psychologists (see Derry 2008). His distinction was between two kinds of concepts – theoretical (or scientific) and everyday (or common sense). As concepts, they have some remarkable similarities to Durkheim's 'sacred' and 'profane', although Vygotsky gave them a very different significance. The task of the curriculum, and schooling more generally, for Vygotsky, was to provide students with access to theoretical concepts in all their different forms from history and literature to the sciences and mathematics. Furthermore, he saw that access to higher order concepts was a complex two-way pedagogic process. Initially, the learner's everyday concepts are extended and transformed by pedagogy through engaging with the theoretical concepts of the curriculum. The process is then reversed; learners draw on their newly acquired theoretical concepts to re-engage with and transform their everyday concepts. Differentiating theoretical knowledge from experience was therefore central to his concept of pedagogy in ways barely touched on by Durkheim.

These two thinkers, despite their limitations, help us to establish the distinction between specialized and non-specialized forms of knowledge as a basis for the curriculum (from Durkheim) and pedagogy (from Vygotsky). We now turn to an analysis of some properties of specialized knowledge. It will soon become evident that specialized knowledge takes various forms.

Some properties of specialized knowledge

In an earlier chapter (Chapter 8) Michael Young drew from Rob Moore (2007) four principal properties of what in this chapter we are referring to as 'powerful knowledge'. It will be evident that different disciplines display these properties in differing respects. Nevertheless, in each of them, specialized knowledge differs in a significant way from what we have called non-specialized knowledge (for example, topical and everyday problems and themes):

Specialized knowledge is systematically revisable

In order for revisions to take place in a systematic and accountable way, there has to be a robust and generally agreed-upon way to distinguish the best proposition from other likely contenders. Disciplinary fields or traditions develop criteria over time which allow their disciplinary community to arrive, with a greater or lesser degree of consensus, at a judgement of this 'bestness', or the nearest we have to truth at any time. Even disciplinary communities that are characterized by sharp disagreements about the criteria for judging 'bestness' can still usually judge innovations in their disciplines with a considerable degree of agreement (Muller 2010). This is a mark of all specialized forms on knowledge.

Different criteria of 'bestness' have been differentially influential over the ages. The criterion we normally take as dominant today is the epistemic tradition of 'bestness' associated with explanations in the natural sciences. Since Popper and Lakatos (both in Lakatos and Musgrave 1970), epistemic 'bestness' distinguishes truth from non-truth in a revisable, non-absolute manner. Two other traditions have, however, been dominant in their turn, and continue to operate in the contemporary academy. The first, and the first that was historically hegemonic in the academy, was the moral or religious tradition of revealed truth. In the ancient European universities Aristotelian philosophy cohabited and prospered alongside theology. But theology was taken as the undisputed key to the intelligibility of man and the universe, hence the priority of the Trivium (the disciplines of the mind and the spirit – the nascent humanities) over the Quadrivium (the nascent sciences of the natural world) (Durkheim 1977). More recent, although certainly less hegemonic, versions of this tradition are found in Newman's famous statement on universities (1996) and in MacIntyre's writings (1981).

In the Middle Ages, at least in Europe, aspects of theology were gradually naturalized, humanized and secularized, and an aesthetic humanism came to rule the criteria for 'bestness'. Only with the Scientific Revolution, from the seventeenth century onwards, did epistemic criteria begin to trump ethical and aesthetic criteria and a regulatory concept of truth came to replace an absolutist concept based on revelation. The principal ethical and aesthetic disciplines are of course an integral part of the contemporary academy, but seen through an epistemic lens, they have come under attack for not meeting two key epistemic virtues: first, they do not constitute what Turner (2011) following Collingwood (1993) calls 'compulsive proof'; and, second, even in terms of their own criteria of 'bestness', ethical or aesthetic judgements do not have the same agreement and reliability as epistemic judgements.

We will return to interrogate these charges more closely later in the chapter. We would like to make two points to conclude this section. First, on the primary charge that the humanities and social sciences do not satisfactorily fulfil natural scientific criteria of epistemic 'bestness', we will argue, that it is based on a category mistake. Irreducible sets of robustness criteria – epistemic, ethical and aesthetic – have always contested for dominance in the academy as we saw above. Each has had its day of dominance. This should not mean that their natural disciplinary carriers should fall from favour simply because one set dominates at any given historical moment. This is to throw the baby out with the bathwater, which is to say, it risks evicting certain forms of powerful knowledge from consideration simply because they do not conform to the currently dominant definition of criterial robustness.

Specialized knowledge is emergent

This means two things. One is that specialized knowledge is produced by social conditions and contexts but cannot be reduced to them. The originating contexts may leave their mark on the knowledge; what kind of a mark and how significant the mark can be disputed. However, the value of the knowledge is *independent* of these originary contexts and their agents. If it is not, if knowledge remains 'contextual', then specialization and therefore the reliability and (and in the sense we have used the term up to now) the 'power' of the knowledge will in a determinable sense remain limited.[6] The human and social sciences are in a certain sense more 'contextual' than the natural sciences. But even here there is 'emergence' from context such that social knowledge, in order to become knowledge, must meet the criterial rules for acceptability of the discipline concerned. Even if these rules or norms are contextually sensitive, they are themselves not contextual, or else they will not be able to function as disciplinary norms.[7] It is then these social norms, not the particularities of the context or the interests or peculiarities of the agents that govern the judgement of knowledge as both specialized and reliable (Weber, in Whimster 2004).

There is a second meaning of 'emergence' that has a particular significance for the social sciences, which was first articulated by Durkheim. Although social events such as crowds, strikes, riots and institutions are constituted by the actions of individuals, Durkheim argued that such events have a 'social' reality that we can have knowledge of that is not reducible to the actions of individuals. This was the burden of Durkheim's argument in his famous study of that most individual of acts, suicide.

There is a position in the philosophy of the human and social sciences which argues that no knowledge, even natural scientific knowledge, can emerge as fully independent from its context, and that all knowledge is in some sense contextual, reducible to its context and the agents of its production (for example, Haslanger 2008). This is an argument *against* the distinction between specialized and non-specialized knowledge that we have drawn on. We would just note that the sense in which knowledge might be claimed to be 'contextual' in physics has a very precise, limited and measurable meaning[8] which hardly warrants the description 'contextual' and is very different from the meaning of same word when it is applied to knowledge in the social or human sciences. We can therefore disregard this claim and focus on the degree of 'contextuality' of concepts in the social sciences.

Specialized knowledge is real

It is about something other than itself about which it says something in a robustly reliable way (see the revisability criterion above). Ever since the Scientific Revolution, the test of this reality has been whether 'the world' answers to knowledge claims. However, all too often this is taken to mean that all specialized knowledge is knowledge about natural kinds – that is, knowledge about nature. From the writing of Giambattista Vico in the sixteenth century, through to the German *methodenstreit* debates[9], the argument of some about the human and social sciences has been that they represent knowledge about cultural or social kinds (phenomena), not natural kinds (phenomena). The debate has revolved about whether knowledge about cultural kinds can indeed be emergent – separable from context – or whether it can only become reflexively – that is partly – distanced from it (Bourdieu 2004). The debate is not settled. Conceding that the human and social sciences are about cultural kinds, however, does not mean that that they cannot be objective, nor that the worlds that they provide an account of are not real.

Specialized knowledge is material and social

All specialized knowledge is produced in particular socio-epistemic formations. These have traditionally taken the form of disciplines which are located mostly, but not only, in universities, with particular rules of formation or, as Durkheim would express it, with their own internal rules of solidarity, hierarchy, and truth norms. Disciplines differ in terms of their internal material cultures (their 'cultural styles' in Becher's (1994) terms). It is this material culture that holds in place the criterial or disciplinary norms (Becher's 'cognitive styles') constitutive of specialized knowledge.

From the above analysis an argument has begun to emerge about different forms of specialized knowledge, and hence of different forms of powerful knowledge. Nevertheless, there is one line of argument from the above that could lead to the conclusion that some forms of specialized knowledge are intrinsically less powerful than other forms, and hence may be less deserving of curricular inclusion. We take this argument very seriously, and present it in the section that follows, before we go on to indicate its limits, and ways in which powerful knowledge can be more broadly and inclusively considered.

Theoretical progression and empirical confirmation as criteria for powerful knowledge: the view from 'Bleak House'

The strongest post-Durkheimian account in the sociology of knowledge is that of Basil Bernstein (2000), and much of the on-going work in the sociology of education derives directly or indirectly from this quarter. This work attempts to flesh out the variations of specialized knowledge and their implications for curricular transmission (see Hoadley and Muller 2010 for a recent review). There are two principal criteria for differentiating forms of specialized knowledge that can be drawn from Bernstein's work, as follows.

Differences in the internal relations of the knowledge

This criterion describes two typical ways in which the internal relations of the knowledge – the body of theory or groups of concepts and methods derived from them – hang together.

- The first is that they build *cumulatively and progressively*, with earlier formulations being subsumed by later formulations. Bernstein called this form a *hierarchical* knowledge structure, in terms of which different knowledge structures and their bodies of theory differ in terms of their degrees of *verticality* (Muller 2007). This clearly describes the family of the natural sciences and in a slightly different way is expressed more broadly by one of Vygotsky's successors, V.V. Davidov (see Gamble 2011; Chapter 3).
- The second typical form is that the internal relations – theories and relations between sets of concepts – accrue not by one subsuming the other, but by the *addition of parallel theories* (languages, or sets of concepts), or in Bernstein's terms, *horizontally*. These parallel languages (bearing in mind that variants like historical narrative also belong here) co-exist uncomfortably but necessarily, because the unavoidable context-boundedness of their concepts limits inter-translatability and hence their epistemic guarantees. This clearly describes many of the social sciences and, somewhat more ambiguously and in some cases in different ways, the humanities.

It is not hard to see why the more subsumptive[10] theoretical disciplines are regarded as powerful. Setting aside the power of their utilitarian applications for the moment – certainly not an inconsiderable power – Weber thought this was the defining feature of modernity. He argued that those theoretical edifices which rested upon a deep base of accepted knowledge have a projective capacity that augments the capacity of scientists to imagine the previously unimaginable, to think the previously un-thought (see Whimster 2004). This is the power of theory in its non-utilitarian aspect, which is not to say that in some cases, such imaginative thinking does not develop practical uses.[11] Yet the question we pose below will be whether theories that do not take this subsumptive or vertical form cannot also have imaginative power, and provide the capacity for thinking the un-thought, albeit in very different ways and perhaps of the kind associated with great art in all its forms (Rosen 2012).

The idea of verticality as a descriptor of knowledge for the curriculum has led to fruitful investigations which have been able to show that curricular subjects with different degrees of verticality require specific kinds of curricular sequencing and pacing to optimize their pedagogic transmission for all learners, but especially those from poor and less privileged households (Reeves and Muller 2005; Hoadley 2011).

Nevertheless, there are assumptions embedded in the criterion of verticality that bear closer scrutiny. The first is that Bernstein explicitly distinguished between two distinct knowledge *structures* of vertical (that is, specialized) discourse, hierarchical and horizontal. He is not further explicit about why he does this, but he can be read to be saying that these forms of discourse are not reducible to one another; in other words, that they are in principal formally distinct. Tantalisingly, he never spelt out what distinguished them, beyond the distinctions already made above. If this reading of Bernstein has merit, and we will argue below that it has, then the nominalization of *verticality* could lead to the conclusion that all knowledge structure, hierarchical or horizontal, can be ranked in terms of their degree of verticality, leading unwittingly to a reductive reading of kinds of knowledge structure, and ineluctably to a view of the horizontal family of knowledge structures as deficit hierarchical knowledges. It is this construal that leads to what we term the Bleak House view. We will return to this non-reductive reading of Bernstein below.

Differences in the external relations of the knowledge

This criterion describes a capacity of the theory to describe, stably and reliably, something other than itself – an aspect of the natural or social world. Bernstein referred to knowledge forms as having strong or weak grammars, and once again, the nominalization of *grammaticality* (Muller 2007) can be read to suggest that all knowledges have either strong or weak grammars. A more nuanced reading of Bernstein will show that he meant 'grammar' to refer only to horizontal knowledge structures (Bernstein 2000: 168). Hierarchical knowledge structures do not have 'grammars' separate from their theories, at least not their accepted theories. What is subsumed in a hierarchical knowledge structure is a set of propositions governing the precise description of a range of phenomena. There can be no degrees of grammaticality here; either the proposition is or is not disconfirmed. Of course these propositions can be revised, but they will be revised from a relatively stable base of accepted propositions, and they will not be revised until an equally or more precise proposition is accepted. In other words, knowledge in hierarchical knowledge structures has a reality that is not separable from the phenomena it explains at least in terms of the current state of the discipline concerned.

Take the case of heat. *Hot* as horizontal discourse is located in the everyday. It does have a separate grammar, based loosely on experience. But *temperature* is part of a hierarchical knowledge structure (a theory of heat) and its grammar and instruments (the thermometer) are integral to its meaning. It is not that horizontal knowledge structures do not have discursive external relations; rather, it is that in hierarchical structures the external and internal relations are not separated.

The grammaticality issue only arises in cases when theory is weak, where integration is not possible, as is the case in the social sciences, in some borderline sciences such as parts of epidemiology, and when as in the case of neuroscience, some attempt to extend the remit of the concepts beyond the capacities of the theory. Once again, why some theories are inescapably weak is not very clearly addressed by Bernstein, and we will return to this again below.

The reading of Bernstein given here suggests then that a certain use of his distinctions can lead to what we have called a reductive view of knowledge forms. It is possible one of us has contributed to this reading (Muller 2007). If 'verticality' and 'grammaticality' are read as qualities of all specialized knowledge forms, albeit to varying degrees, then the distinction between hierarchical and horizontal knowledge structures collapses. The logical consequence of this reduction is that horizontal knowledge structures, primarily found in the social sciences, are seen as deficit hierarchical knowledges, or deficit natural sciences. This reading is powerfully abetted by a reductive move on the social sciences from another direction as well, derived from the explosion in cognitive neuroscience (Turner 2007b) that has been driven by new observational technologies like fMRI scans. This intellectual movement implies that the social sciences are indeed nascent 'immature' natural sciences and that their future as 'real' sciences depends entirely on further developments in neuroscience. Our argument, in concert with our reading of Bernstein, some neuroscientists (Tallis 2014) and philosophers (Bakhurst 2012), and traced back again to Durkheim, seeks to recover the specificity of the social sciences and humanities and thereby their distinctive senses of power.

Beyond naturalism?

How then are the human and social sciences different from the natural sciences? The question has traditionally been seen as 'the problem of other minds'. What the social sciences study is not a chunk of inert nature, what Bertrand Russell in droll fashion once called 'medium sized dry goods' (Laugier 2013). Rather, the social sciences study subjects that are *minded* (McDowell 2007), with their own intentions and understandings of the situation at hand. We can observe what they do, but we cannot directly observe the meanings they attach to those actions; we can only infer them. This is particularly the case for understanding actions in the past, but it also pertains to actions in the present, even when we are in a position to ask the actors. This argument was canonized in Weber's famous distinction between *direct* understanding (or *verstehen* in German), which has come to mean understanding from the actor's point of view; and *causal* or indirect understanding, which requires a rational reconstruction, evidence and a process of inference[12] (in Whimster 2004: 315, 316; see also Turner 2011: 246, 247). It is this indirect or interpretive inference and the relationship between the two kinds of inference that that has become a bone of contention and underlies at least some of the issues in the debate about powerful knowledge and the curriculum.

In the early to middle decades of the twentieth century the 'problem of other minds' was brought home forcefully to the social scientific community from at least three different directions. The first was the collapse of behaviourism as an explanatory theory that had tried to ignore the meanings of social subjects.[13] This was paired with an increasingly ferocious attack on 'positivism' that continues unabated today. The second arose from the difficulties experienced by anthropologists from colonial countries in their imperial task of trying to 'understand' the subjugated populations of the European empires that were then on their last legs (see, for example, Kuper 2005).[14] Third, as the century wore on, a series of social movements fed into a growing confluence: to name but a few – anti-colonial struggles and the emergence of an assertive Third World; the eventual success of the civil rights movement in the USA; the student revolts in Europe and elsewhere; the emergence of 'youth', gender and ethnicity as significant new social categories, peaking in the counter-cultural movement of the hippies in the 1960s and 1970s. 'Anti-establishmentarianism', or a ubiquitous anti-authoritarianism was in the air, what Geoff Whitty presciently called 'naïve possibilitarianism' (Whitty 1974). It is no accident that sociology of education's own mini-movement to 'make it new' (modernism's battle cry) was dubbed the 'new sociology of education', no accident either that it prominently featured a forthright anti-positivism and an experiential empathy with 'other minds' via an adoptive phenomenology from Schutz and Merleau-Ponty (see inter alia Young 1971).

All of these movements had in common, albeit often only implicitly, a particular reading of Kant (Turner 2011). For Kant, understanding always involved 'presuppositions' on the part of the one doing the understanding; the understander always brought to the act of understanding a presuppositional surplus that underlay and ultimately shaped understanding. We return, in a slightly different way to Durkheim's issue with Kant referred to earlier in this chapter. The question was; wherein did this surplus consist? The intellectual mainstream underlying much of the liberatory anti-establishmentarianism sketched above drew on certain strong currents of neo-Kantianism[15] running from Nietzsche through to Heidegger, the German hermeneutists, the American pragmatists and certain kinds of neo-Marxism. Most crucially for the social sciences and how they were appropriated in educational studies, it was through Kuhn's 'paradigms', that 'presuppositions' were to be understood in a non-cognitive or anti-intellectual way, at best as 'culture', at worst as contextual bias or ideology. The resultant 'hermeneutics of suspicion' was precisely that any act of understanding of social activity was constitutively an act of ideological imposition, and often a covert attempt at mastery or 'symbolic violence'.

It was taken as read that this ideological contamination was inescapable and could not but permeate the inferences of the social scientific observer or analyst. This constitutive contamination meant not only that social science was seen as a different sort to natural science,[16] but that it masked an attempt at domination that required resistance, where resistance meant valorising the viewpoint of the 'other' and unmasking the interests of social science.

It goes without saying that this non-cognitive surplus would also mean that social science could necessarily only aspire at best to partial truths,[17] because they would always preclude cognitive closure between data and theory, would always hijack 'epistemic finality' (Turner 2011: 231), and thus remain unobjective and open to ideological bias. As Robert Merton, perhaps the most revered of all American sociologists, was to put it, sociology was destined to be a discipline of 'many approaches but few arrivals' (quoted in Turner 2009).

This 'retreat from the cognitive' (Turner 2012) always had strong voices standing against it, a 'retreat' we have earlier called 'Future 2' in the context of an analysis of directions in the sociology of education (Chapter 5). We would like briefly to return to two strong counter-voices discussed earlier, Max Weber and R.G. Collingwood, both of whom, while accepting that social science would always consist in different perspectives, argued nevertheless that sociology and history, respectively, could both be objective and therefore truthful (Turner 2011).

This claim for objectivity depended for both Weber and Collingwood on a position that held that there were elements of social life and action in the past that could be considered as objectively true and separable from the perspectival entry point of the investigator which was the hidden abode of his or her presuppositions. The value of the perspective, either narrative in the case of history (for Collingwood) or theory in the case of sociology (for Weber), could then be assessed as to how well it could account for the facts as could be agreed from and across different perspectives. That Weber's explanation of the rise of capitalism and his account of forms of authority survive and remain credible a century later, albeit not without criticisms, is testament to their objective longevity. As Bernstein might have put it, we might concede that theories or narrative approaches – the different horizontal languages – embed a certain one-sidedness that reflects the situatedness of the investigator without also having to concede either that one-sidedness was all that could be said about the theory or that the facts of the matter were also therefore necessarily biased. Because the perspectives were plural did not mean that the grammaticality – rules for making judgements in terms of them – had to be weak. For both Weber and Collingwood, explanatory theories were detachable from the facts of the matter, necessarily so for any accountable investigation to be able to take place. In his most famous book, *The Protestant Ethic and the Spirit of Capitalism*, Weber *et al.* (2002) argued that we (and we must assume that at that time he meant 'we Europeans and Americans') need to come to terms with the fact that: 'In Western civilization, and in Western civilization only, cultural phenomena have appeared which (as we like to think) lie in a line of development having universal significance and validity'.

As Weber liked to say, the thoughts of Caesar do not depend on the questions we ask (Turner 2011: 237). But how do we know that we have got Caesar's thoughts right? Here we see the unfortunate consequences of the 'retreat from the cognitive'. If presuppositions are not detachable to some extent from observational understanding or interpretation, there are no resources left to guide or steer the act of direct understanding, and no one person can be 'better' or 'worse' at it than another. Exit knowledge; exit expertise. With the allocation of presuppositions to bias, there is no cognitive basis left for a tutored or expert observational gaze. That this is untenable can be seen by considering the case of expert professional action. The skilled and knowledgeable surgeon knows where to insert the scalpel both because she has the resource of specialized anatomical and physiological knowledge and because she has a repertoire of practical knowledge she has learnt from experience. So too the expert social scientist learns how to make social scientific inferences by learning the specialized knowledge base of the discipline and learning the observational and interpretive techniques taught by adepts. The actions of both the surgeon and the social scientist are, at some point, policed by a knowledgeable scholarly community through the myriad processes of peer review. What this example makes apparent is that the non-detachability thesis has the effect not only of ideologizing all social scientific statements barring presumably the ones unmasking the ideological presuppositions, but more deleteriously, evacuating the possibility not only of expert action (Collins and Evans 2007; Winch 2010) but the possibility of specialized knowledge, and hence of powerful knowledge, in the social sciences.

Weber held to the view that presuppositions (value relevance) were – had to be – detachable from scholarly acts (value freedom), but he never provided a conclusive argument for why or how this could happen. His was ultimately a moral position that he located in his account of the professional vocation of the social scientist (Weber 1958). The approach taken in this chapter begins at a slightly different starting point. As we said in the introduction, and went on to elaborate, the distinction between non-specialized and specialized knowledge is absolutely crucial. Brought to bear on this problem, this implies that presuppositions – which predate the specialized scholarly or professional act – consist in non-specialized elements *as well as* in specialized knowledge elements. Both together form the basis of specialized acts or judgements. It is when pre-predicative specialized knowledge is excluded from consideration that social science can be regarded as irreducibly ideological. If the social sciences are to retrieve their specializations as the basis of their claims to be a form of powerful knowledge, they have to re-introduce the task implied by Cassirer but interrupted by the Heideggerians – that of 'socializing the epistemic and epistemologizing the social' (Turner 2012: 474). That is another way of expressing what we mean by a socio-epistemic theory of 'powerful knowledge'.

The next question becomes: how to ensure that the non-specialized contaminants do not crowd out the specialized elements, which is where methodological rigour (or grammaticality) is critical; that is, methodological rigour as policed by the relevant peer community. We should admit that it is only relatively recently that some of the social sciences have moderated their previously sceptical and even dismissive attitudes towards peer review (part of the heritage of neo-Kantian anti-intellectualism) and taken the responsible step of tightening up on the importance of ensuring anonymity in patrolling the boundaries of what is and what is not admissible as social science. The social – here, the disciplinary community – returns as an executor and guarantor of professional or disciplinary judgement. The sloppier the peer collective is in patrolling the specialized/non-specialized boundary, the weaker will be the specializedness of the resultant knowledge, and the weaker will be the public trust in the resultant knowledge. It is in this way that society adjudges powerful from less powerful knowledge, not only in the verticality of its parent knowledge corpus.

Where does this leave the distinction between natural and social kinds? It is likely that this distinction will turn out to be a red herring. The problem with dichotomising 'natural' and 'social' kinds lies in the implications that are inevitably conveyed, that 'not natural' means not only 'not determined by physical reality' but, as a consequence, 'not fully rational'. The distinction, in other words, accords specialized knowledge to the 'natural' and consigns the 'social' to non-specialized knowledge, folkways, common sense and ideology. From the 'knowledge' position adopted in this chapter, it is not necessary or relevant to make a distinction between 'natural' and 'social' kinds. Besides the reductive freight it carries, attention is distracted away from the kernel of the issue. This is that all specialized knowledge communities have an onus to strengthen their methods, the better to strengthen their attendant theories and the coherence of their concepts.

This in no way denies the differences between the various forms of specialized knowledge that we have discussed. Nor does it claim that some are merely 'immature' versions, which may one day 'catch up', nor deny that the social sciences differ widely in the degree of shared agreement among peers. All these differences reflect the extent to which, as we have expressed it, the relations between specialized and non-specialized knowledge differ in different disciplines. The boundaries between the two are for all practical purposes unbridgeable in physics and in the chemical and, increasingly, in the biological sciences, not the least as a result of the lack of ambiguity of the mathematics they use and the abilities they have developed to express the relationships between their concepts in precise mathematical form. In the social sciences, if we take Cassirer's point about the intrinsic limits to the extent social phenomena are subsumable by concepts this will never be true. However, despite these differences, *all* disciplines deal with the world we face which is inescapably both natural and social. The distinction that matters is between those disciplines that, irrespective of their received conceptual reservoirs, are robust enough to gain public trust and those that do not. This is the social heart of powerful knowledge.

Whither the arts?

We started from the idea that knowledge is 'powerful' because it frees those who have access to it and enables them to envisage alternative and new possibilities.

We focused on how this is exemplified by STEM subjects, and, in different but no less important ways, by the social sciences including history. But what about the arts – performing, visual and literary? Are they specialized knowledge in the sense we have discussed the idea? And are they differentiated from everyday experience as we have argued is true of the sciences and social sciences? And if not, are they, as some current funding and curriculum policies in England seem to imply, to be cast into the dustbin of history?

We reject this view. At the same time, we do not claim that specialized 'powerful' knowledges are distinct from everyday experience only in degree. When we conceived the title of this chapter as the treating of 'powers' and not just of 'power' in the singular, we explicitly recognized that there are different forms of power associated with different forms of specialized knowledge. The STEM subjects are 'powerful' because they offer predictions and explanations beyond any that are possible for those who have to rely only on everyday thinking. The social sciences inherit some of these features: they provide generalizations that are tied, sometimes only weakly, to specific contexts; they generate facts grounded in the relatively objective methods of their peer communities. Their findings become a resource for debates about alternative policies, and they contribute in some cases to a society's conversations about itself. Furthermore, they make testable predictions, albeit in most cases as probabilities not certainties, and remind policy makers and politicians that the consequences of their decisions may be more 'powerful' than their intentions. The point we have made is that only if they take their rules of argument and evidence seriously, only if they treat their boundaries between disciplines and between specialized and non-specialized knowledge as sources of greater generative power, and not just as barriers to innovation, will their accounts come to be trusted and not dismissed merely as a set of competing ideologies.

Having made the point about the power of different types of specialized knowledge, we turn briefly to another dimension of 'power', for example, the power to imagine moral and aesthetic alternatives, which do not represent generalizations in the sense we have discussed, but which may be universal in the sense of connecting people to a larger humanity. There is every reason why access to such powers, expressed in literary, visual, musical or kinesthetic forms, should likewise be an entitlement for all. They are specialized and separate from everyday experiences; they are located in specialist communities that define their concepts, rules and practices, and the boundaries that distinguish them, define their objects and provide constraints that can be sources of innovation and creativity. If they share features in common with other forms of powerful knowledge, what are those features and why is it important to distinguish them from forms made popular by the market?

In a recent comment, the music critic Charles Rosen (2012), whose work we referred to briefly earlier, points us in a fruitful direction, although we can do no more than hint at the possibilities here. Rosen reminds us that the arts, while not liberating us completely from conventional meanings, let alone being without conventions themselves, provide a certain freedom from mundane certainties and conventions. What distinguishes arts from the sciences and social sciences is that although they are specialized and subject to the constraints and the boundaries associated with other types of specialized knowledge, they are not exclusive to specialist practitioners. You do not need to play the violin to appreciate Mozart, to write a novel to read Jane Austen, or to be able to dance to enjoy the Bolshoi Ballet. In each case though, it is possible to gain a kind of freedom from everyday melodies, texts and movements, and to imagine an enhanced set of possibilities in each of those domains.

Whereas the sciences speak to the particular from the general, the arts speak to the universal in the particular, and can enable people to feel part of a larger humanity. It is this freedom that Bernstein (2000) is referring to when he argues that disciplines are resources for 'thinking the un-thinkable' and the 'not yet thought'. Rosen reminds us of the links between the innate aesthetic impulses of human beings and the most obvious characteristic of every form of artistic endeavour, that at some point it inevitably draws attention away from its specific meaning and function to the form of expression and hence to the universal. What distinguishes the arts from other forms of 'powerful knowledge' is that although they have conventions, they are explicitly licensed to violate them, 'to entertain, to surprise, to outrage, to be original'. This he says is their inherent subversiveness and why political regimes, especially dictatorial ones, try periodically to repress them.

There is one important similarity with other forms of 'powerful' knowledge that we have discussed. It is that the conventions (or boundaries) of the discipline, for arts and sciences alike, provide the conditions for being able to transcend them. This returns to our initial definition of 'powerful knowledge' – that it is specialized and differentiated from everyday thinking. At the same time we have extended the meaning and range of 'power' from the more obvious predictive powers of the STEM subjects to those subjects and disciplines that are not sources of generalization or prediction but sources of the power to 'shock, outrage, and surprise' and hence transcend the limits in every present. That surely has to be part of any curriculum entitlement.

Conclusion

It is clear we have not solved all the conundrums that beset the idea of 'powerful knowledge', but we hope to have clarified at least some of them. This is not least because the philosophical community has yet to find a way out of the dead end of the split between the two traditions of neo-Kantianism represented by Heidegger and Cassirer. Positivism tried and failed, by defining science in a way that no scientist could accept and excluding everything else. Constructivism simply attenuated its relativistic implications.

Other attempts like Latour's 'actor network theory' appeared to solve the problem of relativism but at the expense of losing both knowledge and the social (Turner 2012). The social realist spirit that we inherit from Durkheim and attempt to revivify here rehabilitates specialized knowledge and binds it back into a social framework on which it depends. We think however that the long shadow of constructivism – an aspect of what we called Future 2 in Chapter 5 – will be with us yet for some time, not least because, as John Searle (2009: 89) has had occasion to remark, 'People who are convinced by social constructivism typically have a deep metaphysical vision and detailed refutations do not address that vision'. This is a vision of creating the conditions for freedom, which they see threatened by 'objectivity', 'rationality' and 'science'. We too share that vision of freedom, but for us, as we hope to have shown, it is only through the boundaries of the disciplines that genuine freedom, unforeseen expanded possibilities, can be generated. In the meantime, we can but emphasize the importance of powerful specialized knowledge in its diverse forms as the best, and most just, basis for curricular decision-making. Nothing else seems to be on offer.

Notes

1 For example, conferences for head teachers organized by the Prince's Teaching Institute and pamphlets published in the Education Forum of the Institute of Ideas (see Roberts 2012).

2 We need, we will argue, the concept 'powerful knowledge' to distinguish differentiated meanings of the word knowledge; for example, to distinguish knowledge as it is used in everyday conversations (for example, 'he has no knowledge of the city of Tokyo') from the theoretical knowledge of cities associated with the discipline of geography.

3 Ironically, readers will note that White himself uses a version of the thesis that the curriculum represents 'knowledge of the powerful' in linking the origins of school subjects to the economic interests of the rising Protestant middle class in England in the eighteenth and early nineteenth centuries.

4 Emile Durkheim was a French sociologist. He was Professor of Sociology and Pedagogy at the University of Bordeaux and at the Sorbonne, now part of the University of Paris. His clearest, though too little known statement of his social theory of knowledge is found in the lectures he gave to future secondary school teachers at the Sorbonne. They were collected and later translated into English as *Pragmatism and Sociology* (Durkheim 1983).

5 It is important to note that Durkheim's, like Vygotsky's use of 'science', was much more akin to the rigour and objectivity that they saw as a feature of all intellectual scholarship, rather than the narrower contemporary view of science as exclusively natural science.

6 It is on this point that we would differ from Shapin and his famous history of Robert Boyle and the origins of his gas law (1996).

7 A social norm in the critical rationalism of Canguilhem (1989, 1990) is a regulative principle that produces continuity for grounds of judgement. In this sense, to be a discipline is to be grounded in norms. See also Elder-Vass (2010).

8 Nearly 400 years since he discovered them, Newton's laws of motion hold with very high levels of accuracy except near the speed of light when Einstein's theory of relativity applies.

9 Literally, the 'method wars'. This was essentially a debate between the Austrian school economists and the historical school historians on the possibility of a science of human action. Under the influence of Rickert, Max Weber joined in the debate. We deal with his substantive contribution below.

10 We take the idea of subsumptability – the degree to which a phenomenon can be subsumed by the concept (or concepts) of a discipline – from Cassirer (see 1969, 1996, 2000). It is developed more fully in Chapters 2 and 8.

11 A good example is how questioning of the assumptions of Euclidean geometry, untested for almost 2000 years, led to previously unimaginable ways of thinking about space.

12 This distinction has been sharpened in the critical realist tradition, which distinguishes between the *actual* (the thing itself); the *empirical* (the experience of the thing); and the *real* (the generative mechanisms that produce the objective and subjective events). See, for example, Wheelahan (2010) and Collier (1994).

13 One of the earliest researchers to make this argument was, interestingly, Vygotsky whose influence we referred to earlier and whose work has been so misrepresented as the precursor of activity theory (Derry 2008).

14 The anthropologists' ideas, however, have survived the demise of empire and another debate has opened up around the value of 'indigenous knowledge' (see, for example, Rata 2011, 2012).

15 There was, of course another neo-Kantian tradition, associated with Ernst Cassirer, which we referred to earlier. Its marginalization and near demise is discussed by Skidelsky (2008).

16 Indeed the natural and social sciences were often treated as a 'common enemy' in the arguments for anti-racist, heterosexist and feminist knowledge – the latter neatly skewered by means of a penetrating focus on the materiality of gender inequalities by Martha Nussbaum (1999).

17 In many cases, at least in the 1970s and 1980s, this led some to dismiss the idea of truth altogether. In this regard, see Paul Boghossian's (2006) *Fear of Knowledge* and Harry Frankfurt's (2005) *On Bullshit*.

10

OVERCOMING THE CRISIS IN CURRICULUM THEORY

Introduction

What questions should a curriculum theory address? My starting point, at least for the last decade (see Chapter 8) has been: What do students have an entitlement to learn whether they are at primary or secondary school, attending university, or following a programme of vocational or professional education that aims to prepare them for employment? Such questions have no 'once and for all' answers; societies change, so every generation has to ask those questions again – and they are not easy. On the one hand, as educators, we have the responsibility to hand on to the next generation the knowledge discovered by earlier generations. It is this element of continuity between generations which distinguishes us from animals; it is a way of saying that we are always part of history. By contrast, the purpose of the curriculum, at least in modern societies, is not only to transmit past knowledge; it is to enable the next generation to build on that knowledge and create new knowledge, for that is how human societies progress and how individuals develop. The earliest societies, which did not have schools, remained virtually unchanged for centuries. However, we have inherited one important feature from these societies and from the first societies with schools; although the knowledge schools transmitted was largely religious (and assumed to be fixed), it was clearly differentiated from pupils' everyday experience. This is a point this chapter will return to in the contemporary context.

The interdependence of the two purposes of 'transmitting past knowledge' and 'being able to use that knowledge to create new knowledge', as well as spreading this capacity to an ever wider proportion of each cohort, raises difficult problems for curriculum theorists, curriculum designers and teachers. It requires a break from or at least a 'moving beyond' the two most prevalent approaches to education that we have inherited from the past.

One approach has characterized the European traditions but has parallels in those parts of the world which draw on the Confucian tradition and, if we go further back in history, on Islam as well. It inherits a view of the curriculum as a source of the 'sacred'[1] which, since the nineteenth century, has been progressively secularized to form the familiar disciplines of the university and the subjects of the school with their increasingly global reach (Meyer 1992). However, despite the massive expansion, both of new knowledge and of educational opportunities that these traditions have led to, they have not, at least up to now, become fully democratic and lead to 'education for all'. As a consequence, these traditions have inspired critiques and alternatives that have rejected the idea of the 'sacred' and put their trust not in 'knowledge building on knowledge' but in the innate capacities of all learners, and for some, all cultures. This progressive, learner-centred tradition can be traced back to Rousseau and took its most sophisticated form in writings of those influenced by Dewey.[2] It argues that only if learners are freed from the constraints of endorsing the 'sacred', and from what are felt to be the inherently exclusive traditions of the past, will their 'natural' potential be realized. Two very different models of the emancipatory possibilities of education follow. One puts its trust in *knowledge*, and for some, in its inherent openness – that the more we know, the more we are aware how little we know. For this tradition, teachers are not merely 'facilitators of learning' but pedagogic authorities in whatever field they have specialized in. The fault line and vulnerability of this tradition relates, on the one hand, to the increasingly specialized forms that knowledge takes and the limits which this places on its accessibility. On the other hand, it tends to forget how much we have still to discover about pedagogy, as itself a specialist field of knowledge, and how relatively few resources we invest in this task.

The second model puts its trust in the emancipatory capacities of learners, if only we knew how to realize them. It has been massively, although in my view misleadingly, boosted by the assumed potential of digital technologies to enhance learning. If only, some argue, teachers allowed learners unfettered access to the enormous information resource available on the internet, successful learning would become the norm for all and not restricted to the few. Despite the superficial persuasiveness of this argument, we still have no evidence that an information resource – however extensive and accessible – can, on its own, promote *real* learning. The mistake of all such theories is to use the amazing capacity everyone has for experiential or informal learning as a model for the quite different task of moving beyond our experience – the opportunity that schools and teachers uniquely provide.

The task of curriculum theory, I suggest, is to transcend these two models. From 'the sacred' tradition, it must take not only the idea of a 'store of knowledge' but those peculiarly human values of inwardness and inner dedication that shape and are associated with disciplined study and enquiry. In response to the critics of the 'sacred's' exclusiveness, it must argue that the exclusiveness of disciplines is not fixed or given but has a purpose – the discovery of truth – which is, in principle, open to all who are prepared to make the effort and are adequately supported in their commitment. This does not, of course, imply that in today's societies, it is only effort that distinguishes those who progress as learners from those who do not; there are massive political factors shaping the distribution of opportunities. My argument is that a major task of curriculum theory is to identify the constraints[3] that limit curriculum choices and to explore the pedagogic implications that follow.

So far, I have outlined what I take to be the role of curriculum theory – specifically in relation to the issue of 'access to knowledge'. It is a role that for a variety of reasons has, in my view, been largely neglected. That neglect is 'the crisis' referred to in the title of this chapter. This is not to say that curriculum theory or strands of curriculum studies have neglected the question of knowledge content (Deng and Luke 2008). My argument is that this 'crisis' is expressed in the reluctance of curriculum theory, at least since Hirst and Peters (1970), to address *epistemological* issues concerning questions of the truth, and reliability of different forms of knowledge and how such issues have both philosophical and sociological dimensions.

What is the important knowledge that pupils should be able to acquire at school? If as curriculum theorists, we cannot answer this question, it is unclear who can, and it is more likely that it will be left to the pragmatic and ideological decisions of administrators and politicians. Following a brief discussion of possible reasons why the question of knowledge has been avoided by scholars in curriculum theory, I will go on to suggest what might be involved if curriculum theory did start with the question of knowledge; I will then briefly illustrate how such an approach might be applied concretely in schools. The chapter concludes with a brief consideration to why the question of knowledge has been almost systematically avoided by educationalists as a whole and not just by those in the specialist field of curriculum theory. This is certainly true in the UK, where the current debates about knowledge and the curriculum are led almost entirely by government politicians (Young 2011c). However, this tendency is not restricted to one country (Yates and Young 2010).

Origins of curriculum studies as a field

Raymond Callaghan argues in his brilliant and not well enough known book, *Education and the Cult of Efficiency* (Callaghan 1964), that curriculum theory arose, initially in the United States, to solve problems faced by school principals. Early curriculum theorists, such as Bobbitt (1918), who had applied F.W. Taylor's 'scientific management' to improving productivity in factories were confident that the lessons from manufacturing could be successfully applied to schools. The goal of schools – in other words 'what was to be learned' – was taken for granted, so the curriculum was interpreted as the instruction and efficient organization of teaching resources. Instruction was understood by these early curriculum theorists and those that followed such as Tyler and Taba in a highly prescriptive way. The first critics of the model were Apple (2004 [1975]) and Pinar (1978). Together their early works transformed and literally 'emancipated' the field from the rigidities and aridities of the models associated with Bobbitt, Tyler and Taba.

In the UK, we were fortunate to avoid the American obsession with instructional objectives. However, as pervasive in its way was the concept of 'liberal education' associated with the fee-paying 'public' schools such as Eton and Harrow. As a curriculum, the concept of 'liberal education' was given more formal expression in England by the philosophers Hirst and Peters (1970) and it was their formulation that was challenged, from an explicitly sociological perspective by what became known as the 'new sociology of education' (Young 1971).[4]

The significance of mentioning these developments in the 1970s is that while opening up the field of curriculum studies in quite new ways and leading to a variety of innovative empirical studies (Goodson 1987), they also politicized the field (Young and Whitty 1977) and paved the way for its absorption into the radical rhetoric of 'critical pedagogy' that still retains a significant following in education faculties (Giroux 1983; McLaren 1995). The strength of these strands of critical curriculum theory was that they made explicit the way that curricula are not given but always embody prevailing power relations. I have described this as a focus on the curriculum as 'knowledge of the powerful' (Young 2008). However, by its one-dimensional focus on who had the power to define the curriculum, this tradition neglected the extent to which some forms of knowledge give greater power than others to those with access to them, *irrespective of their origins*. A focus on 'knowledge of the powerful', despite its strengths, almost inevitably shifts the analysis from what goes on in schools to the distribution of power in the wider society and offers little either to teachers or to political movements seeking a more equitable approach to the curriculum. It made the assumption that the existing curriculum, based on 'knowledge of the powerful' could be replaced as a result of political changes – without providing any indication as to what such a new curriculum might be like. As politicians have found, in contexts not limited to education, on the few occasions in history when the left have gained power, without such alternatives, they are reduced to some variant of the old models that they had previously opposed.

Let me summarize my argument so far. It is that in moving from a technicist model of instruction, associated with earlier strands of curriculum theory, to an ideology critique, curriculum theory lost (or is fast losing) its primary object – *what is taught and learned in school*. Arguably, as a result, it loses its distinctive role in educational studies. This 'loss of object' – the specificity of schools – has had two consequences. First, it has opened the door in curriculum theory to a whole range of writers in philosophy, literature and cultural studies who raise serious questions about culture and identity in modern society but have little specific to say about the school curriculum. The second consequence is that governments and curriculum designers – at least in the UK – pay less and less attention to curriculum theorists as specialists in the curriculum field. This may be a straightforward reflection of disagreement between policy makers and theorists, but I suspect that it is also a consequence of curriculum theorists renouncing their distinctive specialist role. It is easy to bemoan the forces of neo-liberalism, and academics sometimes seem most comfortable criticizing governments for their policies; however, given curriculum theory's renunciation of its object, we must take at least some of the blame. Despite the neglect by educational researchers of what is taught and why so many pupils learn so little in school, these are issues that will not go away and are issues that, in principle, curriculum theory is in the best position to address. Developing a more adequate theory, it follows, is a major task which this chapter aims to be a contribution to.

Origins of the crisis in curriculum theory

Why then has this crisis in curriculum theory arisen? I want to suggest three reasons. Firstly, and arising from the previous analysis, is the distrust in specialization as the primary source of new knowledge in any field – in this, I will argue that educational studies is no exception. Both the English critique of the elitist legacy of 'liberal education' (Williams 1961) and the American critique of the narrow instructional models referred to what earlier began by questioning their taken for granted assumptions about knowledge. However, neither had a theory of knowledge (and, therefore, of the curriculum) of its own which might have led to a focus on the different forms that curriculum knowledge might take. Thus, they led the field away from a theoretical focus on the different forms that the curriculum might take to a political focus on issues of power, politics and as in the work of some like Pinar, to issues of identity. However, a focus on the curriculum as, in Bourdieu's terms, 'the arbitrary impositioning of the dominant cultural arbitrary' (Bourdieu and Passeron 1990: 22) does not advance our knowledge of curriculum alternatives. There is a place for theories of the struggle for power in intellectual fields of the kind that Bourdieu inspired but in not addressing the limits on arbitrariness that teachers and curriculum designers inevitably face, they do not address the difficult issue of curriculum alternatives in a modern society. This requires us to take the curriculum seriously as an object of practice and enquiry that operates within two kinds of constraints; those of power and politics and the epistemological constraints that tell us that regardless of the distribution of power, how knowledge 'is selected, paced and sequenced' (to use Bernstein's well-known phrase) has consequences for who learns and what they learn in school.

A second reason, I will suggest is that the massive expansion of schooling has led, in a contradictory way, to a loss of confidence in its potentially emancipatory role. This is, in part, a product, under the pressures of global capitalism, of the increased focus on the 'means' rather than the ends of education. From a younger and younger age, school students are encouraged to think of successful learning in terms of their future career or at least in terms of progressing to the next stage of education (primary to secondary or secondary to higher). This focus on 'means' shifts the motivation of learners from *internal ends* – often expressed as 'learning for its own sake' and dismissed as elitist, but crucial to the intellectual development of all students – to *external ends* such as employability. However, educational studies itself has played its part – especially those trends in the sociology of education which tell us that the role of schools in a capitalist society is the reproduction of class relations and by the interpreters of Foucault (1977) who draw parallels between schools, asylums, and prisons. It is not that these ideas are false or do not offer important insights. The problem is that they can too easily become one-dimensional descriptions of 'what schooling does'– a kind of left functionalism which leaves very little space for considering the politically less 'oppositional' but no less important learning opportunities that schooling can offer to all students. School subjects, such as physics and history, always offer contradictory possibilities. If learners are to succeed, they are required to follow prescribed rules and sequences that are laid down externally and can be experienced as imposed and even alienating; on the other hand, with a well-qualified teacher, it is in submitting to such rules that students gain access to alternatives and a wider sense of their own capabilities. This tension between 'compliance with rules' and 'going beyond them' is lost in a curriculum theory that dismisses such rules as only expressions of power or ideology or equally misleadingly, a theory that sees learning anything that does not have short term economic benefits as 'merely academic'.

The third reason for the crisis in curriculum theory that I want to suggest is the increasingly widespread acceptance among educational researchers of the idea that knowledge itself has no intrinsic significance or validity. It follows from this view that the question that teachers are faced with becomes limited to 'is this curriculum meaningful to my students?' rather than 'what are the meanings that this curriculum gives my students access to?' or 'does this curriculum take my students beyond their experience and enable to envisage alternatives that have some basis in the real world?'

University colleagues of mine who visit student teachers in schools report something akin to a 'fear of knowledge' in the schools they visit – knowledge is either not mentioned or seen as something intimidating and dominating. As a consequence, if curriculum theorists do not themselves have theory of knowledge, it is not surprising that teachers interpret expressions of cultural resistance among students as celebrating their subjective meanings and identities. This has led either to an over-psychological approach to identity focusing on the learner as an individual person rather than as a social being (Ecclestone and Hayes 2009), or to the romantic politicizing of some critical pedagogy. What such approaches neglect is firstly that teachers cannot escape the instructional element of their role. Parents send their children to school expecting them to acquire the specialist knowledge that they would not have access to at home. Second, it fails to recognize that although knowledge can be experienced as oppressive and alienating, this is not a property of knowledge itself. An appropriate pedagogy, which engages the commitment of the learner to a relationship to knowledge (Charlot 2012), can have the opposite consequences – it can free the learner to have new thoughts and even think the 'not yet thought'.

I conclude that curriculum theory and, therefore, the curriculum must start not from the student as learner but from a student's entitlement or access to knowledge. Curriculum theory needs a theory of knowledge (Chapter 3) if it is to analyse and criticize existing curricula, and to explore the different forms that they can take. Curriculum theorists do not themselves make curricula; however, at least they can broaden the possibilities that curriculum designers have available to them.

My discipline (the sociology of education and more specifically the sociology of the curriculum) and specifically my own early work – has spent too much time on the political question – who defines the knowledge base of the curriculum? Important though that question is, it has led to a neglect of the knowledge question itself and what a curriculum would be like if an 'entitlement to knowledge' was its goal?

Assumptions of a knowledge-based approach to the curriculum

The framework for curriculum theory that I will outline is an initial attempt to address the question 'what is the knowledge that school students are entitled to have access to?' Before doing this, I will describe briefly the assumptions that I make and which shape both the framework and how I address the question of curriculum knowledge.

- In all fields of enquiry, there is *better* knowledge, more reliable knowledge, knowledge nearer to truth about the world we live in and to what it is to be human. At the same time, this knowledge is not fixed or given; it is always fallible and open to challenge. The difficulty this epistemological claim poses is how to hold these two ideas together – 'there is the better knowledge' and 'this knowledge is fallible'. Fallibility does not mean 'anything goes' but that in any specialist knowledge community, there are rules and concepts which always leave open some questions. This means that in order to experience the fallibility of knowledge, you have to be part of or engaged with the community in question. The natural sciences and the social sciences and humanities pose contrary difficulties. At the school and even at the undergraduate level, students of the natural sciences have to take the idea of fallibility 'on trust'; they are unlikely to have progressed sufficiently in mathematics to make the idea of knowledge being 'fallible' real to them, except in the case of statistics. In the case of disciplines outside the natural sciences, there is often little agreement among specialists about what the rules and concepts of a discipline are. However, even in such fields, there is likely to be a degree of agreement on the range of meanings that would be recognized as open to debate within the discipline, and hence fallible. It is this knowledge, however highly differentiated though it is, that I refer to as 'powerful knowledge'.

Powerful knowledge has two key characteristics and both are expressed in the form of boundaries.

- It is *specialized*, in how it is produced (in workshops, seminars and labs) and in how it is transmitted (in schools, colleges and universities) and this specialization is expressed in the boundaries between disciplines and subjects which define their focus and objects of study. In other words, it is not *general* knowledge. This does not mean that boundaries are fixed and not changeable. However, it does mean that cross–disciplinary research and learning depend on discipline-based knowledge.
- It is *differentiated* from the experiences that pupils bring to school or older learners bring to college or university. This differentiation is expressed in the conceptual boundaries between school and everyday knowledge.

These characteristics of 'powerful knowledge' are not restricted to what in England we call STEM (science, technology, engineering and mathematics) disciplines and subjects, although STEM disciplines and subjects express the features of powerful knowledge least ambiguously (Young and Muller 2013). Although powerful knowledge is not general knowledge, powerful knowledge has generalizing capacities. The concept applies to:

- *Ethics* – for example, Kant's famous principle – 'treat everyone as an end in themselves and not as a means to your ends' is 'powerful', not because it explains or predicts, but because it is as near to being a generalizable (or universal) principle for how human beings should treat others as we can get. Almost identical principles can be found in other great works of philosophy such as those of Confucius.
- *Literature and the arts* – great art works are 'powerful' because they engage with feelings such as guilt, remorse, regret, responsibility and joy that are emotions experienced in particular contexts but common to all human beings.
- *History, geography and the social sciences.*

In each discipline there are those (not all) who have a commitment to the goal of searching for the best, and most reliable accounts of phenomena, to the idea of shared rules and concepts and to the idea that knowledge progresses by building on past knowledge, even when that knowledge is rejected as in the case of much modern art and music. On the other hand, the phenomena they are concerned with are different from those that the natural sciences focus on and not only are their methods and concepts different, but they inevitably do not claim the same reliability.

I assume that the curriculum question 'what knowledge?' is both an epistemological issue that defines what should constitute the entitlement for students at different stages and in different specialist fields and a social justice issue about the entitlement to knowledge of all students regardless of whether they reject it or find it difficult. If some knowledge is 'better', how can we deny it to all pupils and allow some, as we do in England, to be limited to what in effect is 'powerless knowledge' from the age of 14 or 16?

A knowledge-based approach to curriculum

With these assumptions in mind, I turn in the next section to the main principles that need to be taken account of in designing a knowledge-based curriculum. These will include as follows.

Its form of specialization

From my assumption that 'powerful knowledge' is specialized, it follows that specialization in the university curriculum takes the form of the boundaries between disciplines and that such boundaries are defined by concepts, and rules for inclusion/exclusion, inference and argument and for sequencing of concepts. School curricula, by contrast, have pedagogic rather than research goals. Subjects which are 're-contextualized' from disciplines are the form they take.

Recontextualization, in this sense, means (in Bernstein's terms) the selection, sequencing and pacing of contents that takes into account both the coherence of the discipline subject and the limits on what can be learned by students at different stages of their development. In other words, while researchers and university teachers will be largely limited to epistemic criteria, school teachers also have to take account of pedagogic criteria and their knowledge of the capabilities, experience and potential of the students. This difference is one of structure and sequencing, not of content; the concepts of school physics are always specific cases of the concepts of physics itself (for example, a student will learn that 'mass = force/acceleration' at school and 'mass = energy/speed of light (squared)' at university, but the former is a special case of the latter). How recontextualization is done will vary widely across different disciplines and subjects. Furthermore, a disciplinary/subject-based approach does not preclude students gaining sufficient confidence by working within the boundaries of a discipline or a subject to able to challenge them.

The relationship between a national curriculum and the individual curricula of schools

A National Curriculum should limit itself to the key concepts of the core subjects and be designed in close collaboration with the subject specialists. This limit on National Curricula guarantees autonomy to individual schools and specialist subject teachers, and takes account of schools with different cultural and other resources, different histories and in different contexts (for example, schools in cities and rural areas). At the same time, it ensures a common knowledge base for all students when some may move from school to school.

The difference between conceptual (curriculum) knowledge and content (everyday) knowledge

The difference between school knowledge (in other words, the curriculum) and everyday knowledge is that they are constituted by concepts that are different in both structure and purpose. The everyday concepts that children acquire in growing up enable them to make sense of the world in relation to specific contexts. They are context-specific but are flexible and endlessly adaptable to new contexts and new experiences. Experience, in this sense, can be understood as the acquisition of more and more context-specific concepts. However, the coherence of everyday concepts, such as it is, is tied to particular contexts, and without the opportunity to engage with the concepts of a subject-based curriculum, children's understandings are inevitably limited to those contexts and those experiences. In contrast, the concepts associated with a subject-based curriculum are not tied to specific contexts; they are linked to each other and the underlying theories associated with the subject in question and underpinned by the community of subject specialists. It is this difference in structure that enables students with access to subject-based concepts to generalize beyond their experience and provides the educational rationale for the curriculum and its links to the broader purposes of schooling. Here is an example to illustrate this simple but rather abstract point:

> Pupils live in a city like London—they know about the part of the city they live in, cops and so on. This is an example of the non-school knowledge that pupils bring to school—it will be different for each pupil and limited by their experiences in growing up. Acquiring such knowledge is not dependent on going to school. At some point, however, pupils will meet a geography teacher. Geography teachers have a very different kind of knowledge about cities which relates to how they differ, their history and how they change. This is school knowledge—in this case, the conceptual knowledge of geography—the city is one example of a geographical concept. It does not replace a pupil's everyday experience; it extends that experience and enables the pupil to generalize about it. Other examples could be taken from literature or history. In the case of the sciences, pupils are likely to come to school with some knowledge of the natural and material world. However, most science does not relate to directly to their non-school knowledge. In science classes, laboratory experiments play the part of the everyday world to generalize from for the student. The concepts of physics and chemistry enable them to think beyond the specific activities they undertake in the laboratory.
>
> *(abridged from Young 2011c)*

The difference between pedagogy and curriculum

Pedagogy,[5] in the sense, I am using it in this chapter, refers to what teachers do, and get pupils to do; however, teaching is not just a practical activity (or a craft, as some English politicians claim). Teaching depends on both the knowledge that teachers have of their subject, the knowledge that they have about individual pupils and how they learn – and the knowledge that informs what they require their pupils to do. In contrast, although the curriculum refers to the knowledge that pupils are entitled to know, it does not include pupil experiences. Pupil experiences are a crucial learning resource for both student and teacher; however they vary widely, and furthermore, pupils do not come to school to know what they already know from experience.

Assessment as 'feedback to pupil and teacher' and assessment as the 'driver of the curriculum'

It is pertinent to distinguish between *assessment as feedback on pupil progress* – to pupils, teachers, parents and government – and *assessment as a driver of the curriculum and pedagogy*. Teachers are increasingly under pressure to shift the balance from the feedback role of assessment towards its accountability role as a policy or curriculum driver.

Practical implications – an example

I have been having discussions over a period of perhaps 18 months with a head teacher of a large mixed secondary school (over 80 staff) in England; they initially arose out of her reading my book (Young 2008) and led to some of the issues raised in this chapter. She has written a manifesto for her school staff titled a *Knowledge-driven School* (see Appendix). I am not suggesting that her ideas derived in any direct way from our discussions. However, I think her manifesto does illustrate how ideas often dismissed as abstract can be constructive in supporting a head teacher's role as curriculum leader and how difficult theoretical and often abstract issues in the sociology of the curriculum can be expressed in ways that are accessible to non-specialists. Her next step is that she intends to ask her heads of department to respond to the manifesto from the point of view of their subjects.

Objections to a knowledge-based approach

The approach to the curriculum which I have outlined is widely rejected in England, not only by teachers but by many educationalists in university faculties and the majority of those who see themselves as 'on the left' politically. I want to conclude, therefore, by considering three of the commonest types of objection to a knowledge-led curriculum that I have faced as a curriculum theorist in the UK.

I find it useful to distinguish three types of objection, the practical, the epistemological, and the political; inevitably, of course, they overlap.

Practical objections

Even in developed and relatively well-resourced countries like the UK, a significant proportion of secondary school pupils fail to achieve a reasonable educational level by the age of 16. The kind of knowledge-based curriculum that I am proposing could, if there were no other changes in staffing of schools or the preparation of teachers, almost certainly increase this proportion of failing pupils and encourage more disaffection and drop out.

It follows, for some educationists and many teachers, that such a curriculum is not practical for all students. It does not recognize the real difficulties teachers would face in engaging more than a minority of pupils on the basis of such a curriculum. Many students, it is argued, need a curriculum more related to their interests and capabilities. Conversely, there is considerable evidence that while programmes based more on pupils' immediate interests may make them happier at school, at the same time, they deny them access to the very knowledge they need if they are to progress to further study or have a reasonable chance of employment.

That is the inescapable practical dilemma of mass secondary education, at least in western capitalist societies, which community-oriented or employment-oriented programmes do not fully face up to. What such programmes do, however, is to mask the problem of educational failure and limit the likelihood that it will be addressed at its origins which are, substantially, not in the schools but in the wider inequalities of society. As I will come back to, this leads us beyond the curriculum to political questions. The practical dilemma stands more as a critique of a type of society than of a curriculum theory.

Epistemological objections

The knowledge-led approach to the curriculum is criticized by some educationalists in two quite distinct ways. Those endorsing postmodernist and poststructuralist theories of knowledge claim that all knowledge is unavoidably 'from a standpoint'. It follows that from such a perspective identifying some knowledge as 'powerful' is little different from accepting the dominant definitions of knowledge found in elite schools.[6] Again, from such a perspective, a knowledge-led approach is ideological. It asserts that as all knowledge is arbitrary, a knowledge-led approach is no more than the imposition of special interests. Student interests or preferences are, from such a perspective, as good criteria for a curriculum as any others. As I indicated earlier, denying the potential universalism and generalizability of 'powerful knowledge' means that all that is possible for curriculum theory is critique. The only alternative such a perspective offers to teachers is that they should help students find some meaning in their lives, regardless of the limited possibilities this may leave open to them.

The epistemological objection to a knowledge-based curriculum that is made by some philosophers (e.g. White 2012) is that 'school subjects' are out of date and inappropriate in a world in which knowledge is changing so fast. However, this confuses the content with the structure of the curriculum (Chapter 3). The historical fact that secondary school students in England in 1870 studied history and physics, and still do, does not mean their content has remained unchanged. Subjects are educational resources that topics and interdisciplinary themes (like the environment) important though they are, can never be. Subjects are:

- sources of stability for schools, students and teachers. This is important as part of the role of the school is to 'transmit' knowledge acquired by previous generations;
- sources of national (and international) coherence. Families move and students go to a new school in the same country or another country. Subjects give some guarantee (some subjects more than others) that a student will be able to continue and further his/her studies in a class of a similar age group in another school. Students taking non-subject-based courses, based on themes and topics, often find themselves repeating the same things year after year with no sense of progress;

- sources of identity for both students and teachers. For teachers, they have been developed by specialist professional associations (for teachers of mathematics, for example) where they can share and discuss new approaches. For pupils, the role of subjects is analogous but different. They initially enter what for many will be an alien world of the curriculum; their prior experience has not been subject-based. However, subjects with their clear boundaries and rules offer them an opportunity to develop new identities as part of new communities of learners and so become keen to follow questions defined by the boundaries of subjects that take them further in a subject and, in some cases, allow them to challenge those boundaries; and
- re-contextualized (I argued earlier) from disciplines which are a society's primary source of new knowledge. The link between subjects and disciplines provides the best guarantee that we have that the knowledge acquired by students at school does not rely solely on the authority of the individual teacher but on the teacher as a member of a specialist subject community.

Political objections

In the UK, the curriculum proposals of the last Government (DFE 2011) placed a considerable emphasis on a specific and narrow range of subjects, effectively limiting choice for both schools and students. These proposals, as I indicated earlier, have been opposed by virtually all those 'on the left'. They are seen as elitist and promoting social injustice and greater inequalities. Like the poststructuralists I discussed earlier, these critics accept, by implication, the relativist argument that there is no such thing as 'powerful knowledge' that is represented by subjects which should therefore be the entitlement of all pupils to have access to. They assume that 'access to subject knowledge' can be discarded as a priority for perhaps a third of each cohort by the age of 14 or 16 on the grounds that those pupils are not interested or find it too difficult or that it puts impossible demands on teachers. The disturbing lesson that I take from this objection is that many of these critics are somehow able to rationalize their avoidance of the question of 'knowledge', or perhaps are reluctant to accept a realist position that recognizes that epistemological constraints are for all practical purposes inescapable.

The dilemma is easier for those on the right as they do not believe in even the possibility of the progressive reduction of inequalities. They can accept a version of 'powerful knowledge' as the basis of the curriculum and locate the levels of failure it could lead to entirely in the choices of individual pupils (they don't work hard enough or their parents do not support the teachers). Morally and politically, I do not find the argument that rests on individual choice tenable; the possibilities of choice are not evenly distributed. However, that does not help resolve the dilemma faced by those on the left who are committed to greater equality.

My own view is that no curriculum can, on its own, significantly reduce educational inequalities. In our capitalist societies, schools will reproduce those inequalities – acutely in some countries, less so in others. However, reducing social inequalities is primarily a political task of establishing a more equal society, not an educational task. In England, a primary source of *educational* inequality is the opportunity that wealthy parents have to buy a 'better' education[7] for their children in private fee-paying schools which charge up to and over £30,000 per year. It is a sad comment on the Labour Party, as the main party of the left, that twice in 1945 and 1997 when they had large majorities in Parliament, they avoided the 'private school issue'. However, this is a political, not an educational issue; it is only a task for educators in our role as citizens. There is a real division of labour. I am no longer convinced, as I was in the 1970s, that it is helpful to see everything as political. I may have views about private schooling, but I have no political space to act on such views; the Labour Party are light years away from tackling the issue and there is no longer even the possibility of a socialist left or any idea as to what kind of alternative it could offer. For those of us who are curriculum theorists and our colleagues in the schools, our task, whatever our politics as citizens, is to develop curriculum principles that maximize the chances that all pupils will have *epistemic access* (Morrow 2009), or access to the best knowledge we have in any field of study they engage in. Denying access to this knowledge to some pupils, because they find it difficult, is like denying the equivalent of our Hippocratic Oath – to make available to them the 'best knowledge' that we can. At least a knowledge-based curriculum will highlight and not mask the inequalities in our society as so-called pre-vocational programmes invariably do. The *political* message of a knowledge-based curriculum is that inequalities in the distribution of resources of all kinds must be reduced if educational opportunities are really to be improved – and that, in the contemporary phrase is 'a big ask.' Meanwhile a better curriculum, supported by good teachers who believe in it remains the highest priority. The struggle over schooling has always has been a struggle for knowledge; that is what the debate about the curriculum should be about. Curriculum theorists are, I have argued, education's experts on knowledge; for this, we draw on sociology and philosophy and sometimes psychology. Political parties and the governments that they elect need our expertise, even if they do not recognize it, if their curriculum policies are going to support such claims as education for all and equal opportunities.

Appendix: A knowledge-driven school

In the teeth of structural change, we remember our role as society's educators and guardians of the young. While Teachers' Standards are expectations of our professionalism, what of our purpose? We are the people who offer powerful and shared knowledge to the nation's children. That knowledge comes from centuries of learning, and from the universities and subject associations. It is powerful because it enables children to interpret and control the world: it is shared because all our children should be exposed to it. It is fair and just that this should be so. It is unfair and unjust when children are offered poor quality knowledge which fails to lift them out of their experience.

Here are 10 things to remember.

1   Knowledge is worthwhile in itself. Tell children this: never apologize that they need to learn things.
2   Schools transmit shared and powerful knowledge on behalf of society. We teach what they need to make sense of and improve the world.
3   Shared and powerful knowledge is verified through learned communities. We need to keep in touch with universities, research and subject associations.
4   Children need powerful knowledge to understand and interpret the world. Without it they remain dependent upon those who have it.
5   Powerful knowledge is cognitively superior to that needed for daily life. It transcends and liberates children from their daily experience.
6   Shared and powerful knowledge enables children to grow into useful citizens. As adults they can understand, cooperate and shape the world together.
7   Shared knowledge is a foundation for a just and sustainable democracy. Citizens educated together share an understanding of the common good.
8   It is fair and just that all children should have access to this knowledge. Powerful knowledge opens doors: it must be available to all children.
9   Accepted adult authority is required for shared knowledge transmission. The teacher's authority to transmit knowledge is given and valued by society.
10 Pedagogy links adult authority, powerful knowledge and its transmission. We need quality professionals to achieve all this for all our children.

Notes

1   I use the term 'sacred' in the broader sense introduced by Durkheim (1995) which is not limited to religion, but refers to any meanings that are separated from the problems of everyday life such as obtaining food and shelter.
2   This is not to imply that Dewey was unaware of the limitations of a child or learner-centred approach. However, it cannot be denied that this is how many of his followers have interpreted him (Egan 2004), or that despite what he wrote, his own pragmatist epistemology lays him open to such a critique (Durkheim 1983).
3   Here, I am focusing epistemological constraints on a curriculum if it is to enable students to access what we referred to as 'powerful knowledge' in Chapter 9. Curricula are also determined by external constraints which take us to political questions and beyond the scope of curriculum theory.
4   Of greater conceptual depth and more lasting significance for curriculum theory, as well as the sociology of education was the early work of Bernstein (1971). It is through a paper on knowledge structures (Bernstein 1999) written towards the end of his life, that the importance of Bernstein's early work has fully been recognized (Moore 2004; Muller 2000; Wheelahan 2010; Young 2008).
5   I am using the term 'pedagogy' analytically rather than descriptively to refer to teachers' practices and the theories (often implicit) on which they are based. In Latin languages like Portuguese, this can be confusing as the meaning of pedagogy is almost equivalent to the broader English word 'education'.
6   I have referred earlier to this view as seeing the curriculum as an expression of 'Knowledge of the powerful'; in other words, those in positions of power define the curriculum for elite schools to suit their children's needs and in effect (if not explicitly in intention) to

discriminate against the rest. This focus on elite schools is important, but it is necessary to distinguish elite schools from elite curricula; the former focuses on unequal access, the latter claims that knowledge itself can be reconstructed – that, for example, a non-elite state school should teach different physics to a private school. This is a point I will return to in the concluding section. This is the unresolved dilemma of all social constructivist approaches to the curriculum.

7   Or at least one that gives their children the best chance to achieve high grades and progress to a top university.

11

THE PROMISE AND PATHOS OF SPECIALIZED KNOWLEDGE

All societies, at all times, distinguish between two broad classes or forms of knowledge: a specialized form and a general or generic form. In all societies the specialized form develops in specialized for-purpose institutions, and is distributed selectively in the population. The general form is distributed to whoever is an inhabitant of the relevant context where the knowledge is located. Everybody has some of both kinds of knowledge; but some, always a smaller number, have more specialized knowledge than others. This distinction between specialized and unspecialized knowledge is a constitutive one, and doesn't tell us in itself what the specialization is a specialization *of*. Some struggles are about what the dominant specialization should be – theology, classics or science, for example. Other struggles are about specialization itself, and the degree to which it is desirable and therefore merits inclusion in the curriculum. Both bear on the value society comes to place on specialization.

In most traditional societies, the initial specialization is religious or at least otherworldly, a form of sacred knowledge, which is why Durkheim (1995) called it sacred, in contrast to profane or everyday knowledge. Sacred knowledge has to do with questions of ultimate worth; profane knowledge deals with how things work, with useful knowledge of all kinds. Over time, of course, so-called profane knowledge also becomes specialized, but it specializes in a way distinct from the way sacred knowledge specializes. Profane knowledge becomes specialized to a particular external problem or set of problems in a particular context, and the raison d'etre for its dynamism is exhausted by the solution to the problem. Sacred knowledge is addressed to larger questions, ultimately universal ones, which, in their pure form can only be answered by recourse to first, fundamental, or ineffable principles: What does it mean? What is virtue? Where did it all start? Rather than being merely useful, the answers address question of aesthetics (about the beautiful); ethics (about the good); or much later, epistemology (about what is true). It is necessary to stress that these are tendential characteristics; the degree of focus on external purpose, or the degree of presumed universality or particularity will clearly vary from context to context. At key points in history, these become productively blurred, as we will see. Between the two, a proliferating variety of hybrid forms are to be found as we can see in the contemporary university (Gamble 2009; Muller 2009; Shay *et al.* 2011).

The first steps towards a non-religious specialized knowledge were taken by the Babylonians and Chinese, then consolidated in Greece and Egypt, the cradle of mathematics and the first home of schools for its advancement and propagation. The great Greek scholars like Euclid and Archimedes travelled to learn and teach in Alexandria, which is where abstract mathematics as a hypothetico-deductive system emerged, parting company with the empirical geometry used by the Egyptian surveyors (Raven 2011). Later, algebra (from al-Jabr) and trigonometry flourished under the Abbasid caliphs between the eighth and the thirteenth centuries in Baghdad, where the Persian astronomer Nasir al-Din al-Tusi invented trigonometry, anticipating the work of Copernicus (Cohen 2010). Through all these developments, and from the earliest times, it was theoretical knowledge rather than its practical applications that the scholars prized. So impressed with the beauty and power of the new form of knowledge was Archimedes, the father of mechanics and engineering, so it is said, that he died, in 212 BCE, preventing his calculations of cylinders and circles from being effaced by a Roman centurion. His face on the one side, and his famous cylinder inscribed in a circle, adorns the Fields medal to this day, the Nobel Prize of the global mathematics community.

Mathematics, philosophy and other forms of abstract theoretical knowledge were, before the seventeenth century, with rare exceptions, linked to and legitimized by the moral order, by the spiritual tradition of society. Theoretical knowledge developed, sometimes in concert with a specializing practical knowledge, as in Archimedes' case; more often insulated from it. Knowledge growth before the seventeenth century was 'in classical and Hellenistic worlds, China, the medieval Islamic world, and medieval Paris and Oxford' all characterized by a pattern 'of slow, irregular, intermittent growth, alternating with substantial periods of stagnation, in which interest shifts to political, economic, technological, moral, or other questions' (Gaukroger 2006: 18). After all, in a divinely-appointed world, of what purpose is new knowledge, or knowledge for its own sake? In this way, and in all civilizations, the sacred order not only legitimized what was accepted as knowledge but also put a brake on the development of new knowledge. Gaukroger characterized this as a 'boom-bust' pattern, which only changed in Europe to a pattern of steady, cumulative knowledge growth in the seventeenth century.

As schools and then universities developed – in the Confucian East, in the Islamic world, in Latin Europe, for example – practical and theoretical specializations developed slowly in boom-bust fashion over time, giving rise to the crafts and the disciplines in an uneven manner. In each case, the disciplines of the 'inner' or higher world ruled the schools. Which discipline became the queen of the disciplines (*regina scientiae*) differed: up to the middle ages, it was history in China, jurisprudence in the Islamic countries and theology in Latin Europe (Raven 2011). What they had in common was that they were all disciplines of the word and the book, and all were linked by a strong bond to the spiritual values of society which, as I said above, gave them a social tethering but also dampened the pace of development, because the disciplines of the inner and outer were strictly bounded, and the inner disciplines insulated, to a greater or lesser extent, from profane reasons.

The practical crafts like boatbuilding, calligraphy, healing and agriculture, highly sophisticated as some were becoming, were not considered worthy of entry to the university in the medieval universities of Latin Europe. When the dominance of theology gradually began to wane there, through the strenuous efforts of the Humanists, it was replaced by the humanities – grammar, philosophy, the classics and history. All of them nevertheless maintained a strong bond to the moral order, beholden to the Catholic Church which retained absolute authority, even over early scientists like Galileo, as he learnt to his cost. The moral order retained the power to grant final legitimation to all mere worldly knowledge because it alone could articulate the essential spiritual unity of the population. The worldly disiplines, even then, were seen as dissipative in nature, and hence dangerous if they were not first circumscribed by the essential spiritual and unifying core of society. First the inner, then the outer; abstract thought before worldly deployment and use: this was the strict order in Islamic scholarship and the European universities up until the so-called scientific revolution of the seventeenth century (Durkheim 1977).

I have so far sought to establish that the first great cleavage in formal knowledge in all societies known to us is the cleavage between sacred and profane – with the domination of the former over the latter – which morphed over a period of centuries into the dominance of abstract knowledge over the practical arts and crafts. This was not a static ahistorical dominance. It was and is contested, no more so than today as we can see from the current demands for 'relevance' and 'usefulness' coming from the marketplace which try to suggest that theoretical or abstract knowledge has passed its sell-by date and the universities should focus more on relevant and practical skills (see Chapter 13 below). Nevertheless, while the theoretical and abstract disciplines remained tethered to the spiritual traditions of society, the profane empirical disciplines took a back seat, and justified themselves in the name of the spiritual tradition. The empirical arts were not granted the latitude to contradict the eternal truths.

All this was to change between the seventeenth to nineteenth centuries in Europe with the scientific revolution. The inductive experimental procedures of the crafts and the 'natural philosophers' had gradually grown more elaborate and, at their most sophisticated, they had evolved into inductive experimental disciplines of some precision, in optics, for example. When these operations became fused to a, by now, highly developed mathematics, two things happened. First, theoretical experimental science was born – a fusion of the speculative and the experimental – with the development of theory the first prize. Second, this cleared the way for this powerful new theoretical knowledge of nature to be put at the service of the most developed crafts, and new forms of applied knowledge developed rapidly, soon giving way to technological professions with increasingly powerful applied scientific knowledge bases, like medicine and engineering. This is how Francis Bacon, 'that peer of scientific propagandists' (Merton 2001: 43) put it in his illuminating parable of the spider, the ant and the bee in his *New Organon*:

> Those who have handled the sciences have been either Empricists (men of experiment) or Rationalists (men of dogmas). Empiricists, like ants, merely collect things and use them. The Rationalists, like spiders, spin webs out of themselves. The middle way is that of the bee, which gathers its material from the flowers of the garden and field, but then transforms and digests it by a power of its own.
>
> *(Bacon 1620/1994: 95)*

Bacon continues with visionary understatement: 'From a closer and purer league between these two faculties, the experimental and the rational (such as has never yet been made), much may be hoped' (1620/1994: 95).

Bacon was not some born-again secularist. The blueprint for the *New Organon* that he forged was rooted in a biblical narrative, that of the Fall of man as described in *Genesis* 3, which led to a loss of knowledge and a restriction of human control over nature. The New Instauration was precisely to restore the dominion of man that had been lost at the Fall (Harrison 2007: 12), and in so doing to revive and continue God's original purpose.

I will not labour the point that the new sciences developed, in very short order, a formidable power in both a conceptual and technological sense, soon displacing the till-then dominant humanities in the European universities, with physics, that 'favourite Puritan scientific discipline' (Merton 2001: 69) taking over the mantel of queen of the sciences on behalf of the emerging disciplinary cluster of 'nature-knowledge', the now enlarged family of natural and technological sciences (Cohen 2010).

We might ask what happened in China and the Islamic states where many of the fundamental breakthroughs were first made. Weber's famous explanation pointed to the lack of an inner-worldly asceticism as carried specifically by Puritan doctrine (Weber in Whimster 2004: 25–34; see also Merton 2001). Weber thought, for example, that Confucianism disdained the aescetic attitude to the world, as did the ancient Greeks (ibid.).

This is partly backed up by Elman (2009) who points to the dissolution of the Jesuit order in China at the time. Other historians point to agricultural stagnation (Elvin 1983) or the lack of an activist bourgeoisie (Needham 1954). More generally, they were never as obsessed with nature-knowledge as were the Christian countries, a legacy of their particular sacred traditions (Cohen 2010). It is certainly not the case that they did not possess the necessary basic knowledge; in many cases, they made the original breakthrough but forewent the possibility of worldly exploitation, letting the invention lie intellectually fallow. What history makes clear, then, is that intellectual invention and developmental elaboration do not necessarily run in tandem.

Some consequences of the rapid growth of knowledge in seventeenth-century Europe deserve comment. Science-based technology first accelerated in the West (and parts of the North) but not in the East or South, nor in Africa. An extension into these continents was to come later as techno-science became the basis for the global innovation economy. Second, both the theoretical sciences and the science-based professions like medicine and engineering more and more rapidly developed new knowledge, building on existing knowledge and rapidly superseding it. This was aided by the rapid evolution of a new kind of applied knowledge, where theoretical predictions were used in the design of useful artefacts – science-driven practical knowledge, spelling the end of the traditionally powerful crafts which had been strictly inductive and often refused to record their traditions in an effort to protect them.

Specialized knowledge increased exponentially on the basis of the new disciplinary queens, maths and physics, then chemistry. This changed the balance of power within the orbit of reflective knowledge from the ethical and aesthetic to the epistemological: henceforth, knowledge with 'truth' credentials would carry more weight than knowledge that did not. This did not happen overnight, largely because of the ethos of Puritanism which through its tenets of glorification of God retained an integrating, but dimnishingly so, hold over knowledge specialization. But it did mean that the moral grounding of scientific knowledge in the West began to be displaced, creating a slow-burning crisis of legitimation of scientific knowledge to which I will return – the price to be paid for knowledge acceleration. Indeed, a number of distinguished commentators have for this reason blamed knowledge specialization itself for the 'disenchantment' of the scientific world picture, none more so than Weber himself, with his deathless aphorism: 'Specialists without spirit, sensualists without heart: this nullity imagines that it has attained a level of civilization never before achieved' (op cit.: 33). This aversion to specialization is today widespread.

Despite a number of rear-guard actions by the Humanists,[1] they were never able to re-establish absolute legitimacy on their own terms, and were increasingly driven into marginal positions in the academy. Sadly, that is still the case today, and probably accounts for some of the specialization-aversion. So, although it did not happen immediately, with science now dominant, the link between the epistemological and the ethical – the moral guarantor for knowledge up till then – first strained then broke.

The significance of this break should not be under-estimated. Modern science depends on the fact that our destiny is in the hands of impersonal causal laws founded in mathematical regularities, not of Divine Will or otherworldly direction. For some with a religious bent, this remains shocking, not to say an affront, one which is more or less successfully being opposed in many states in the USA today around the issue of evolution and intelligent design in the school curriculum. But there is a second consequence of the break. The untethering of the now-dominant specialized natural sciences from the sacred makes visible a latent and complex tension between specialization, on the one hand, and social cohesion and integration, on the other; a tension that the ethico-spiritual link had hitherto, with greater or lesser success, managed to keep in check. In a rapidly specializing world, with no intrinsic ethical check, we must confront the question of how social integration is to be managed. In a world of growing heterogeneity and low solidarity, what will stop durable social relationships giving way to ephemeral transactions and 'normative shrinkage'? (Archer 2013). How are imaginaries of community and nation sustained when the force that prevented specialization from sliding into fragmentation and the erosion of meaningful social bonds has been disabled? This is discussed further below.

Before I return to the issue of values and science, it may be useful to reflect on where this has left knowledge in our contemporary world. If the account briefly sketched so far has merit, the sacred-profane distinction gives way to at least four emblematic ways of arriving at knowledge about the world in addition, of course, to the overriding faculty of imagination:

- deductively, to answer purely conceptual questions, whether validated by empirical warrant or not: conceptual knowledge;
- deductively, by using principles to generate new useful and practical knowledge: applied conceptual knowledge;
- inductively, via procedural and practical knowledge, underpinned by some conceptual knowledge: principalled procedural knowledge; and
- trial and error everyday knowledge – knowledge by acquaintance: procedural knowledge.

The conceptual knowledge bundle is rooted in a body of concepts interrelated by a governing theory; the procedural knowledge bundle is rooted in empirical experience and held together by its supervening purpose. The more interesting forms are the middle two. This is where most of the formal knowledge in our educational institutions is found. Here a key point becomes plain: both procedural knowledge and conceptual knowledge can be principled, but the principles are differently grounded. In principled procedural knowledge the principles emerge from the procedures themselves: the principles are what make the procedures cohere; but this can best be seen, and learnt, in practice. In the case of conceptual knowledge, the principles arise from the way the concepts are connected in a body of theory.

The force of the distinction between the middle two knowledge bundles lies in the fact that, with their animating principles arising from different roots, they hang together differently. This has an important implication for the curriculum based on these different kinds of knowledge because they have different curricula configuration and coherence requirements.

The more contextually relevant the bundle to be learnt is, the more it will stress the kind of knowledge that inheres in specialized practice; the more conceptually relevant the knowledge to be learnt is, the more it will stress knowledge that fits the conceptual and theoretical framework to be learnt. The more task specific the proficiency, the more contextually relevant and coherent the curriculum must be; the more knowledge-specialized, the more conceptually relevant it must be.

This has many implications for curriculum design and development (see, for example, Shay *et al.* 2011; Muller 2009). For present purposes, though, the following bears on the discussion of specialization. If in earlier times specialization was the province of the sacred/conceptual domain of knowledge, and the profane domain was relegated to empirically accreted particulars for particular purposes, this is no longer the case. Knowledge specialization now occurs regularly in all three knowledge domains where concepts have been integrated, albeit differently. It may be that accretion is driven primarily empirically, as it is in kinds of experimental chemistry and in medical and pharmaceutical work; or it may be driven by theoretical breakthoughs; or indeed by many combinations of them. Conceptuality though remains key to knowledge specialization, and though the boundary between the different knowledge forms may have been breached, this remains the 'golden thread' of specialization.

To return to the question: why has specialization provoked such a negative reaction? One form of reaction can be traced to a perrenial complaint that the humanities have made against the natural sciences ever since they were de-throned as the queen of the sciences (discussed above). The argument rests upon the original Trivium argument for its precedence over the Quadrivium, namely, that it provided the moral anchor for the potentially promiscuous sciences, without which their practitioners become, in Weber's words quoted above, 'Specialists without spirit, sensualists without heart'. This view lies too behind F.R. Leavis' extraordinary attack on C.P. Snow in the so-called *Two Cultures* debate (see Muller 2011b: 211–2). Bernstein expressed dismay at what he saw as the untethering of technical and professional knowledge, which, in his words, had become 'divorced from inwardness' (Bernstein 1996: 87; see also Chapter 12 below). Durkheim too warned about the potential for aridity in sciences preoccupied only with the external world, thereby cutting themselves off from means to become 'humanized and revitalized' (Durkheim 1977: 337). All of these views warn of the instrumental dangers of specialization, particularly in the sciences. Only the extreme voices take that to entail a blanket rejection of specialization.

A version of 'specialization-aversion' can be found within the humanities, not infrequently paired with an aversion to 'disciplines' in favour of interdisciplinarity or pan-disciplinarity, on the medieval grounds of the indivisibility of knowledge. Colin Burrow gives expression to both views in his review of a book on philology by James Turner:

> And in the dark nether reaches of the academic mind it can become a form of ego-building in which the accumulation of increasingly complex historical details as a proxy for understanding creates a little zone in which the scholar believes him or herself to be the only person who possesses proper knowledge.'
>
> *(Burrow 2014: 37)*

and a little further, 'disciplines are a wet sock to the imagination' (ibid.). These are forms of 'specialization-aversion' bound up in a complex way with the age-old 'contest of the faculties', all of them decrying the spiritual loss, real or potential, in the wake of the scientific revolution and the secularization of specialized knowledge. These are bound up, in turn, in a complex way with issues of social justice.

There are three things worth noting. The first is that specialized knowledge is, as already noted, always selectively distributed. There is an issue of equity involved here: to decide how much specialized knowledge every learner should be offered for each fit-for-purpose qualification (Wheelahan 2010), and then to exercise political will in ensuring that this is properly delivered. It is not a new issue, of course, but increased specialization raises it anew. This is a matter of social justice, with which this book is centrally concerned. Pedagogical research which takes this seriously will continue to map the pedagogic conditions which will optimise the learning opportunities for children from disadvantaged communities (Hoadley and Muller 2010). But it is an unavoidable fact that, as ladders of specialization grow ever higher, fewer and fewer learner-citizens will have the wherewithal to stick it out to reach the apex. For some, this is by itself a negative consequence and one that should be decried. I will briefly below visit the ethical consequences of specialized knowledge before I try to connect these issues back to the issue of an inner spiritual core to specialized knowledge.

Second, specialized knowledge is, for the foreseeable future, likely to grow, not lessen, in importance. A new problem then arises: how will schools cope with those pupils who, for various reasons, simply have no interest in the specialized knowledges on offer, or who choose not to put in the endeavour required to succeed? How will education deal with those who find themselves epistemically disaffected from specialized knowledge? In the past they were diverted into less specialized streams; but today these too are increasingly becoming more specialized (Yates 2013).

I will now return to the rift between the epistemological and the moral, to the seemingly thorough-going secularization of the dominant conception of knowledge. This conception has reduced questions of worth to epistemology and fused this with the quest for empirical validation and utilitarian application. The result has been a powerful self-elaborating socio-epistemological engine that operates outside of guiding moral-ethical precepts except the constitutive norms of science (Merton 1992; Turner 2007a). What gives this engine a spiritual or transcendent rationale beyond its scientific elegance and its technical usefulness; virtues apparent largely to its initiates? For the seventeenth-century English Puritans, science was the discovery of 'divine Reason', the 'Wisdom of God', as it still is for Islamic scholars (see Cohen 2010; Muller 2011a). In the bastions of science in the West, the meaning underlying this link has long evaporated.

Or has it? This deserves a little more attention. Earlier, the stance of Francis Bacon was cited, insisting on the religious or 'higher' mission of an experimental natural philosophy. This view was to become the rule in seventeenth-century scientific circles, the idea that science was a religious vocation. As Boyle once said: natural philosophy was the 'philosophical worship of God' (cited by Harrison 2007: 15), or as Newton put it in the fourth edition of the *Opticks*, 'natural philosophy, or science, was enlarging the bounds of moral philosophy, and of shedding light on the nature of the "first cause" – God' (ibid.: 15, 16).

As for the material benefits of science, this was nothing more than Christian charity in action. Of course, this view also came in for a fair degree of lampooning at the time from those who felt that profane nature-knowledge was either trivial or dangerous, or both. Political commentator James Harrington wrote that the new scientists were good 'at two things, at diminishing a Commonwealth, and multiplying a Louse' (ibid.: 2), the first slur being a reference to the challenge to the divine right of the King posed by the new 'democratic' authority of science, the second refering to the the lowly preoccupations of the experimentalists. Thomas Shadwell wrote a play, *The Virtuoso*, mocking the uselessness of science, and Swift's *Gulliver's Travels* takes a savage side swipe at scientific academies.

This opposition came from various quarters and was by no means all of peace. Some thought that Aristotle's natural philosophy had a firmer ethical base than that of the new philosophy. Yet others saw, correctly, that science presaged a greater challenge to the authority of the clerisy than to theology, which over time became conflated with religion in toto. Nevertheless, Baconian ideals of a redemptive better world paired with Puritan piety proved for a good while a potent glue to weld together the nascent epistemological strengths of science and an otherworldly higher moral purpose.

By the time of the nineteenth century, natural philosophy had morphed almost unrecognizably into modern science and, at least rhetorically, had shed its external religious trappings. This also had the unfortunate effect of weaning science from its connection to inner piety, and the link to the inner was lost. As Harrison (2007) shows, science had by this time gained in confidence to stand on its own, and with the professionalization of science came determined efforts from scientists to distance themselves from religion, creating in the process an unfortunate and misleading polarization between science and religion that persists to this day. Harrison also shows that it was not only science, but also religion that changed its character at this time, and with the instantiation of 'religion' as an organized belief system came 'an objectification of the inner disposition' (ibid.: 19), effectively the reification of religion, which probably also contributed to the burgeoning polarization.

There is a further issue which should not be overlooked. This is that in polities where science is at its most specialized, liberalism of one kind or another is probably the reigning belief system. If Siedentop (2014) is right that the idea of equality and justice is the real moral legacy of Christianity, then rights-based politics stands on a sacred base. This poses a special problem for state rule in liberal polities, since with social and cultural differences burgeoning, how can a state elicit an adequate degree of loyalty and legitimacy without some form of state-led attempt to corral support – and thereby violate is own liberal precepts? In Nussbaum's recent address of the problem, this can only be done by engaging the sentiments (or 'emotions') on behalf of justice.

The changing of the institutional landscape of both religion and science is part of the reason why attempts to re-invoke a religious spirit and to yoke this to statecraft and purposes of social integration have failed so dismally. Robespierre's attempt to replace Christianity with the 'cult of the Supreme Being' never got off the ground, and most thinkers, in puzzling over this matter, have followed the line of some sort of 'civic religion', starting with Rousseau, the original social contract theorist. Notable was the attempt by the father of positivism, Auguste Comte, to found a secular religion of 'humanity' with all the ritualistic trappings, 'Catholicism without Christianity' as the English biologist, Julian Huxley, called it, and sharply criticized by J.S. Mill who otherwise agreed with him. Both Rousseau and Comte imagined their civic religion to be hierarchical, instilling obedience, and in Rousseau's case, mandatory (see Nussbaum, 2013). As Nussbaum comments, this is just the sort of thing we do not want, commending instead Herder's more 'feminine' position which stressed reciprocity and compassion.

This is the point for Nussbaum: in modern instrumental liberal society, citizens, left to themselves, will revert to a 'narrow sympathy' (ibid.: 3), a selfish and competitive individualism antithetical to social integration and to an appreciation of a common fate. How is this to be inspired? Nussbaum's answer is through love, and its vehicles, the arts (ibid.: 388).

Though her book reviews the contractual tradition started by Rousseau, Nussbaum appears to conceive of interdependence at the level of the nation and exclusively through the medium of sentiments. Durkheim agreed with the need for contemporary institutions that foster sentiments through common rituals, but increasingly thought that, in a specializing world, this would be best mediated through professional associations that promote the supreme virtue of cooperation within specialization.

There will doubtless be on-going efforts by thinkers to re-articulate a common spiritual bond that resides in no religious dogma. Dworkin's (2013) book on 'religion without god', a plea for a 'secular atheism' is a case in point. It seems like a steep and stony path. In the meantime, the requirements of social justice pose a question that educational philosophy has wrestled with in the wake of specialization. This is: does the fact of specialized knowledge pose a special challenge to egalitarianism? To what extent should we consider it unfair not to provide equal access to specialized knowledge? Is the matter of ever-restrictive access to specializing knowledge an offence against natural individual rights? For many commentators, the mere fact of restricted access brands it as unfair. But is it?

The question of equality is tricky because there is not only one kind of objection to equality. These are based in turn on different sorts of values which may require trade-offs for their realization. The debate is complex (see Brighouse 2014 for an admirable map of the territory). What matters for this chapter is that addressing the most demanding or weightiest of the values helps us to chart a way forward on questions of justice with respect to education and specialized knowledge. For instance, what would best promote fair equality of opportunity when applying for a job, asks Scanlon (2004)? That all candidates have access to the same specialized knowledge which is a requirement for the job? Or access to the same quality basic education which would enable all children to develop intellectually and therefore be able to make use of later opportunities to develop their talents further? For Scanlon, the answer is plainly the latter. 'Substantive equality of opportunity is …

based on the obligation of a state to provide certain kinds of education to all its citizens' (ibid.: 29). In other words, for the contemporary contractarian position, the principal issue of educational fairness and equality speaks to the ideal of comprehensive education and the older ideal of the 'common school' (ibid.: 29). While restricted access to specialized knowledge is hardly fair, it is overridden by a more stringent and demanding requirement for common basic education – and, we daresay, without which any hope of integrative social bonds of either a religious or secular sort is a vain hope. This will not be the last word on the matter.

This chapter has sought to describe some of the features of specialization and its discontents which lie at the heart of our contemporary condition, and to weigh the extent of the issues at stake. This is the promise and pathos of specialization: its potential both to liberate and to alienate, to open up new worlds and to create new inequalities. It emerges from successive cleavages in the evolution of our cultural heritage and is thus indissolubly part of it. As such, as Derrida said of the *pharmakon*, it is neither wholly remedy nor wholly poison. To regard it as wholly one or the other, to praise it unreservedly, or to denigrate it absolutely 'reduces it to one of its simple elements by interpreting it, paradoxically, in the light of the ulterior developments it itself has made possible'. Derrida continues: 'Such an interpretative translation is thus as violent as it is impotent: it destroys … but at the same time forbids itself access to it, leaving it untouched in its reserve' (Derrida 1981: 99). The pathos of specialization is thus also a romance, and the whole story is by no means told.

Note

1 The so-called 'Science Wars' involved the humanities redescribing scientific discovery in constructive terms, in essence reasserting the primacy of a human-centered world – the one originally designed by God as described in *Genesis*. This is the essential humanist credo, a view most fully developed in nineteenth-century Romantic thought. The scientists for their part took this to be an assault on the objective truth of their enterprise, that is, they took it as an epistemological challenge. The debate rumbles on in the more esoteric reaches of epistemology and the philosophy of mind, but for now the humanities have been effectively repelled (see Phillips 2000 for a witty and deflationary view of these matters).

SECTION 4

Universities, professions and specialized knowledge

12

THE BODY OF KNOWLEDGE

Introduction

Sociology of education has never had a satisfactory way of talking about knowledge. Its overriding concern has been with social action, with the social forces impinging on curriculum and pedagogy, and with their distributional consequences. A concern with the 'stuff' of learning was not considered germane to sociological theorization or investigation. In many cases, including Bernsteinian circles (see Tyler 2010) it still isn't. As Bernstein was to put it, in relation specifically to Bourdieu, sociology of education has largely concerned itself with the relay, not with what is relayed.

This tiptoeing around the stuff of learning could be partly understood in terms of the traditional object of social analysis – action, not thought. But was some action not more thoughtful – more knowledgeable or expert – than other action? And what was it that made the difference, or rather, what was it that one had to have for there to be a difference? Sociologists did not ask this question. At least they could agree that it was not inherited intelligence; beyond that, it was terra incognita. The assumption seemed to be that 'knowledge', insofar as it was anything at all, was some kind of tacitly acquired capability that became infused into the synapses (see Perraton and Tarrant 2007; Kotzee 2012 for sceptical responses). What mattered for sociology was, in the first instance, the social location of the learners which governed what it was they could show they knew in the final examination, and therefore governed on-going inequalities. This seemed to be irrespective of what it was they were learning.

Sociologists of education were thus not a great help to educators struggling with what the curriculum should comprise in the last quarter of the twentieth century. But neither were philosophers and psychologists. The former seemed to be bitten on all sides by the pragmatist bug; following Wittgenstein, for whom *knowing* something was *doing* something – usually, following a rule. It was what learners *did* that mattered. A host of practice-based psychologies arose, to be followed by sociologists and their varied communities of practice. In the background, 'knowing how' preoccupied the philosophers, and 'knowing that' seemed to have dropped off the intellectual agenda.

This marked swing to practice, in all its sociological, psychological and philosophical varieties, has been variously diagnosed. From within Bernsteinian ranks, a critique has been mounted that (some of the) practice-centred approaches reduce all questions of knowledge to social position. In Moore's pithy phrase, this 'conflates *what* is known with *who* knows – knowledge with knowers' (Moore 2012: 345). This of course does not apply to all approaches that deal with practice, but it does mark a tendency that holds the theoretical high ground in the social sciences (see Beck 2002; Reckwitz 2002). For writers like Moore and Young (2001), this results in relativism, which, despite its democratic intents, undermines a powerful view of knowledge, and at the same time undermines the social justice argument for entitlement to powerful knowledge for all. For them, it was precisely the denial that some knowledge was more powerful than other knowledge that validated the social justice demand for equality of distribution, and made its inequitable distribution visible; it was precisely the denial of powerful knowledge that rendered the inequality opaque.

For another group of more classroom-focused Bernsteinians, following middle period Bernstein, the result of the practice turn was the naturalization of an invisible pedagogic regime. Put more prosaically, the focus on learners and what they can do licensed a swing away from what learners were entitled to learn, focusing instead on what kinds of skills they should be able to exercise – a focus which legitimated and continues to legitimate the stipulation of the curriculum in skill and outcome-based terms. The result was invariably an under-stipulated curriculum and under-signalled pedagogy that directly disadvantaged those already disadvantaged, a fact brought out graphically by a series of conceptually-informed empirical studies reported in the second Bernsteinian symposium and beyond (see, for example, Muller, Davies and Morais 2004).

Bernstein had of course presciently put his finger on this issue. For him, generic 'skills-talk', which he called 'generic modes', originated in further and vocational education, but had been extended much more widely 'partly in response to the perceived need to functionalize education for a world in which futures are held to be increasingly unpredictable' as Beck put it (Beck 2002: 89). Generic skills-talk thus denotes a weakening of classification of knowledge boundaries; a new receptiveness to instrumental concerns that aim not at specialization but at 'trainability', an empty openness to future requirements as and when they occur. This 'emptiness' denotes empty in two senses: one, conceptually empty, that is, without content; and two, socially empty in that the decontextualization of generic skill also cuts the skill-holder off from any common community of practice.

Most critically, as Beck goes on to point out, generic skill modes 'insidiously suppress recognition of their own discursive base, that is, they suppress awareness of the fact that they are themselves tacitly rooted in theory, notwithstanding their claims to be based on practice' (Beck 2002: 90; Bernstein 2000: 53). But what is that theory? And why is it so persistent? This chapter aims to explore this issue beyond simply dismissing it as an ideological error.

This trend to skills-talk has if anything become more marked since Bernstein wrote in the late 1990s, propelled by the current global vogue for qualifications frameworks which, proclaiming a new 'pedagogic right' of 'transferability', require learning outcomes to be stipulated in 'outcomes', which invariably means generic skills rather than knowledge terms (Allais 2012). Generic skills have been taken to task for decontextualizing context – specific know-how, for atomizing what is to be learnt and hence undermining coherence, as well as for effectively disguising that which is to be learnt. Critiques range from studies on the effects of generic skill stipulations on disciplinary knowledge (Jones 2009), on vocational qualifications (Brockmann, Clarke and Winch 2008) and on doctoral programmes (Gewirtz 2008). Skills-talk in the curriculum – stipulating what you should be able to do rather than what you should know – has become hegemonic.

It was against this emergent current that Bernstein, together with his critique of 'generic modes', launched his sociological analysis of discourses and knowledge structures in the mid 1990s with the question: what was knowledge before it became the curriculum? – wherein consisted the 'discourses subject to pedagogic transformation' (Bernstein 2000: 155). His answer is almost too familiar now, but I shall revisit it again below from a different angle.

Before I do that, I want to turn to the idea of *knowledgeable action* because, for all the persistence of the skills-talk, we are no closer to understanding what kind of knowledge we have when we can, or can't, do something. The question is present whenever we consider what it means to perform well at school or university, but it is brought into even sharper relief when we consider the professions and professional expertise; what does it mean, as a knowledgeable professional or skilled craftsman or woman, to do something expertly, or innovatively? What is it we know when we know how to do something? Conceptual knowledge of some sort? Some or other procedural knowledge? Or something else altogether?

In the next section I will turn, necessarily schematically, to some debates in philosophy where, it turns out, arguments rage over the nature of 'how to' knowledge, which, in the light of the above, is not too surprising. I will then return to Bernstein to see whether his account stands in need of elaboration in order to cope with knowledgeable action in its socially distributed ramifications.

1 Know-how and know that or, what must you know in order to can do?

Consider the following:

1   An illiterate farmworker, Mr Hendriks, with no formal training, is able to design wagons to the specification of his farmer. When asked how he does it, he just says that he 'visualizes' the new design. He is able to apply knowledge

that he did not formally acquire, and he is able to innovate, but on the basis of what is not clear (Muller 2000).

2 'Industrial chicken-sexers can, I am told, reliably sort hatchlings into males and females by inspecting them, without having the least idea how they do it. With enough training, they just catch on' (Brandom 1998: 375).

3 The baseball player Knoblauch was reputedly the fastest second baseman of his time. When asked to reflect on how he did it, he mysteriously lost the knack (Dreyfus 2006).

With some variation, these examples pose the question as to what it is we know (or don't know) when we can (or can't) do something. The chicken-sexers claim that their accurate judgement is based on intuition, not knowledge. And the hapless Knoblauch didn't know he knew anything at all until he was asked to think about it, at which point he lost what he didn't know he had. Nor is it only expert performance in the craft or vocational sector of expertise that is viewed through the lens of 'fluent action' (Kotzee 2014). If Gladwell (2005) is to be believed, the doctors of Cook County have mastered the art of intuitive diagnosis of heart problems. They don't reflect upon it, they just diagnose. Gladwell advocates this approach, called 'thin slicing', as a general and efficacious way to save cognition time while preserving accuracy.

Philosophers of a certain persuasion use examples such as these to make the argument that in much expert action – some like Dreyfus would say in all of it – it is fluent action or 'know-how' that governs our actions; not 'know that', or conceptual knowledge. It is practice not understanding that makes perfect, it is skills not knowledge that matters. In fact, for philosophers of this persuasion, knowledge or thinking about it (or as Dreyfus contends, knowledge of an expert action and thinking about an expert action) positively gets in the way, as in the case of Knoblauch; or at least the verbalization of it does – a phenomenon cognitive psychologists call 'verbal overshadowing' (Stanley 2011: 159).

It is worth a brief glance to the origin of this way of thinking in Gilbert Ryle's distinction (Ryle 1945: 6). Here is how he sets up the problem, actually an ancient dilemma called the dilemma of the *Hare and the Tortoise* by Lewis Carroll:

> A pupil fails to follow an argument. He understands the premises and he understands the conclusion. But he fails to see the conclusion follows from the premises. The teacher thinks him rather dull [!] but tries to help. So he tells him that there is an ulterior proposition, which he has not considered, namely, that *if these premises are true, the conclusion is true*. The pupil understands this and dutifully recites it alongside the premises ... And still the pupil fails to see. And so on forever. He accepts rules in theory but this does not force him to apply them in practice. He considers reasons, but he fails to reason.
>
> *(Ryle 1945: 6)*

Ryle concludes that knowing a rule means knowing how to infer, not simply being able to state the rule: 'Rules, like birds, must live before they can be stuffed' (Ryle, 1945: 11). A sizeable cohort of analytical philosophers has followed Ryle down this path. 'Knowing that' is best considered together with 'knowing how', without which it ('knowing that') is simply inert. Or as Peter Winch (1958: 58) was to put it a little later: 'Learning to infer is not a matter of being taught about explicit logical relations between propositions; it is learning to do something'.

It is useful at this point to briefly recall the two principal positions that this view was set against. Both of them put their faith in conceptual knowledge which is 'in the head', so to speak, something that one knows is the case. For the rationalists (sometimes called intellectualists, or Cartesians), knowledge is a set of logical relations, a set of propositions about the world. These are the outcome of reason, which can then be brought to bear on experience. For the empiricists, knowledge is something one absorbs through experience. Both sides have over the centuries traded choice insults: rationalists stand accused of the 'myth of the mental'; empiricists, of the 'myth of the given'. Neither are however in any doubt that knowledge in the end resides in propositional form in the beliefs of the knower, or that truth is a matter of reference, that these propositions are 'about' something that we can check and confirm. With the Ryleans, and after Wittgenstein, we have another possibility: knowledge is a kind of skill or ability, knowledge is as knowledge can do. All 'know that' is a kind of 'know-how'.

Two kinds of Rylean should be distinguished. The first kind, following phenomenology, believe that philosophers have spent too much time considering the 'conceptual upper floors' and have ignored the embodied coping going on on the ground floor. For Dreyfus, the Knoblauch example shows not just that verbalization 'overshadows' action, but that 'thought' is 'the enemy of expertise' (Dreyfus 2007: 354). This branch of the 'practical knowledge' philosophers is in this sense anti-intellectual, having also an affinity with the proponents of 'tacit' knowledge like Schön and Polanyi (Kotzee 2014). As Kotzee goes on to show, such accounts are unable to account for differences in expert performance between experts and novices, but are more crucially unable to account for differences between unspecialized forms of expertise in everyday life like driving a car well, and highly specialized forms of expert performance such as complex surgery. Besides, what help can an anti-intellectualist be to scholars of curriculum? We are back here with the central problem of skills-talk.

A second kind of pragmatist is more interesting, promising far more for a sociological account. This is the inferential approach of Robert Brandom and the 'Pittsburgh School'. Brandom's (2001) is a complex position, owing as much to Hegel as to the analytical tradition. If the modern Dreyfusards have defined all intelligent action as fluency, Brandom, and his colleague McDowell (1996), define all action as having conceptual content: in McDowell's phrase, all action is 'minded', or in Brandom's phrase, takes place 'in the space of reasons'.

'Mindedness' is rendered stable and objective by the 'game of reasons'. Conceptual knowledge in this account is that which can be offered as, and by itself stand in need of, reasons.

Understanding or grasping such propositional content is a kind of know-how, or practical mastery of the game of giving and asking for reasons: being able to tell what is a reason, for what, distinguishes good reasons from bad.

(Keeler 2004: 250)

To be able to play the game is to be able to keep score on what you, and other players, are committed and entitled to. Evaluating a claim means understanding how it would change the score. This sets up a chain of inferential relations, which, if made explicit, is what Brandom would call a 'conceptual structure'. The reliability of concepts is underwritten by scorekeeping. Rational activity is thus a thoroughly normative, that is to say social, activity.

There is much that is attractive in this account. If the rational referentialists turn all-knowing into 'knowing that', inferentialism turns all 'knowing that' into 'knowing how' – to give reasons. It is a thoroughly social activity, and could appeal to sociologists who seek an objective way to define knowledge in social terms. It also emphasizes the systemic character of conceptual relations. Two thoughtful papers seek to persuade us that this is indeed just what we need in thinking about curriculum and pedagogy. Derry (2008) outlines the affinities the inferentialist view has for Vygotsky and his view of the cultural-historical understanding of human practice. The 'abstract rationality' that writers like Wertsch dislike in Vygotsky, Derry thinks we should rather see as the objective and systemic quality of concepts. Derry goes on to say, 'Effective teaching involves providing the opportunity for learners to operate with a concept in the space of reasons within which it falls' (Derry 2008: 58), which means for Brandom understanding the 'norms implicit in concept use' (Derry, 2008: 60). Clearly an inferential account could provide one kind of tool to flesh out what Bernstein allusively called the 'recontextualizing principle' of vertical discourse that binds concepts into a knowledge structure.

Winch (2013) broadly takes this approach into curriculum description. If knowing a concept is best described as an 'epistemic ability', what a curriculum must then do is be able to describe the systematic conceptual elements of a subject and the relationships between them, 'but also in terms of the procedures required to gain and to validate knowledge' (Winch 2013: 13). Winch means that individual concepts do not (only) have empirical reference; more importantly, they refer to other concepts that are deeply implicated in their meaning. Knowing which concepts refer to which other concepts, and their implications, are what knowing a subject is about. Induction into 'concept mongering' – knowing how to move confidently around the space of reasons – is then the core business of education.

Does it solve the problem of intelligent action? It is hard to see what Brandom could offer Knoblauch, and it would offer cold comfort to Ryle's schoolmaster who knows the schoolboy can't reason, but still doesn't know why, except for saying there is something he can't do instead of know. Above all, one should be clear that objectivity is one thing – Habermas (2000) has called Brandom's position an 'objective idealism' – but, like all pragmatists, Brandom gives up on truth. Reasoning appropriately is as objective as it gets. Concepts only infer, they do not refer.

Pragmatists say 'appropriate' when rationalists say 'true'. As Fodor and Lepore (2007: 470) retort: 'Thunder follows lightning not because that's the way we play the language game, but because of the laws of meteorology', or as Horace said more grimly long before that: '*Naturam expellas furca, usque recurret*', which translated means: 'You can drive out Nature with a pitchfork, but she will be back'.

The inferentialists helpfully draw our attention to the joined-up nature of concepts and the social basis of this joined-upness. How does the Bernsteinian notion of knowledge deal with this? Do we need inferential first aid? And by defining conceptual knowledge as inferential ability, do they help us with the two main problems that frame this chapter: the problem of intelligent action, and the problem of how to write curricular specifications in a 'non-inert' way that does not collapse back into skills-talk? Or the prior question: can the Bernsteinian framework deal with these questions adequately? It is to this that I now turn.

Bernstein in the workshop of knowledge

This section looks at Bernstein's theoretical toolkit for looking at knowledge from the vantage point of the above. Let us start by looking at Bernstein's first distinction, that of horizontal and vertical discourses. Horizontal discourse is 'context dependent and specific' (Bernstein 2000: 157) and is composed of 'strategies' and 'procedures' that are segmentally organized, whereas vertical discourse is 'principled'. The inferentialists have troubled this distinction between 'procedural' and 'principled' forms of knowledge, in two ways. All knowledge, horizontal or vertical, is conceptual; and however 'principled' the knowledge might be, it is always also a form of 'know-how'. The first point is not a problem for Bernstein's theory. Each segment might have conceptual ballast, but the segments are functionally, not conceptually, related in horizontal discourse. Their form of integration is *functional*. The point about vertical discourse is that the integration of knowledge 'bits' is at the level of meanings: the form of integration is *conceptual*. The *principle of integration* – functional or conceptual – is thus that which distinguishes horizontal discourse from vertical discourse. This can be scaled with reference to subsumptability, after Cassirer (Chapter 2) in terms of discursive saturation with Dowling (1998) or semantic density with Maton (2010); all point to one or other feature of the integration or internal relations of horizontal or vertical discourses.

On this analysis, Bernstein is not an inferentialist in the normal sense, indeed his account of internal symbolic relations is closer to what rationalists would call declarative knowledge. For the inferentialists, the connectedness principle is the inferential network. For Bernstein, the connectedness principle they are talking about is the *external* not the internal relations of discourse. This is usually discussed under the notion of strength of syntax or grammaticality, more recently in terms of semantic gravity, but can also be fruitfully considered in terms of Bernstein's notion of an 'external language of description' (ELOD). The ELOD describes something other than itself, a referent that is empirical or textual. Both of the notions (grammaticality and ELOD) describe the connection between the internal symbol structure and the concrete case, the empirical instance, to an instantiation of *context*. I would like to suggest that we can think about intelligent action, for example, of a professional (doctor, a teacher or a lawyer), in the same way as we think about doing research. The surgeon is connecting what she knows about the anatomical body to an instance of a real body.

Expertise in doing this consists in rigorous tracking: as firm and accountable a chain as possible must be constructed between the 'invariants' of the conceptual pile and the variabilities of the empirical instance. In research, the ideal is to stabilize the context of the instance so as to minimize unforeseens. This can take the form of a specially constructed environment like a laboratory. In naturalistic research, the context of the instance can't easily be stabilized and produces surprises. Analogously, the operating theatre is designed to minimize external contextual variation; of course, the heart could still be in the wrong place. The law court is far less stabilized, and here the opposing actors in the environment aim to produce surprises. In such cases, intelligent action requires an inferential suppleness that we call 'thinking on your feet'. Likewise, actuaries and engineers deal directly, and accurately, with margins of variability.

So far I have been discussing intelligent action in terms of a syntactic tracking from the conceptual pile to an instance. This can be considered in terms of inferential chains. Either way, a successful enactment is called intelligent action, or expertise. The guiding idea here is one of *accuracy*, which means eliminating error on the internal side of the symbolic relation and variability on the external side, as well as making well-formed connections between them. But accuracy is a reproductive guiding ideal. In research, the ideal is to produce *novelty*, even if genuine novelty is hard to come by. Analogously, in professional or intelligent action novelty is not infrequently called for, as in architectural design, for example. To put the issue another way, knowledge pile and a stabilized context can seem pretty deterministic. Wherein does the possibility for producing genuine novelty reside (Ramognino 2011)?

I suggest that it can be found in three sites, all of which are central to an exploration not only of scientific innovation but also of transcending accuracy in intelligent action, towards a consideration of the bases for virtuosity. The three sites are: the generative capacity of the conceptual pile; the generative capacity of the discursive gap; and the generative capacity of the social base of the knowledge practice.

Innovation and virtuosity

Referring to hierarchical knowledge structure, Bernstein comments that:

> In the end, it is the theory that counts and it counts both for its imaginative conceptual projection and the empirical power of the projection
>
> *(Bernstein 2000: 164–5)*

With 'imaginative projection', Bernstein is following Durkheim in pointing to the idealizing capacity of theory, its capacity to project possibilities not yet thought. This might be rephrased to say that a theory with appropriately generalizing power always has the capacity to generalize to a case not yet imagined. The possibilities realized by all of today's computer software and smart phone apps were unlocked, in principle, when Alan Turing as an undergraduate in 1936 solved Leibnitz's 'decision problem' in mathematical logic and constructed the Turing 'universal' machine to give it form. This is evidence of the 'power' of the theory (Chapter 10).

The phrase 'discursive gap' is usually associated with the external relations. The ELOD, as Moore explained, attempts to 'close the discursive gap between concept and data' (Moore 2006: 38). To 'close the gap' is thus a normative moment in the research act. It can be extended to the range of intelligent professional action. The surgeon must 'close the gap' between the ailing body and the conceptually driven diagnosis by making the cut in the right place. Closing the gap is thus a pre-condition for the normative ideal of accuracy.

There is a second normative moment alongside the accuracy imperative that Bernstein outlines in his interview with Joseph Solomon in giving a somewhat different slant to the discursive gap (Bernstein 2000; see also Moore and Muller 2002). Bernstein here emphasizes the point that the encounter with the empirical world via the ELOD always produces a surplus, one that bears within its excess a productive potential. Under the scrutiny of the theoretical model, the empirical object will always generate, or have the capacity to generate, greater ranges of information than the model calls for (Bernstein 2000: 209). This is occasioned by the:

> discursive gap between the rules specified by the model and the realization rules for transforming information ... This gap enables the something, so to speak, to announce itself, it enables the something to re-describe the descriptions of the model's own realization rules and so change.
>
> *(Bernstein 2000: 209)*

We may say that a zone of freedom and of risk is thus situated both at the site furthest from the context – at the cutting edge of the theory, and the site nearest to it – at the point of interaction with the context; both when the boundary is at its most productively taut and when its egress has been breached. It is the latter that most concerns intelligent action. This can be most graphically seen in the world of professional sport, where the sportsman responds not to a world captured in the snapshot of a theoretical model, but one dynamically changing. To watch a master sportsman respond effortlessly to this situation is one of the pleasures of watching competitive sport. The same goes for professionals who have to respond daily to the exigencies of the surplus, the kitchen dramas of context. This is the stuff of hospital and courtroom television drama series, watching professionals setting aside their personal dramas (mostly, not always) and coping with the smaller and larger surprises of context. Such is the romance of professionalism in our society.

What all this makes clear is that the 'knowledge' of a professional domain such as law, medicine or teaching, for example, cannot be adequately accounted for if there is not also an account of the more or less dynamic exchange between the existing conceptual pile or reservoir and the ceaselessly generated case-by-case knowledge generated in encounters with contextual instances, for example, case law, legal precedents, medical cases, new software code, patents etc. This knowledge has the potential to fill in the gaps in the epistemic rainbow between the primary colours of the conceptual pile. To see what is at stake, I will return once more to Bernstein and his account of how novelty is assimilated into the reservoir in horizontal discourse.

The socialization of professional knowledge and the social base

Dealing with context, as Bernstein makes clear in his account of horizontal discourse, is often but not always a solitary affair. The teacher stumbles on innovation behind the classroom door, the doctor behind the consulting room door, and so on. How does this novelty circulate? – only by a reduction of isolation and exclusion. 'Any restriction to circulation specializes, classifies and privatizes knowledge' (Bernstein 2000: 158). The greater the privatization, the more static is the exchange between repertoire and reservoir; the greater the privatization, the 'weaker the social base' (Bernstein 2000: 158).

This deserves underlining. There is a direct relation between the promotion of circulation between repertoires and reservoir and the strength of the social base, and consequently the social power of the profession. Consider the different way in which the professions deal with knowledge from contextual encounters. Surgery, law, engineering, architecture, biotechnology and transport are regarded by economists of innovation as 'structurally progressive' domains because there is fruitful traffic between the case-based innovations in horizontal discourse and the conceptual pile in vertical discourse. Education, by contrast, is regarded as 'structurally unprogressive' (Foray 2011), which means that there is a very small canonized conceptual reservoir in education; it is revitalized very slowly by basic research; and the contextuality of teaching means that it is very difficult to do grammatically stabilized evidence-based research with generalizable import. Classrooms are rich sites of innovation but much of the innovation in education does not get beyond the classroom where it has been generated (Foray and Hargreaves 2003). It rarely gets codified, and even more rarely disseminated through dedicated casework journals, as is the case in law and medicine. There is restricted feedback from contextual innovation to the conceptual reservoir and thus the innovations lodge in the private repertoires of teachers. Teachers are simply 'artisans' engaged in trial and error tinkering and teaching has yet to become a fully-fledged craft.

What student teachers learn, in the absence of a robust and dynamic knowledge system, is usually siloed 'theory' from singulars borrowed from the social sciences, and procedural prescripts that, as Beck remarked earlier, 'suppress recognition of their own discursive base' (Beck 2002: 90). Theory and practice is to be integrated, not in the parent reservoir via socialized procedures of peer vetting and collegial endorsement as with other professions, but in 'practice' – which is to say, in private. In the teaching profession, the restricted traffic between context-based innovation and the knowledge base is partly underwritten, and held in place, by a professional identity narrative that celebrates 'learning by experience' and decries codification as somehow stultifying. Skills-talk, the language of artisanal practice with its under-current of anti-intellectualism, is centrally part of this complex.

Conclusion

This chapter has argued that what the referentialists call knowledge is best consid-ered as the internal relations of the knowledge structure, the consolidated concep-tual pile 'for now' socialized in vertical discourse. What the inferentialists call chains of inferences is best considered as the external relations of the knowledge structure, the two-way traffic between the socialized reservoir and the practitioner repertoires. Distributive rules govern the traffic in both directions:

- from the reservoir to neophytes, which as the above has tried to clarify, distrib-ute both the internal relations of the conceptual pile and a particular connec-tive path to its deployment in real contexts. An implication is that there can be more than one inferential path for each set of internal knowledge relations; and
- from the case-based contextual encounters to the reservoir in vertical discourse. If the social base is under-socialized and the distributive rules undeveloped, the traffic back will be restricted, innovation will be privatized and change in the profession will be restricted, leaving change to be driven by the state. There will be national differences in this dispensation.

Novelty can be produced by the projective power of the internal relations – gener-alizing to the 'unthought' – and at the site where the classification must be relaxed to deal with contextual particulars. Unless both forms of innovation can feed back into the parent knowledge structure and circulate relatively unrestrictedly, the social collective that composes the social base of the knowledge structure and its practices cannot prosper.

I conclude that Bernstein's theory, when lifted out in this fashion, can deal fruit-fully with intelligent action and professional practice. This after all was his original intention, as he says in the closing paragraphs of the 'Discourses' paper:

> The analysis ... reveals the inter-dependence between properties internal to the discourse and the social context ... Briefly, 'relations with' and 'relations to' should be integrated in the analysis.
>
> *(Bernstein 2000: 170)*

'Skills-talk', in this view, is an account of the stuff of learning that focuses on the external relations of the knowledge structure as if that was all there was, rendering the internal relations and the socialized knowledge structures invisible. As Bernstein (2000) says, when both are 'integrated in the analysis', we get an immeasurably richer picture of the living body of knowledge.

13

DISCIPLINES, SKILLS AND THE UNIVERSITY

Introduction

Writing in the introduction to a recent volume with the rather ominous sub-title 'The breakdown of scientific thought', the editors set themselves the task of anatomizing the latest epochal transformation in the global system of higher education and research. What is happening, say the editors, is 'a reorganization of knowledge production that opens the university sector to market mechanisms, with the result of making universities in effect, suppliers of knowledge within a global knowledge economy' (Hasselberg *et al.* 2013: 2). This has been variously designated as 'academic capitalism' (Slaughter and Rhoades 2004), and 'epistemic drift' (Elzinga 1997) to mention only two. Central to this transformation is the blurring of boundaries between science and the other domains of society such that the special norms and interests of science are dissolved into those of politics, civil society and the market.

Thorsten Nybom puts it as follows: the nineteenth century social contract between science (or the university) and society, was formulated in terms of science *as such* in relation to society 'the *entire scientific endeavor* (that) was considered to be relevant and useful' (Nybom 2013: 26, 27). We now have, says he, a 'perversion' 'where "relevance" and "usefulness" gradually became synonymous with the ability to fulfill the more or less immediate and often short-term needs and demands of different societal "stakeholders", purchasers, or principal funders' (ibid.: 27). Basic disciplinary knowledge is, in this critique, being 'crowded out' of the university – out of its heretofore privileged place in the curriculum, as well as out of prized and rewarded kinds of research.

The stage is set for a conflict of perceptions. Useful, applied, relevant knowledge is, in Nybom's account, viewed as inimical to basic, conceptual, traditional scholarship. The proponents of relevance, on the other hand, are, if anything, even more vociferous and adamant as we will discuss further below. The way the dispute is all too often cast, as a bitter zero-sum game, means that the polarized positions attempt to trump one another. This can happen in one of two ways; first, they can attempt to supplant the offending position (for example, problem-based *instead of* traditional curriculum); or the forms and arrangement propitious for the one stifle the 'voice' of the other, even unintentionally. Our position will be that none of this is in the longer-term interests of the university, and that we need to move to a scenario which lies beyond the unproductive standoff, towards a third position or 'future' (Chapter 5).

The dispute between 'disciplinary knowledge' and 'relevant skills and knowledge' goes to the heart of any debate about the purpose of universities, and indeed about the purpose of education. It raises questions about what universities should be about, what they should be researching, what they should be teaching, and how this is to be stipulated. Our approach in what follows will be to follow the trail from the originary tensions embedded in the medieval universities to the present dispute, and to trace how these have changed over the years. We thus begin with the disciplines.

Roots of the disciplines

Disciplines have traditionally been associated with universities in two quite distinct ways. One has been as part of the idea of a liberal education for the elite, mostly expressed by the humanities such as classics, history, philosophy, language and literature. In Europe, the humanities (including theology) had a long and unchallenged dominance since the founding of the first universities in the thirteenth and fourteenth centuries. With the legacy of their religious roots, the humanities disciplines became the primary curriculum of elite education and were, by the nineteenth and early twentieth century, unquestioned as the best way of preparing men of the appropriate lineage to rise to positions of power at home and abroad. The basis of their legitimacy was moral and intellectual; and advanced training in the classics was thought to train both mind and spirit.

The German reforms of the early nineteenth century led to the idea of research-based universities, principally of a scientific and technological bent (Turner 1971, 1975). Since then, universities and the natural and technological sciences have been seen as the main source of higher level knowledge workers for what is now referred to as the knowledge economy. As a consequence, the humanities have become progressively displaced. Their claims to offer 'powerful knowledge' now had a competitor in the emerging STEM (science, technology, engineering and mathematics) subjects that appeared increasingly attractive to governments as a result of the remarkable success of the natural sciences in their technological applications in industry and medicine which rested on an increasingly firm scientific basis.

Today's disciplines can best be understood as secularized forms of those established initially by the medieval university in the form of the Trivium and the Quadrivium (Durkheim 1977; Muller 2009). It is from this legacy that we get such ideas as knowledge and learning 'for their own sake' and of course, academic freedom. Academic freedom is underpinned by two key dicta. The first is associated with 'freedom of conscience', immortalized by Cardinal Newman (Cornwell 2011). In this sense, academic freedom is a distinctly limited freedom. It is not freedom to do or think anything, as it is sometimes erroneously thought. It is freedom within a particular discipline and its rules. In the case of academic disciplines these rules are epistemic – concerned with concepts, arguments and methods. However they are also moral rules that bind disciplinary communities together and determine appropriate modes for conjecture and refutation (Abbott 2001; Young 2011d).

The second rationale on which freedom of expression rests has to do with the freedom and autonomy necessary to pursue innovation, where the freedom to pursue intellectual clues that might lead nowhere, and the freedom to make mistakes, are both part of the undecideability of true scholarly innovation. In this sense freedom entails the freedom to transgress the rules when claims to novelty are made, invoking what Lakatos (1976) called the 'stretchability' of concepts. This is how disciplines grow and change (Muller 2000).

Disciplines are not just about 'truth seeking'; they are about power, promotion and prestige. However, as the philosopher Polanyi pointed out about science, what makes disciplines distinct is that 'truth seeking' is their raison d'être even if sometimes power-seeking and practical exigencies seem to take precedence (Polanyi 1962). But because scientists frequently are venal does not mean we are therefore entitled to reduce all cognitive to personal interests, as Bourdieu (2004) said, even less does it mean that we can dismiss science as just another power game.

Disciplinary enquiry, in the broadest sense of Polanyian 'truth seeking', has proved itself, over the last two or more centuries, as an enduring form for organizing enquiries in the search for truth in stable communities with their own rules for internal self-government, truth in the sense of both 'standing the test of time' and of leading to the most reliable knowledge we have at any one time.

A social theory of knowledge

Durkheim traced the origins of disciplines as a form of curriculum organization to the distinction between the 'sacred' and the 'profane' that he found in the studies of aboriginal societies that he drew on for his book *The Elementary Forms of Religious Life* (Durkheim 1995) and which he saw expressed in the curriculum of the medieval universities (Durkheim 1977; Bernstein 2000). For Durkheim, the distinction between the 'sacred' and its concern with the fundamental questions of 'who we are' and 'what happens when we die', and the 'profane', the practical problems about how people feed themselves, find shelter and survive from day to day, is found in all societies. It was the basis, he argued, for the conditions for social progress and the key agents of that progress that are closely linked to disciplines as a source of new knowledge.

For Durkheim then, 'sacred' knowledge is knowledge that is not tied to specific contexts; it is knowledge that takes one beyond immediate needs and experience. In contrast, 'profane' knowledge is knowledge concerned with the material survival of societies – initially food, shelter and security. It is knowledge that is tied to specific contexts, valuable in those contexts but of limited generalizability outside them.

In the earliest societies that Durkheim studied, 'sacred' knowledge took the form of religion, generally ideas about the after-life or ideas about a parallel magical world. The sociological importance of religion as an expression of the sacred lay not in its content, in specific beliefs about God or gods, for example, but in its structure, its independence from particular contexts and in the internal consistency of its concepts. His argument was that the structure of the sacred not only provided the basis for ideas about the after-life as it does in the case of theology, but, as it became secularized, as a cognitive tool for projecting beyond the immediate, for generalizing about the world and our experience. For Durkheim, secularization did not just mean the progressive loss of credibility of religion and the growth of science, but the transformation of the sacred as it appropriated more and more domains such as nature and the universe that had previously been subordinate to a religious or otherworldly explanation. Through the cumulative successes of science, theology in the eighteenth-century universities was forced to renounce its claims to absolute truth outside the narrow domain of the after-life. In other words, social progress gradually became dominated by secularized 'sacred' knowledge principally of the natural sciences, less and less by the original religious 'sacred'. This has caused a crisis of meaning in Western societies, far less so than in Islam and the Confucian societies (Cohen 2010), which will however not be pursued here.

For Durkheim, then, 'sacred' knowledge consisted in what he called the 'collective representations' that allow a society to develop shared knowledge that is beyond individual experience. As we said above, its distinctiveness lay both in its non-context boundedness and in its internal connections that relied on ties internal to the body of knowledge itself, not on external relevance or utilities. A basis was thus laid for these bodies of knowledge first to endure stably across time and specific collections of people, and, after the printing press, to be disseminated and absorbed in locales geographically remote from the place of their production. These organized bodies grew into disciplines of different types – the natural sciences both theoretical and applied, where theories could be put to rigorous test; the social sciences, which offer weaker forms of corroborative legitimation and thereby laid the grounds for a greater, recurrent, undecidable conflict within their specialist communities. The humanities, in which different forms of human experience such as literature, music and art were the focus of contemplation became conceptualized and the subject of debate among specialists.

Disciplines, as an expression of Durkheim's collective representations, have been preserved and developed by specialist communities and have defined the parameters of thinking of what is of greater or lesser worth, true or false in different fields at any particular time. Euclid's geometry as an example of the secular 'sacred' was treated as 'true' for 2000 years, but it was not until the mid-nineteenth century that mathematicians made explicit Euclid's fallibility and developed non-Euclidean geometries, which have led to space travel, geographical positioning systems and mobile phones. Durkheim thus provided the basis for a social theory of knowledge that locates the historical roots of systematic knowledge in the early religions. He did not theorize this further in the sense of specifying the axes of variation on which various different forms of knowledge might vary. For this, we have to move briefly to the work of the exemplary English Durkheimian, Basil Bernstein.

Two forms of disciplinary organization: Singulars and regions

Bernstein developed Durkheim's ideas in two ways that extend the social theory of knowledge. The first is by theorising the internal properties of knowledge forms, which we will not go into here (Bernstein 2000). The second is by theorising two different forms in which the internal relations of knowledge relate to external concerns, which is of more direct concern in the present chapter. The first he called 'singulars', the second 'regions'. We could say that whereas singulars represent conceptually derived and empirically buttressed symbolic orders, regions represent a fusing of this internal symbolic order with external orders of a more immediately practical kind. This deserves elaboration.

Singulars

Singulars are the general form of disciplines. In Bernstein's words:

> Singulars are knowledge structures whose creators have appropriated a space to give themselves a unique name, a specialized discrete discourse with its own intellectual field of texts, practices, rules of entry, examinations, licences to practice, distribution of rewards and punishments … Singulars are, on the whole, narcissistic, oriented to their own development, protected by strong boundaries and hierarchies.
>
> *(Bernstein 2000: 52)*

Their key characteristics are:

- they construct clear boundaries between themselves, other singulars, and the everyday world;
- they construct specialized identities by means of 'introjection'. By this, Bernstein seems to mean symbolic identification with the discipline though attaining mastery. Introjected identities are distinct and highly calibrated. Physicists are not only distinct from each other, but especially distinct from, say, historians or from the person-in-the-street; and
- on the basis of this, they exhibit strong inner commitments which are simultaneously epistemic and moral. A strong disciplinary identity thus entails both the possession of specialized knowledge and of a specialized disposition to certain forms of conduct regarding disciplinary matters. As scholars like Becher (1989) have pointed out, disciplines differ as to the strength of their insulation and therefore as to the strength of their attendant disciplinary identities (see also Henkel 2000).

Until the eighteenth century, singulars dominated the university curriculum in the form of disciplines, which had roots in the medieval distinction between the Trivium and the Quadrivium, disciplines of the inner life (of the word) and of the outer world (the world) respectively. Up to then, most scientific and all technological developments took place outside the university. Since then, singulars of the natural sciences have developed exponentially, and next to them a new form of knowledge organization, the 'region'.

Regions

The Scientific Revolution, that phenomenon of the seventeenth century that designates the rapid, exponential growth of knowledge about the natural world, did not occur simply as a great bootstrapped leap forward in abstract conceptual thought. Advances in abstract knowledge, like trigonometry, were known far earlier in the Islamic countries. However, on their own, they did not propel a marked advance in natural scientific knowledge (Raven 2011; Gaukroger 2008). Francis Bacon, its most effective and persuasive propagandist, described it as the synthesis of the virtues of the scholastic spider – the abstract theorists spinning purely mental webs – and the empiric ant – experimentalists of all kinds, from the backstreet apothecaries to the alchemists like Newton – combining in the superior virtues of the bee, thus opening the way for experimental science, but especially experimental physics. At the same time, the empiric crafts, which had up until then been proceeding largely in a trial and error fashion, sometimes joining forces with theoretical knowledge (as in the iconic example of Archimedes), more often not, also received a renewed impetus, and the field of scientifically propelled professional knowledge emerged alongside the pure experimental sciences, pre-eminently medicine and engineering, the first generation of professions.

Professional knowledge displayed a new form of organization. As it absorbed and recontextualized contextual knowledge from the sciences, usually more than once, it had perforce to attend internally to the growing theoretical knowledge structures of basic science. But because it's very raison d'être lay with specific problems in the world and the technologies needed to solve them, it simultaneously had to face outwards to construct solutions in tandem with them. Bernstein called this Janus-faced form of knowledge organization a region. 'Regions are the interface between disciplines (singulars) and the technologies they make possible' (ibid.: 52). We may rephrase this by saying that regions connect internal conceptual orders (singulars) to external constructed orders and technological worlds. A number of features distinguished the emerging 'regions' from singulars.

- They involved more than one singular – for example, engineering involved mathematics, physics and chemistry, and the new medicine involved anatomy, physiology and chemistry.
- The success of the early regions and the growth of the professions associated with them led to similar attempts to regionalize the social sciences and render

them of service to the worlds of commerce and government. Groups of the new singulars such as economics, psychology and sociology were brought together to form regions such as social work, business and public administration, teaching and so on. A key difference between the new social science-based disciplines and the older natural science-based disciplines was the relative unreliability of their knowledge base and the lack of agreement on shared epistemic rules within the social science disciplinary communities. This inevitably raised questions about the credibility of their graduates as members of the new and emerging professions. It is partly for this reason that these disciplines have been more vulnerable to challenge and criticism both from their peers within the academy and from their sponsoring agents in government. This internal instability led also to a continual fractiousness within the disciplinary community itself, a further continuing source of instability.

- The organizational form of these second-generation professional knowledges was thus weaker, in two senses; the singulars they faced inwards to were less robust, but second, the professional bodies they faced outwards towards did not have the political clout of the bodies of the first generation of professions. Less bounded and hence less buffered both on the inside and the outside, the newer social professions have always been more vulnerable to pressures both from inside the academy and from outside forces in the marketplace and in government. They are consequently pervaded by a sense of status anxiety, as Becher (1989, 1994) noted.

- Regions construct specialized identities by projection of the knowledge as a practice in some context. Consequently, professional identity seems to the layperson (and to some human resources managers) to rest largely on what the professional *can do*, an instrumental feature of professional identity at least partly responsible for the pervasive emphasis on know-how or skills in the educational language of the marketplace and government. Skills-talk tends to background the conceptual content of specialized know-how, underplaying the fact that the ability to have specialized skills at all depends on the prior attainment of a specialized identity, and therefore of specialized theoretical knowledge. We will return to this argument at greater length below.

Challenges to disciplinary knowledge

The common strand through all these developments is what might be called the 'disciplinary leadership' of the universities, where disciplines designate both singulars and regions. However, even in institutions where the professions are strong, the basic scientific disciplines tend to claim the epistemic and political high ground, in line with the traditions stretching back to their medieval origins, as we sketched above. This tacit disciplinary hierarchy is increasingly under pressure, as we noted in our introduction. The idea of knowledge for its own sake, the self-image of strong-boundary singulars, no longer has the unquestioned legitimacy it once had, and these disciplines have increasingly to justify themselves in terms of some or other idea of 'relevance', which they can only do by weakening their boundaries with the world, which further weakens their traditional power and legitimacy.

Challenges to their legitimacy come both from without and within. Even where they are from within the academy, the argument is for a greater outward orientation for all forms of knowledge, including the pure disciplines, both sciences and humanities. In what follows, we will briefly discuss two forms, among others, in which the challenge has been framed.

New modes of research?

One of the prominent internal academic challenges is represented by the publication by Michael Gibbons and his colleagues of their book *The New Production of Knowledge* (Gibbons *et al.* 1994).

In this volume, Gibbons and his colleagues made both a descriptive and a prescriptive argument. Descriptively, they argued that the disciplinary-based mode of knowledge production, referred to as 'Mode 1', was becoming superseded by trans- and cross-disciplinary modes which they referred to as 'Mode 2'. Mode 2 crucially involved 'contextualization', that is, the interpenetration of scientific knowledge and social contexts, where not only does science 'speak to society', but where society 'speaks back to science' (Nowotny *et al.* 2001: 50). This meant in turn that knowledge stakeholders would not just be testing and applying knowledge, but influencing how the knowledge was formulated in the first place. The prescriptive implications of their description were the claim that Mode 2 was more efficient in producing the kind of knowledge that a modern knowledge-based economy needed – more problem-centred, more relevant, and more useful. In a word, the call was for knowledge production to become not only more applied and hence useful, but for the traditional first step, basic science or Mode 1, to be skipped entirely.

The Mode 2 model attracted considerable interest within governments, especially in developing countries engaged in social and political transformation, as it appeared to be a way of bringing together academic rigour and the practical needs of the developmental state as well as of workplaces. Gibbons (1998) himself urged its adoption in African universities. However, the evidence for the ambitious claims made for Mode 2 as a new approach to innovation is equivocal. Writers like Peter Weingart (1997) have questioned whether the idea is new at all. Jensen *et al.* (2008) show that it is the researchers most interested in worldly problems that are also the most prolific contributors to basic scientific research publications; the two can co-exist happily together without the one having to eclipse the other.

What Gibbons and his colleagues did not initially foresee was that weakening the epistemic rules of the disciplines in the move from Mode 1 to Mode 2 might weaken the features of disciplinary knowledge that made it a unique source of innovation (Shinn 1999). The problem, more in the natural than the social science disciplines, turns out to be that innovations even in applied fields like engineering are often conceptual as much as they are practical. This means that if all research moves to Mode 2 practices in the face of practical exigencies, the wellsprings of innovation are likely to be diminished rather than increased. Nevertheless the book undoubtedly put down a marker for a more activist and less hierarchical and 'engaged' role for universities, and one which has fed into a more recent version of the debate in the curriculum field, that between knowledge and skills, which we discuss below.

There are signs that the Gibbons group has realized belatedly that, in advocating a bold transition from Mode 1 to Mode 2, they might have painted themselves into something of a corner. Indeed, unexpected scholarly bedfellows of every stripe have flocked to the Mode 2 banner. Nowotny *et al.* ruefully note:

> If nurse researchers pounced on 'Mode 2' to reduce their subordination to medical research, or if global accountancy companies placed 'Mode 2' at the heart of newly established 'Centres of Business Knowledge' – both of which are actual examples – who were we, the authors, to complain? We had fallen into our own post-modern trap.
>
> *(Nowotny et al. 2003: 180)*

Above all, the starkness of the alternatives seemed in hindsight a false choice. While the innovation economy does indeed need useful applied research, most research and development managers understand that this does not happen without simultaneous advances in basic science, and while they look to the technological universities for applied knowledge, they still look to the universities for basic conceptual advance, as David Cooper's (2011) empirical study shows. Moreover, Donald Stokes' (1997) notion of 'use-inspired basic research' more accurately captures what the high-tech research and development laboratories are doing, more often than not with the help of seconded academics as studies like those of Steven Shapin (2008) show.

We may conclude that in the real world of research, Mode 2 has not so much superseded Mode 1 as new kinds of research groupings have emerged where the issue of conceptual innovation nevertheless remains critical. What this ought to mean is that the integrity of the singulars in the universities should be safeguarded, since this is where the conceptual breakthroughs are distilled into the evolving canon and transmitted to new generations of students. All too often, however, under pressure from the 'engaged' lobby still in thrall to the lure of Mode 2 (Hall 2010), and the 'outcomes' or 'problems based' curriculum reformers, they remain under threat in many sectors of higher education today. It is to the latter that we now turn.

The challenge of outcomes and skills

Despite these reservations, which are becoming acknowledged in some of the academic work on innovation and relevance (Shapin 2008), they are not widely acknowledged by educational policy makers, and the drive to make universities more efficient and to speak directly to external demands continues together with attempts to make learning more practically meaningful to students. A central way to give this effect has been an outcomes-based[1] of curriculum stipulation. This is most manifest in the policies and influence of major international organizations such as the OECD, the EU and the World Bank (for example, OECD 2005; CEDEFOP 2008; EU 2012).

This move to outcomes seems to be prompted from at least two different, though interrelated, quarters. The first is the growing apprehension on the part of employers about what newly-qualified employees 'can do', whether they can 'hit the ground running'. This is of course a long-standing preoccupation with employers but seems to have intensified over the last decade (Case 2011). The second is from an alliance of learning theorists and curriculum and qualifications designers concerned to improve the learning opportunities for learners and to boost their prospects for cross-qualification and cross-country mobility. A few examples:

- the drive to introduce national outcomes-based qualification frameworks at all levels up to doctorates. There were 138 such frameworks at the last count (Allais 2011);
- the European Higher Education Area regulations which aim to ensure common outcomes of all degree qualifications in the Eurozone (Brockmann et al. 2008); and
- the extension of competence-based curricula to higher education. An example is *Tomorrow's Doctors* (GMC 2009), the curriculum framework newly approved by the General Medical Council for the professional education of doctors in England. We will examine this framework in a little more detail below.

This has placed the focus squarely on 'what is to be learnt' and how this is to be represented in the curriculum. Outcomes-based stipulations do two things. First, they assume that there are multiple routes to mastery of an outcome, hence de-privileging the epistemic ladder that scaffolds the outcomes; second, they privilege what students *can do* ('know-how') rather than what they *know* (conceptual knowledge). As we hope to show, both together silence the role of specialist knowledge and as a consequence the role of the specialist communities associated with them (Allais 2012). To bring this out it is useful to reflect briefly on one prominent conceptual basis for this move. The English philosopher Gilbert Ryle offers the following dilemma:

> A pupil fails to follow an argument. He understands the premises and he understands the conclusion. But he fails to see the conclusion follows from the premises. The teacher thinks him rather dull but tries to help. So he tells him that there is an ulterior proposition, which he has not considered, namely, that if these premises are true, the conclusion is true. The pupil understands this and dutifully recites it alongside the premises ... And still the pupil fails to see. And so on forever. He accepts rules in theory but this does not force him to apply them in practice. *He considers reasons, but he fails to reason.*
>
> *(Ryle 1945: 9)*

Ryle is saying that knowing the content knowledge of the curriculum, while important, does not on its own lead to mastery. The propositions alone are inert.

What the learner also needs is the *know-how* to make his or her way through the propositions. In Wittgensteinian vein, the learner must know how to do something with the propositions. In this way Ryle launches his famous distinction between 'knowing that' and 'knowing how', in the process complicating the distinction between knowledge and practice.

But what does it mean to 'know how' to do something? What exactly is that knowledge and how should it be described? Christopher Winch (2010), in an important recent book, helpfully describes two kinds of 'know-how' knowledge, both of which, over and above propositional knowledge he regards as integral to 'systematically organized knowledge', which is the bedrock of a subject or discipline. They are:

- knowledge of the *inferential relations* between the propositions. It is not enough to know the propositions in themselves. Neophytes, to be adept, must also know what the reach and power of the propositions are, and how to make their way around and between them. This involves knowing which normative rules are non-negotiable and which admit of latitudes of discretion (are defeasible). This is facility with *existing knowledge*; and
- knowledge of the *procedures* in assessing, testing and acquiring new knowledge. For any field of knowledge, this is knowing how warrants work, what their scope and limits are, and how to put them to work in judgements that produce something novel. This is facility with *new knowledge*.

Winch (2013) has gone on to unpack 'know-how' further, and distinguishes between techniques, skills, second-order (or 'transversal') abilities and 'project management'. We will not pursue this further here, but there are two points to stress. The first is that the various kinds of 'know-how' supplement and depend upon the 'know that' or conceptual knowledge. They do not *replace* it. To do so is to put the learning cart before the horse.[2] The second point is that there are various kinds of 'know-how' knowledge, all relating in different ways to conceptual content, only a small part warranting the name 'skills' proper (Winch 2013). Much 'outcomes' talk equivocates about the first point, and, by defining everything in outcomes terms, irons out the distinctions Winch regards as crucial in the second. The result all too often is a reduction of 'know that' to 'know-how', and a consequent silencing of the 'voice' of knowledge.

Regarding the first point: the equivocation can be seen in policy documents advocating outcomes, for example in a recent document from the OECD's 'Key Competences' project, KeyCoNet (2012). The document begins with a commodious definition of 'competence' as a 'complex combination of knowledge, skills, understanding, values, attitudes and desire', but goes on, on the same page, to define 'key competences' as 'transversal across fields; they refer to a higher order of mental complexity which include an active, reflective and responsible approach to life; and they are multi-dimensional, incorporating know-how, analytical, critical, creative and communication skills, as well as common sense' – in other words, everything but conceptual knowledge.

The English programme for a new medical curriculum *Tomorrow's Doctors* referred to above sets out to stipulate a programme of undergraduate medical education which will develop the outcomes needed by graduates. There are three broad outcomes categories, each designating the competent doctor as an agent of a particular kind: 'the doctor as a scholar and a scientist'; 'the doctor as a practitioner'; 'the doctor as a professional'. Under each, in an ordinal list, is a series of sub-outcomes, 38 for outcome 1, 53 for outcome 2, and 31 for outcome 3. All of them, with one exception, are stipulated in 'can do' terms, for example: 'diagnose and manage'; 'communicate effectively' and so on. The exception is 'know about ethical guidelines'. A high priority is thus accorded to generic skills that could apply to any field of study or occupation; examples are problem solving, thinking skills, learning to learn and communication skills (see also Gewirtz 2008).

The curriculum thus gives a horizontal listing of some 200 outcomes, stated in 'can do' terms. There is no prioritization, so relative importance is not signified. There is no signposting of progression, so that the progression requirements of high-concept knowledge content are not rendered visible. Gradations of cognitive demand are not signalled. In other words, this outcomes listing represents a powerful 'flattening' of the programmatic content and skills to be learnt over the course of the undergraduate medical curriculum. It is hard to avoid the conclusion that in such formats, outcomes or 'know-how' knowledge are intended to replace, not supplement and enhance conceptual disciplinary knowledge. And as Stephanie Allais (2011) has shown, such erasure does not only eclipse the conceptual content of the 'what is to be learnt' but also undermines the specialist knowledge base and hence the legitimacy of specialized knowledge communities in the disciplines.

The demise of singulars?

The skills-based approach to the curriculum retains a high level of appeal for policy makers. Its origins, we have argued, lie less in what we know about pedagogy or curriculum and more in pressures for relevance, utility, efficiency and cost saving, on the one hand, and socio-ethical notions of 'empowering the learner', on the other. The same goes for arguments for contextually relevant research as we saw above. Taken to its logical conclusion, such an approach would lead ultimately to the end of discipline-based research and study as we know it, and remove much of the autonomy that universities still retain. It is this relative autonomy that forms the institutional basis for learning and enquiry being steered not by external demands in the first instance but by the internal configurations of conceptual fields and their parent disciplines.

At this point we would like to summarize the arguments being made in this chapter:

1   We have argued that spiraling specialization does indeed ramp up the anxieties of knowledge-dependent industries which rely on the competency levels of their newly-qualified job entrants; this translates into an anxiety about what

graduates 'can do'; and this in turn renders the notion of skills/competences/attributes/capacities powerfully attractive and plausible.

2   We have argued further that it is indeed the case that graduates need a range of knowledge 'goods' from the curriculum, as we saw with Winch, which includes 'know what' conceptual knowledge and various kinds of 'know-how' – techniques, skills, second order abilities and 'project management'. Crucially, the 'know-how' abilities are *dependent on* the conceptual knowledge of the domain concerned in all but a small number of mechanical skills and techniques. The 'skills-talk' that most worries us is that form of discourse which pays lip service to the importance of knowledge but then goes on to concentrate almost entirely on the 'know-how' requirements of the curriculum. This has the effect of shoehorning the 'know that' part of the curriculum into a 'know-how' box, which obscures the curriculum requirements of the conceptual knowledge – its requirements for sequence, pace, progression and level of difficulty. This not only empties out the curriculum of content, but also generates a special hindrance to acquisition for learners from disadvantaged educational backgrounds.

3   We do not deny that the innovation economy requires innovative practical knowledge to be able to keep innovating. Our argument is simply that it also requires innovative conceptual knowledge to keep on innovating, and that the repositories and safeguarders of this capacity are the disciplinary singulars that are currently taking a bashing in popular media and academic quarters alike.

In other words, this chapter articulates our concern that the legitimate requirements of relevance will lead to counter-productive university reforms and curriculum experiments that could, because of their global scale, prove to be extremely costly in human and financial terms.

In the last part of this chapter we want to broaden the discussion of disciplines by returning to Durkheim. His argument (Durkheim 1964) was that social progress depends on differentiation and specialization (Young 2011d). The growth and development of universities and their disciplinary form of organization is an example of this differentiation and specialization, and is inescapably linked to the broader process of modernization.

To give priority to skills over disciplines in university curricula, whether through outcomes or skills-based stipulations is not only to silence the voice of knowledge in the curriculum and the classroom, but it is also a form of de-differentiation and de-specialization, in two senses. The first sense is that it blurs the distinction between higher and vocational education, and masks the particularity of each. The second sense is that by conflating skills and knowledge it de-differentiates the difference and particularity of 'conceptual' and 'practical' knowledge, two specialized building blocks of the curriculum which are required in different proportions in qualifications that are vocationally or academically oriented (Muller 2009; Shay *et al.* 2011). Finally, it also de-specializes when it emphasizes generic skills at the expense of specialist content.

The alternative does not condemn us to the old elitist and static forms of discipline-based faculty structures. Rather, it means starting from a basic criterion of specialized knowledge as the basis for university curricula, regardless of whether they are based on 'pure' disciplines such as literature and chemistry or 'applied' disciplines such as engineering or teaching, or draw on the natural or the social sciences or the humanities. The criterion is to make a firm distinction between everyday and conceptual or specialized knowledge. Access to, and the production of, specialized, uncommon sense knowledge in any field defines the purpose of higher education and what university students are entitled epistemological access to. This is not an anti-skills, anti-applied knowledge, anti-professional or anti-vocational approach to the curriculum; it applies as much to applied as to basic disciplines (Wheelahan 2010). It is an approach that identifies both what a contemporary democratic society needs and the role the university is best suited to perform as a fundamental institution of such a society. This does not mean that universities will remain static in what they do. Specialization and differentiation are evolutionary processes and they follow no linear evolutionary path, branching off into new disciplinary formations, coalescing into new regions and singulars as new specializations drive new and unexpected differentiated qualification pathways. But it does mean that it is necessary to resist efforts to de-differentiate or de-specialize the curriculum and the university if a differentiated future for the universities, indeed for society, is to be assured.

Notes

1 The terms vary considerably, for example, 'outcomes', 'skills', 'competences', 'graduate attributes', capacities', 'capabilities'. As Winch (2010) has argued, there are real differences between these terms, but the 'family resemblance' they share is that they all denote a kind of 'know-how' (Ryle 1945).

2 Discovery learning and other forms of 'learning by doing' set out to afford epistemological access to a discipline through procedural knowledge. In concept or content-rich fields, this amounts to learning how to recognize or create new knowledge before understanding the normative structure of the existing knowledge. 'Learning by doing' might seem more plausible in learning about forms of occupational knowledge, but it unfortunately all too often operates as an excuse not to provide access to conceptual knowledge (see Winch 2010; Wheelahan 2009).

14

EVERY PICTURE TELLS A STORY

Epistemological access and knowledge

Introduction

The term 'epistemological access' has become ubiquitous in the scholarship of higher education learning in South Africa. Coined in 2002 by the late philosopher of education Wally Morrow,[1] it has since been deployed in numerous papers and publications as a banner to signal intent to move beyond physical or formal access to *meaningful access* to the 'goods' of the university. Latterly, the term has been contracted as 'epistemic access' (e.g. Chapter 4), a term which certainly sounds more elegant but means something quite specific in traditional epistemology as I will show below. Yet what exactly is being designated by the term? The answer is far from straightforward. This chapter is an attempt to shed some light on the issue. I will begin with a reflection on the terms of emergence of 'epistemological access' as a conceptual staple in South African scholarly discourse, by starting with the beginnings of its use with Morrow, in order to see why and how it is relevant to this community today.

Morrow was a prolix and subtle writer despite his deceptively limpid prose. The argument for epistemological access is published in at least five different formats. Nor is it as easy as just reading those texts. One has to discern what exactly he is taking up cudgels against at any particular time, and this shifts. It starts with a 'picture' of small group teaching, which academics overwhelmingly favour, according to Morrow; it moves to the fallacious notion that the concept of teaching is transparent to its ends; then to what Morrow calls 'epistemological bulldozer drivers'; then to outcome-based education; then to the National Commission on Higher Education, and so on. Yet underlying these apparently moving targets was a robust consistency of argument. He was a scholar who wanted to clarify *what it means to teach*. What follows is my attempt to make sense of the strength and the limits of his views. From the limits I will outline what I think a more fruitful way forward might be. I will make the argument that Morrow was a fellow traveller of the 'knowledge' movement in educational studies (see Maton and Moore 2010), but that he also left a legacy that in important ways might have helped to forestall its emergence.

'A picture held us captive': part 1

> A picture held us captive. And we could not get outside it, for it lay in our language and language seemed to repeat it to us inexorably.
>
> *(Wittgenstein 1953: 115)*

'Epistemological access' as a term of critique saw the public light of day in October 1992, first in a presentation to Morrow's colleagues at the University of Limpopo (then the North; in Morrow 2007), then in a presentation to the 1992 Kenton Conference under the title 'A picture holds us captive' (also in Morrow 2007). The title is glossed from Wittgenstein (1953). The 'picture' in question for Wittgenstein was a representational ('picture') theory of language, which holds that ideas are internal representations that accord more or less accurately with external reality. This representational theory runs from Descartes through to Kant, the logical positivists, and remains influential today (among, inter alia, the linguist Noam Chomsky, the philosopher Jerry Fodor and the artificial intelligence community).

The tenaciously false picture Morrow had in mind here was the idea that academics could only teach properly if classes were small. A piece of biography may explain why Morrow felt at this early stage that a prime threat to 'proper' teaching, which he later came to call 'systematic teaching', was this picture. Having moved from the University of the Witwatersrand to the University of the Western Cape (UWC) a few years earlier, and faced with the consequences of UWC's then-famous 'open access' policy, Morrow found himself standing in front of enormous classes for the first time. Realising that a change of teaching strategy was called for, he proposed the idea that a systematic teaching programme could be better presented using modalities of distance education. However, his colleagues at UWC were not nearly as enthusiastic about this idea as he was. The first two papers were thus addressed to those academics who obdurately clung to the traditional ideal of 'co-present' small class teaching, which he called somewhat derisively the 'hothouse picture of teaching' (Morrow 2007: 42–3). The alternative he was offering was one where the 'intelligible structure' of what was 'to be learnt' was expressed in the 'learning package' rather than by the live teacher, a notion novel at the time in higher education circles.[2] Morrow gives only the barest hint as to what the 'intelligible structure' should look like. I will later suggest that Morrow the philosopher of education was pointing to *structured philosophical procedural knowledge*. While the argument is made more fully below, this is of a piece with Wittgenstein's argument that, in the words of Cohen and Miller (2010: 38), 'philosophy is not a body of knowledge. It is not a *discipline*.'

It is worth remarking that nobody else in the community of which Morrow was a part, the Kenton community, was talking about curriculum as a structured learning package at the time, as a quick glance at the Kenton proceedings will show. At the point of Morrow's first usage in 1992 – between the release of Nelson Mandela and the first election in 1994 (see also the timeline in front of Morrow 2007) – times were heady, when possibilities seemed boundless and solutions to all educational ills were simply a matter of getting the policy correct (see National Education Policy Investigation 1993). Those talking about universities were worrying about student 'learning', or rather failing to learn, and no one worried much about school learning, let alone about the curriculum. Morrow was one of the first to sound a warning that, if we were serious about 'opening the doors to learning' as the then fashionable slogan had it, *formal access* was one thing, *epistemological access* another: indeed, they were in 'direct conflict with each other' (Morrow 2007: 19).

In the next iteration of the 'epistemological access' argument, Morrow's tone was more ascerbic (Morrow 1994; also in Morrow 2009). This version provided Morrow's first answer as to what epistemological access was access *to*. Here, the target is not a picture held by academics but a 'culture of entitlement'[3] manifest in the educational demands of students. 'Entitlement' was a 'culture' that demanded access, coupled education and politics unproblematically, inverted the burden of responsibility for failure, and saw entry requirements – indeed, all evaluative criteria – as 'malevolently' placed obstacles to accessing to the qualification (Morrow 2009: 77). Crucially for Morrow, the distinction in this 'culture' between formal and epistemological access was blurred, leading to a devaluation of achievement, a fatal self-imposed impediment to success.

Achievement for Morrow was the result of effort and skill, and educational achievement was achievement in relation to educational activities. 'To learn how to become a participant in an academic practice is to learn the intrinsic disciplines and constitutive standards of the practice' (Morrow 2009: 77). This took time and effort, and no external agent could cancel these requirements: no one could run your race for you; no one could write your exam for you. Gaining access, thus, was *learning how to become a participant in a practice*, and since academic practices have developed around the search for knowledge, access to an academic practice entailed epistemological access. To deny this was 'facile relativism' (Morrow 2009: 70).

Morrow's tone became overtly polemical in his paper on 'epistemic values' (Morrow, 2003; also in Morrow 2009). Epistemic values for Morrow were formal and content-neutral; they guided disinterested enquiry. They could not be re-invented at will, and epistemological access required a prior commitment to them. Morrow discerned severe threats to epistemic values in free South Africa from at least three sources: from the market; from agents of 'epistemological change' (the higher education democratisers); and most critically, from political pressures to promote academic access and success. These pressures came from the 'bulldozer drivers' who threatened to uproot the 'cemetery' of academic enquiry.

With a few exceptions, Morrow was not as concerned about general student learning as he was about teachers – the BEd students that were in-service teachers at UWC. Learning what it meant to be a teacher was Morrow's central concern. It was not so much academic learning as professional learning that was his focus:

'Professional knowledge is practical knowledge harnessed to an ethical ideal' (Morrow 2009: 78). When discussing the 'effort' component necessary to achievement, the examples he gave first were mainly physical skills – climbing a mountain, playing netball, running in the Comrades Marathon. In a later footnote, he added the following: how to weld a steel structure; how to care for the chronically ill; how to read; how to solve problems in maths; how to conduct research in microbiology (Morrow 2007: 6). What these 'how tos' had in common was that they were all examples of learning to become a participant in a practice, and because a practice is, like speaking a language, rooted in a 'tacit framework of meaning' (Morrow 2003: 31), it was practice that made perfect sense, since not everything could be explicitly articulated.

Exactly what Morrow meant by a practice is never made completely clear. Slonimsky (2010: 45) distinguishes usefully between regulative and normative kinds of practice. MacIntyre's (1981) is an influential view of practice as normative of which Morrow was certainly aware, but in the two main collections of his work (Morrow 2007, 2009) he refers only in a footnote to MacIntyre in the course of discussing teaching as a practice (Morrow 2009: 69), and only in general terms to the virtues that for MacIntyre underpin normative practice. Ironically, as Le Grange (2010) shows, MacIntyre explicitly denied that teaching was a practice, on the grounds that it did not have its own distinctive internal 'goods': the normative structure of mathematics teaching derives from the mathematics, not from the teaching (Le Grange 2010: 83). Below, I will discuss a different branch of contemporary philosophy that depends centrally on reasoning as a normative practice, associated with the work of John McDowell and Robert Brandom.

One conclusion from the foregoing account might be that Morrow was operating with what Winch (2010: 138–51) calls a 'fluency' view of expertise that operates at a tangent to a knowledge-based view. One of the potential effects of such a view is to forestall talk about knowledge: as Winch says somewhat drolly, 'A new picture has come to hold the professional and vocational educator captive: that of the tacit expert' (Winch 2010: 136). A concept was something that allowed you to *do* something: 'we should think of concepts not as names but as rules for practical thinking' (Morrow 2009: 3). Still, he also thought that practical 'process without content is vacuous' (Morrow 2009: 65), and he thought that textbooks were an 'indispensible resource' in purveying 'systematic learning' (Morrow 2009). The case that I will argue here is that Morrow was, perhaps for reasons to do with his major concern about teacher professionalism, more often than not focused on *know-how* knowledge, not *know that* knowledge – or what has been called procedural, not propositional, knowledge. This did not render the knowledge he was talking about any the less conceptual, as I will argue below.

After ten or more years of relative neglect by the higher education learning community, epistemological access was picked up in the 2000s and quickly became ubiquitous. On the face of it, this should come as no surprise. By the mid-1990s, the previously white universities, now 'open' in more than just aspiration, were being inundated by students of evident promise who lacked a thorough schooling, students still today referred to as 'previously disadvantaged'. How to provide 'access' to that which they had been denied by their schooling became a foremost question for academic developers in the previously white institutions. Boughey is usually credited with the term's re-introduction (see Boughey 2003, 2005). Kotta's (2008) Masters had epistemological access in the title, but no reference to Morrow in the bibliography, although she does reference Bak. By the time of the 2011 edited publication of Bozalek, Garraway and McKenna, it was clear that the term had found firm purchase in the scholarly community (see also Lotz-Sisitka 2009; Shalem 2010; Arbee 2012). On 5 February 2014, the London-based Society for Research in Higher Education hosted a discussion on 'Epistemic access, powerful knowledge and the role of higher education policy'. In much, but not all, of this work (see Shalem 2010 for an exception), the notion of 'epistemological access' is taken as self-evident and is hardly interrogated.

What has suddenly drawn the attention of this community? Is there more to the appropriation than just as a sexy synonym for 'successful teaching practice', or plainly, good teaching? I can think of two possible reasons for the attraction. The first is in the power of the distinction drawn between 'formal' and 'epistemological access'. This distinction functions in much the same way as does Young's between 'knowledge of the powerful' and 'powerful knowledge':[4] in both cases a clear line in the sand is drawn against a form of anti-intellectualism, and each does it in a clear but defensible way (see Chapter 3). Second, again in common with the notion of 'powerful knowledge', epistemological access is readily associated with talk of 'rights to access', in that the 'good' in question is a 'social' or public good. It is thus a concept that lends itself to deployment in arguments of social justice.

I believe, though, that the affinity the higher education community feels for the term lies at a deeper level. In order to begin to bring this out, I will make a brief detour through the philosophical concept of 'epistemic access'.

How do we know?

Epistemic access points to a core problem in traditional epistemology, which is: how do we know?[5] How do we justify a belief in something? On what grounds do we know it is X rather than Y? When is it knowledge rather than opinion? For centuries after Descartes, the rationalist (or intellectualist) answer had been – by exercising the mind rationally. Earlier than the rationalists, though, in a tradition stretching back to Aristotle, an empirical tradition was influential, given a powerful boost by Francis Bacon and the Scientific Revolution in the seventeenth century when the term 'empiricism' in its modern meaning arose to support the new sciences and to oppose Cartesian rationalism. In contemporary epistemology of scientific knowledge, especially for the experimental scientific community, the appeal to observation still has powerful prima facie attraction: we know because it is directly available to us for verification though our (technologically amplified) senses.

There are a number of virtues to observation:

* it operates independently of us, and is thus robust;
* it allows for adjustment and refinement;
* it permits tracking over time; and
* it allows us to connect what we perceive with what we know (Azzouni 1997).

A remarkable amount of fuss has been kicked up over empiricism as a theory of knowledge. Its adherents claim for it a privileged access to truth and knowledge. However, large questions remain. Where does this leave invisible objects like mathematical 'posits'; can we 'know' them if we cannot 'see' them? More inconveniently, modern science has only been able to progress because it has posited 'unobservables' (quarks, for example, or the Higgs boson), and the positing itself, 'theory' rather than observation, comes under the same scrutiny. Can theory have the same virtues as observation? That is, can theory offer a secure route to epistemic access? (See also Psillos 2004, 2011.)

Contemporary epistemology has wrestled with the imperialism of rationalism, on the one hand, and empiricism, on the other. In the philosophy of natural science, a range of realisms have joined battle with a range of ir- and anti-realisms. Two things are at stake: whether the world to be described is independent of the description or the theory, to satisfy observation's first and most important virtue; and whether unobservables – or even observables for that matter – are independently real.

One anti-realism influential in the 1960s, no longer dominant in the philosophy of the natural sciences but still disproportionately so in social science, stems from Wittgenstein and was made famous by Thomas Kuhn (1962). According to this view, the world is not mind- or theory-independent. Put baldly, this means that what one is committed to, or knows, depends upon the language game one is using. The grammar furnishes the key concepts that structure the language game. Science is by this account a language game, with subgames (or 'paradigms'). Its practices are internal to the game; that is to say, they do not give users purchase on an independent world. Because science in this view is not about the world as such, what it pursues is not 'truth' or 'knowledge', but the solving of puzzles as structured by the conceptual architecture of the game. Scientific realism, on the other hand, sees the *world as already structured*, and it is this that rubs up against our theories and gives them more or less traction.

Scientific realists thus say that epistemic access is access to reality or knowledge of reality; Wittgensteinian anti-realists say that epistemic access is access to practices and their grammar. It is comprehensible thus why Morrow might have been taken for an anti-realist. He comes closest to a Wittgensteinian or regulative view of practice in a paper called 'Scripture and practices' (Morrow 2001, 2009), where he outlined his objections to outcome-based education and laid out his alternative, which involved induction into a web of practices. However, it must be said that, from the vantage point of epistemic access, Morrow was an odd kind of anti-realist.

'Epistemology' in 'epistemological access' thus seems to mean 'the logic of the concepts of the game being played', an internal warranting logic without any external epistemological grounding in reality or its structures. However, by this Morrow mainly meant to point to the logic of teacher professionalism, even though he rarely gave content to what those concepts or their interrelations might look like. By contrast, he appeared to accord an embattled reality to 'the' practices of academic inquiry that could be threatened by various kinds of bulldozer. Also, he took these threats deadly seriously. It was not simply a 'puzzle' to him, and certainly not a 'game' in the colloquial sense. If he was in some moods a non-realist, then he was a decidedly non-sceptical non-realist.

Is it puzzling that this kind of view was taken up by higher education learning scholars? Not if they too were operating with a kind of Kuhnian language game view of academic proficiency or expertise. I will not attempt to demonstrate that this view is ubiquitous in higher education studies, although I believe it has been. Here is one example: Herbert, Conana, Volkwyn and Marshall (2011) quote Sioux McKenna as saying that 'the single most significant factor affecting student success at university is the gap between the *ways of knowing* students come with from school and those which the (university) curriculum exposes them to' (Herbert *et al.* 2011: 8). It is not unreasonable to suppose that such scholarship has dealt with practices like 'ways of knowing' rather than with knowledge. Why 'rather than'? Because this approach locates the failure in the practices that presume a knowledge base, leaving the knowledge base itself uninterrogated. Practices of what, exactly, we might ask? A practices approach all too easily 'black boxes' the knowledge of which the practices are an expression.

This seems to me entirely understandable. After all, a founding rationale for the importance of scholarship in higher education has been that the issue is pedagogical rather than epistemic: that the problem lies with the practices of teaching and learning rather than with the logic of the knowledge or its curricular recontextualization. It is no surprise that the majority of work has tended to follow the 'practices' picture, focusing on the modes of knowing and teaching rather than, in more MacIntyrean vein, on the normative 'goods' of the discipline being learnt or taught. In the next section, I will briefly outline the emergence of the 'knowledge-based' approach in South Africa, one form of its take-up in higher education scholarship, and then turn to some new kinds of problems it has had to confront.

'A picture held us captive': part 2

The 'knowledge-based' perspective entered South African sociology of education scholarship in 1994 when the English sociologist of education Basil Bernstein visited the University of Cape Town to give a series of advanced seminars on his new work. This was published as Bernstein (2000). The seminarians were treated to an early version of his sociological theorization of 'knowledge', which had a profound effect on their subsequent educational scholarship.

The first resonance could be seen in the PhDs produced in the wake of the seminar: the structure of school art (see Bolton 2006), labour law (see Breier 2003,

2004), cabinet making (see Gamble 2004a, 2004b), early grades numeracy (see Reeves and Muller 2005), and a Master's dissertation on architectural knowledge (see Carter 2011). Later PhDs include Bertram (2008) on school history, Johnson (2010) on school biology and Arbee (2012) on marketing. An adapted Bernsteinian analysis anchored the first Review of Curriculum 2005 (Review Committee 2000), launching a series of curricular analyses that spelt out the implications of knowledge and curriculum structure for learning: Bertram's work on history (2009, 2012), Dempster and Hugo (2006) and Johnson, Dempster and Hugo (2011) on life sciences. There have been studies on university history (Shay 2011) and sociology (Luckett 2009). This is to mention only some of the work.[6]

The studies mentioned here are by no means homogeneous, but they all share a core assumption, which is the distinction between everyday and specialized or disciplinary knowledge – between horizontal and vertical discourse, in Bernstein's terms. Where the Kuhnian approach saw cultural or even ideological differences between paradigms, the knowledge-based approach sees a fundamental socio-epistemic discontinuity between specialized and non-specialized forms of discourse. The analytical focus then becomes the form of the particular specialization in question.

There were early key papers using Bernstein to examine higher education curricula (see e.g., Ensor 2006), but the first major study that placed knowledge structure of kinds of curriculum at the centre of an empirical analysis in higher education was Shay, Oosthuizen, Paxton and Van der Merwe (2011). What Shay and her co-authors do is analyse and compare the knowledge components of higher education curricula at the Nelson Mandela Metropolitan University, spanning the academic-professional divide. This extends work previously done by Muller (2006, 2009) and Gamble (2009) to show how curricula differ in terms of their combinations of contextual and conceptual knowledge, showing empirically what others like Hanrahan (2010) had just mentioned: that the two components form not one continuum but two. Shay (2013) has since redescribed this insight using Maton's work.

Yet there are critical issues raised here. The first has to do with conceptual knowledge. After Bernstein, the emblematic structure of conceptual knowledge is taken to be that of physics, that is, progressing hierarchically from a broad base of particulars to an ever more general set of explanatory propositions, forming what I call below a 'conceptual pile'. It is hard to avoid the supposition that all other disciplinary structures are somehow lesser aspirant versions of this natural scientific ideal, which leads in the to the 'bleak house' view of knowledge in the social sciences and humanities (Chapter 9). This is one aporia of Bernstein's 'picture', one that has affinities with the Cartesians and the logical positivists like Nagel (1961). It is a view that, however inadvertently, paints a less than optimistic picture of knowledge growth in the non-natural sciences. After all, who would willingly want to settle for a horizontal congery of squabbling languages – as the humanities are famously depicted to be – when across the corridor is to be found a serene, orderly empire of propositional knowledge, proceeding logically from the most particular to the most general (Maton 2010)?

Gamble's work on the knowledge structure of craft (Gamble 2004b), raises sharply the issue of propositional content or principle in practical knowledge, indeed, the issue of how practical knowledge is to be modelled. Is practical knowledge just horizontal discourse with a lot of principle, and is it only the propositional content that gives it 'verticality'? This is certainly how many would see it. In the knowledge-based professions, where there are high demands for conceptual as well as practical knowledge, this does not take the account very far.

The 'picture', then, of knowledge structure as a higher or lower pile of propositions only stands in need of elaboration. To be sure, modelling the conceptual pile and examining how pedagogy plays it out is a fundamental starting point. Much of the school-based work shows what a disaster the curriculum can become when, through one or other practice-based view – outcome-based education, skills-only curricula, and so on – this first step is neglected or the conceptual ladder suppressed (e.g., Muller 2006). Yet what the newly emerging work in higher education curriculum and learning is posing is this: is that all? Morrow for one did not think so. To show why, I next make a brief detour through some contemporary work that, seemingly at a tangent to Bernstein, speaks directly to this issue.

Knowing that and knowing how

The English philosopher Gilbert Ryle, conducting his own dispute with Cartesian rationalism, offers the following dilemma:

> A pupil fails to follow an argument. He understands the premises and he understands the conclusion. But he fails to see the conclusion follows from the premises. The teacher thinks him rather dull but tries to help. So he tells him that there is an ulterior proposition, which he has not considered, namely, that if these premises are true, the conclusion is true. The pupil understands this and dutifully recites it alongside the premises ... And still the pupil fails to see. And so on forever. He accepts rules in theory but this does not force him to apply them in practice. He considers reasons, but he fails to reason.
>
> *(Ryle 1945: 9)*

Ryle makes the point here that knowing the propositional knowledge, while important, is not enough. The propositions, on their own, are inert. What the learner also needs to have to escape the vicious infinite regress is the *know-how* to make his or her way through the propositions. In Wittgensteinian vein, the learner must know how to do something with the propositions. In this way Ryle launches his famous distinction between 'knowing that' and 'knowing how', and in the process complicating the distinction between knowledge and practice.

However, what does it mean to 'know how' to do something? What exactly is 'know-how' knowledge and how should it be described? Winch (2010), in an important recent book, helpfully describes two kinds of 'know-how' knowledge, both of which, over and above propositional knowledge he regards as integral to 'systematically organised knowledge', which is the bedrock of a subject or discipline. They are:

- Knowledge of the *inferential relations* between the propositions. It is not enough to know the propositions in themselves. Neophytes, to be adept, must also know what the reach and power of the propositions is, and how to make their way around and between them. This involves knowing which normative rules are non-negotiable and which admit of latitudes of discretion (are defeasible). This is facility with *existing knowledge*.
- Knowledge of the *procedures* in assessing, testing and acquiring new knowledge. For any field of knowledge, this is knowing how warrants work, what their scope and limits are, and how to put them to work in judgements that produce something novel. This is facility with *new knowledge*[7] (see also Winch 2012).

In an influential contemporary branch of philosophy, this is known as making your way around the 'space of reasons' – knowing how to play the game of giving and asking for reasons (see, e.g., McDowell 2007; Brandom 2000). Conceptual knowledge in this account is that which can be offered as, and itself stands in need of, reasons. 'Understanding or grasping such propositional content is a kind of know-how, or practical mastery of the game of giving and asking for reasons: being able to tell what is a reason, for what, distinguishes good reasons from bad' (Keeler 2004: 250). To be able to play the game is to be able to keep score on what you, and other players, are committed and entitled to. Evaluating a claim means understanding how it would change the score. The conceit of 'scorekeeping between players', usefully brings out the social nature of 'know that' and 'know-how' knowledge and judgements based on them.

There is a position in philosophy – the intellectualist or Cartesian camp (see Stanley 2011; Stanley and Williamson 2001) – that maintains that all 'knowing how' is a kind of, or can be translated into, propositional knowledge, or 'knowing that'. On the other side of the spectrum, the connectionist camp (e.g., Dreyfus 2006; Schön 1983; Polanyi 1966) seems to be suggesting that all knowledge possessed by expert practitioners is embodied, tacit and exercised in a fluent way without passing through cognition; all knowledge is 'know-how' (Winch 2010; Kotzee 2012). Both positions – the intellectualists and the connectionists – have their defenders but are in the end not helpful for the problem at hand. The Rylean position presents the midway position, as has been persuasively argued by Winch (2010). To sum up so far: there are two kinds of knowledge, 'knowledge that' and 'knowledge how'. It is unhelpful to reduce the one to the other; both are more inter-related than previously thought; and both must be accounted for in the curriculum.

How does this help to amend Bernstein's 'conceptual pile' 'picture'? Let me recap briefly the ground rule separating horizontal discourse from vertical discourse. Bernstein argues that 'a vertical discourse takes the form of a *coherent, explicit and systematically principled* structure' (2000: 157). Yet this is a structure of what? What comprises 'the discourse'? I have said above that it is all too easy to conclude from Bernstein's account of hierarchical knowledge structure that knowledge is defined only as theory, propositional knowledge, 'know that': 'This form of knowledge (hierarchical knowledge structure) attempts to create very general propositions and theories' (Bernstein 2000: 161). Bernstein does not say that is all it does, but the door is opened to conflating knowledge structure with theory, and to consigning practical knowledge to horizontal discourse. Both moves are wrong.

Winch has been persuasive that both kinds of knowledge ('know that' and 'know-how') should be described in the curriculum, in what he calls a 'subject' (Winch 2012). A subject is 'systematically organised knowledge'. We can conclude that subjects are systematically organized ensembles of 'know that' and 'know-how'. This sounds innocent enough, but it has a number of far-reaching entailments:

- When Bernstein speaks about 'a systematically principled structure' he is referring to *two* iterations of vertical discourse, not just one: the *theoretical pile* or conceptual core(s) of the discipline, on the one hand; and the *subject* which is a recontextualization of the pile plus a recontextualization of 'know-how', on the other. There has been a tendency to take the theoretical pile as the subject, and the subject as the theoretical pile. This muddles matters, leaves a great deal unstipulated, and leaves the door open for a return of 'skills', 'outcomes' and perhaps other forms of knowledge-less practice.

- A subject then is composed of two epistemic domains, the 'know that' or propositional domain and the domain of 'know-how' or procedural knowledge (of which there are many subtypes – techniques, transversal skills, and so on, see Winch 2012). Each of the domains stands in need of curricular description. Each of these domains can be more or less hierarchical. To conceive of procedural knowledge as hierarchical might seem foreign, but that is probably because we are used to equating procedural knowledge with contextual or practical knowledge in the corporeal sense. Yet Bernstein was explicit that procedural knowledge could be hierarchical in the sense of part of vertical discourse: 'The procedures of vertical discourse are (then) linked, not by contexts, horizontally (as in horizontal discourse), but the procedures are linked to other procedures hierarchically' (Winch 2012: 160). Hierarchical procedural knowledge is thus not contextual knowledge. Moreover, these domainal hierarchies need not vary in tandem. History, for example, has a lot of empirical content but very little explanatory theory that is indigenous to the discipline. However, it has a highly elaborated, rigorous tradition of procedural knowledge that regulates how empirical claims are evaluated and weighed (Winch's procedural knowledge proper), and narratives composed from masses of particular facts (Winch's inferential knowledge). Both of them are kinds of 'know-how'. Although there is a dispute as to the theoretical explanations most appropriate for the field of history, there is widespread consensus about the 'know-how' tradition and the judgemental appropriacy it affords. One might then fairly then say that the 'know-how' knowledge of historical studies (inferential as well as procedural) is more hierarchical than its propositional 'know that' knowledge base.

- It follows that *all knowledges have procedural knowledge*. It is not the case that procedural knowledge belongs to some fields – like practical/vocational or professional ones – and not to others – like academic ones. Without it there would be no argumentative style or means for evaluating claims to new knowledge. Likewise, *all knowledges amenable to pedagogic transmission have some theoretical knowledge*, as Gamble (2004b) has shown for cabinet making.
- Not all procedural knowledge will be a part of vertical discourse. Whether the procedural knowledge belongs in vertical discourse or horizontal discourse depends on how it is organized, as Bernstein said above. To put that more colloquially, those procedures that have become integrated into the tradition by explicit recontextualizing are thereby socialized by being inserted into vertical discourse. Those procedures that are the possession of practitioners learnt in specific situations – experientially acquired rules of thumb – are often tacit, functionally connected to specific contexts, and are therefore by definition part of horizontal discourse. They are part of the personal repertoire of the professional or craftsperson but have not been socialized into the canonical reservoir.

To return to Morrow: it should now be clearer what he and Bak were trying to do in their quest to render 'epistemological access' to students in their metatheory class via what they saw as an innovative modality – distance, really self-study – but by means of an explicit intelligible structure. Yet this is a structure of what? Morrow was certainly not trying to teach them a hierarchy of philosophical propositions. In an earlier book (Morrow 1989) he called it 'critical thinking'. With 'epistemological access,' he clarifies his intention to induct them into a facility with the warrants of logical argument (see also Shalem and Slonimsky 2010: 13). This was a capacity he intended would serve them well across their educational careers. To be told that styles of reasoning belonged to specific disciplinary formations, as the sociology of knowledge would argue, would have cut no ice with him. The 'epistemological' discourse into which he wanted to afford access was discipline-blind (hence the 'meta' in 'metatheory'). However, Winch may have recognized it as *philosophical procedural knowledge*, more specifically, knowledge of the internal inferential relations of analytical philosophy, and the wisdom of this effort would be underpinned by the fact that philosophy, like history, had stronger – more hierarchical – procedural 'know-how' knowledge than a set of propositions that were hierarchically arranged as they were in physics. Winch may also have approved of Morrow's basic intuition that this needed to be rigorously structured to optimize access. However, he might have added that the students would have had to learn at least some propositional knowledge or common content in order for the inferential relations to have something to work with, a point with which Morrow would probably have agreed. If propositional knowledge without procedural knowledge is inert, then procedural knowledge without conceptual content is blind. Most people who have tried to teach generic skills have had to come to terms with this inconvenient fact.

Conclusion

The main thrust of this chapter, besides reflecting on Morrow's undeniable contribution, has been to restate the case for looking at knowledge, its variational forms and some of the educational implications. The suggestion is made that one of the main ways to short-circuit talk about knowledge is to talk about practice, or practices, as the principal or sole 'goods' of the educational enterprise. This tends to focus on what is done, easily losing sight of the point that the intelligibility of what is done – whether it is intelligently, accurately or expertly done – depends on knowledge acquired rather than on practice made perfect: better yet, practice made perfect *with* knowledge acquired.

That it is important to focus on what is done should also be clear. Yet what is done, at least as far as curricular design is concerned, is a form of knowledge, either inferential, referring to a canonical style of argument and reasoning, or procedural, referring to ways of weighing claims to new knowledge. Both are *doing things with knowledge*. This is the heart of the educational enterprise and it remains tragic how little is known about how it works, circulates and becomes productive. It has also been suggested that higher education studies has, through a well-intentioned focus on practice, at times taken its eye off knowledge. This is understandable. Nevertheless, that is not the only place to look for the solution to 'epistemological access'.

Finally, I have reviewed here three traditional answers to the question, 'what is epistemological access affording access *to*?'

- *Knowledge of theoretical propositions and theoretical systems.* This is the rationalist answer, which leads to a picture of knowledge as theory only.
- *Knowledge of things themselves.* This is the empiricist answer, and one can hear echoes of it in some contemporary neuroscientists' avowals that by direct study of the brain we will discover the answer to the mystery of consciousness. This leads to a naturalistic picture of knowledge as empirical facts only.
- *A practice, its associated rules, norms and customary moves.* This is the practice-based attempt to avoid both empiricism and rationalism, but risks dissolving knowledge into practice, thereby losing sight of its fateful specificity.

I have outlined a fourth answer, after Ryle and after Winch, which attempts to hold in view both the insights of rationalism[8] (knowledge as theory, or 'know that') and the insights of the practice theorists (knowledge as practice, or 'know-how').

Educational scholarship has for too long been embroiled in a polarized argument between the two positions. Since the position of each suppresses important aspects of the other, this has led, not for the first time in educational studies, to a fruitless oscillation from one to the other and back again. The position proposed here attempts to move the debate forward by combining the best features of each and trying to avoid their worst features. The first position led, in mass schooling, to theory learnt as facts and without understanding. The reaction that followed was against force-fed facts and rote learning. This second position dealt with this by shifting theory out of sight and emphasising the practical accomplishments of learning. This opened the door to various forms of educational anti-intellectualism and to attempts to teach procedures without explicitly teaching the theory, which simply disadvantaged the already disadvantaged. It also disabled vocational education (Winch 2009). This chapter has attempted to sketch a way beyond the impasse, a way that Morrow, however abstractly and schematically, had carved open with his notion of 'epistemological access'.

Finally, what, from this perspective, would be the explanatory gain for the issue of 'educational disadvantage'? Morrow left us with tantalisingly few clues as to how we might 'structure' the curriculum to make it more accessible to such students. This chapter has argued that what he did do was stress a neglected part of the curricular package, namely, what I have called above the 'know that' part of the discipline, an insight that has been taken further by Winch and others. This augments a fruitful Bernsteinian tradition of conceptualizing the 'goods' of the curriculum, and by expanding our understanding of the different components of the knowledge to be learnt, alerts us to new possibilities as to where not only 'disadvantaged' students may be going astray.

Notes

1 As far as I know. Robert Merton (1993) reminds us of the inherent perils of attribution, which cannot easily be avoided.
2 Morrow frequently recounted his efforts, together with Nelleke Bak, to teach metatheory to a class of hundreds of BEd students, via distance-delivered 'systematic learning'. Bak's (1998) own account (in Morrow and King 1998), adds the notion of 'epistemological labour' to the account – how to make the knowledge and the language (meaning the argument) 'clear' but not 'easy'. Neither Bak nor Morrow offer evidence for the claim that their course design delivered epistemological access, where others did not. The argument is purely analytical.
3 The phrase echoes Kenneth King's 'climate of entitlement', in his 2003 paper in *Perspectives in Education*. King was frankly alarmed at the devaluing effect activist populism was having on the value of striving to achieve a matric.
4 Incidentally, like Young, Morrow too was critical of the equation of knowledge and power (see, for example, Morrow 2007: 30).
5 I will here be dealing rather narrowly with a few core issues in the epistemology of scientific knowledge, where they are raised most sharply. It is beyond my remit to deal with other contemporary contentious issues, such as the issue of 'epistemic diversity' (for example, Siegel 2006) or 'epistemic injustice' (for example, Fricker 2007), although these surely deserve discussion in a broader account.
6 This Bernsteinian-inspired concentration on knowledge and curriculum is also somewhat unusual. The dominant empirical deployment of Bernstein up until his passing had looked mainly at the classification and framing values of instructional and regulative discourse – which is to say, at pedagogy, an approach that has been influential here in studies of schooling (see Hoadley 2007) but which never really caught on in higher education studies here (but see Case 2011).
7 Discovery learning and other forms of 'learning by doing' set out to afford epistemological access to a discipline through this kind of procedural knowledge. In concept- or proposition-rich fields, this amounts to learning how to recognize or create new knowledge

before understanding the normative structure of the existing knowledge. 'Learning by doing' might seem plausible in learning about forms of occupational knowledge, but in concept-rich fields it puts the cart before the horse, and for vocational fields it unfortunately all too often operates as an excuse not to provide access to conceptual knowledge (see Winch 2010; Wheelahan 2007).

8 For the purposes here, rationalism and empiricism had a roughly similar impact on curriculum thinking – they both buttressed the facts-based traditional curriculum.

15

TOWARDS THE SOCIOLOGY OF PROFESSIONAL KNOWLEDGE

Introduction: Professions and their knowledges

In a review of research on the sociology of work written two decades ago, Andrew Abbott (1993) commented that work on the professions was unusually dominant within the broader field of the sociology of work, and that within that 'theorizing dominates' (ibid.: 203). Notwithstanding this glut of attention, the sociology of professions remains a frustratingly under-specified area, and the demarcation criteria that have emerged to distinguish professions from other occupations – deployment of expert knowledge, technical autonomy, a normative orientation, and social and material rewards (Gorman and Sandefur 2011) – do not unambiguously distinguish between professions and other expert occupations. Nor do they take us much further than Glazer's depiction of 'their hopeless predicament' in analysing occupations that are variously described as 'minor' (Glazer 1974), 'soft' (Becher and Trowler 1989) or 'semi-professions' (Etzioni 1969). Opinion is divided on whether this matters or not. According to Evetts (2006, 2013), the bulk of researchers in the USA have 'moved on' (Evetts 2006: 134) and no longer seek demarcating criteria, since these do not help in understanding the power of some professional groups but not others, nor in understanding the 'contemporary appeal of the discourse of professionalism in all occupations' (ibid.).

For European researchers like Sciulli (2005), it decidedly does matter: how else do we distinguish between expert occupations like haute couture and cuisine, and professions like medicine or law? For Sciulli, it is important to see that

> expert occupations (compared to professions) ... do not bear fiduciary responsibility, and they also do not institutionalize either theory-based instruction or ongoing deliberation. They do not typically establish and then maintain collegial formations, as reflected in on-going behavioural fidelity to the threshold of procedural norms.
>
> *(Sciulli 2005: 937)*

What Sciulli is stressing here are the 'structural' or institutional features of professions. Yet here too, variation is so wide as to elude neat conceptual demarcation, and it is arguably growing wider still. Sciulli concludes, in a phrase that has resonance with the philosopher Robert Brandom, that professions are 'reason-giving collegial formations' (Sciulli 2005: 958), but that too was already established by Abbott (1988).

The centrality of intrinsic normative commitments and responsibilities was established in what Gorman and Sandefur (2011) call the 'Golden Age' of the sociology of professions, by Parsons and Merton who, following Durkheim, emphasized the socially integrative function of professions. Although this was a diminution of Durkheim's contribution, it did foreground the relation between the internal normative commitments of professions and their broader macro social functions. In reaction to the perceived conservatism of this functionalist description, a revisionist period followed, of Marxist, Weberian and later Foucauldian provenance, which put professional bona fides in question and, in an inversion of Parsonian optimism, pointed to the monopolistic and gatekeeping operation of professions and for their broader ideological function. This phase of critique, with its shift of focus from professions as an occupation to professionalism as an ideology, also cast suspicion on the validity and value of expert and professional knowledge, a position that in science studies at least we have yet properly to emerge from, and one which made it difficult to establish the reality and efficacy of 'expert knowledge' (Collins and Evans 2009). Nevertheless, it was in this phase too that Abbott (1988) established the centrality of formal abstract principles for professional formations, as mentioned above.

The phase that followed reinterpreted the Parsonian values, and returned to the normative emphasis of the Golden Age (as in Friedson 2001), but in a 'more balanced and cautious' way (Gorman and Sandefur 2011: 138). There have been a wide variety of case studies, which seem to say more about the occupational niche in question than they do about what professions are, and how they work. Evetts (2013) detects a shift in the occupational structure of professions with corporations and organizations, both private and public, increasingly being the workplace location for all kinds of professions – the long established ones like doctors, lawyers, engineers and accountants, as well as the 'new boys on the block' such as social workers and teachers. This seems to have led to a shrinkage of autonomy and discretion in Evetts' view, fuelling the literature on 'de-professionalization' and even 'proletarianization'. This can be overstated, of course, and is not a major focus for European scholars, except in England.

There are two features that can be distilled from the contemporary work in the sociology of professions that are worth noting. The first is that, in the present discursive climate of the 'knowledge economy', 'knowledge work' and 'expert occupations', there is simultaneously concern about the increase in the riskiness of professional judgement – the threat that codification and standardization poses to the autonomy and discretion of the traditional 'liberal' professional – and a residual suspicion about the probity and trustworthiness of all professions and professional

judgement. Whether this reflects the views of an increasingly informed and sceptical public about the trustworthiness and value of the professions, or is a long hang-
over from the scepticism about knowledge that underlies public attitudes in an age
that has distinct anti-intellectual overtones, is hard to say. Second, the upshot has
been that the nature of professional knowledge has escaped scholarly notice and,
when spoken about at all, is spoken about in terms of professional expert judgement
and what professionals *can do* with the knowledge. What the *knowledge is that professionals have had to acquire to be experts* has, by and large, eluded scholarly attention.

The paradox we are left with is this: in an age where 'knowledge' as a qualifier
is attached to a wide range of categories and actions, when expert occupations proliferate, and the legitimatory discourse of 'professionalization' is deployed across the
occupational spectrum, *knowledge itself*, and above all the sociological study of professional knowledge, goes virtually unremarked. In a nice twist to the paradox,
'knowledge' itself is increasingly used as a legitimatory qualifier for sociological
work – but the knowledge itself is by and large passed over in silence (Chapter 4).

The project we are pursuing by means of this volume is to put the sociological
study of professional knowledge into the centre of scholarly focus in research on
professions and their formation. This is not just a matter of restoring sociological
balance. As educational sociologists, we have also repeatedly come up against the
intellectual lacuna left in discussions around the aims of higher education and the
curriculum (see Chapter 13 above). We have noted in earlier work how the exclusive stress on the 'can do' side of the knowledge equation – on skills and competencies at the expense of knowledge on skills in the design of national qualifications
frameworks (Young and Allais 2013), and on outcomes in national school curricula
(Chapter 4; Muller 2007) – can distort the resultant educational goods, and impair
educational provision. It is the distinctive socio-epistemic properties of different
kinds and bodies of knowledge that are put to use in problem-solving and other
kinds of knowledgeable practice that is our singular concern in this volume.

To say that, however, is not to make a strong split between knowledge and
action; this would, in the case of professional knowledge, be particularly counter-
productive. Indeed, as the various contributions to this book will show, there is a
continuum between these, and it is easy to blur the lines. The distinctions we wish
to refine are analytical. There is an interesting related body of work that focuses on
'knowledge engagement and learning' (Jensen, Lahn and Nerland 2012: 5), which
has carved out new perspectives in understanding the knowledgeable nature of
professional work. It starts however, from our perspective and in terms of our central interest, just too far in the direction of 'can do' and the 'practice' of knowledge-
based professions, and pays little attention to the 'specialized knowledge' involved
in that practice. This perspective has obvious affinities with the work in this volume,
and is represented by the contribution of David Guile, who makes a first stab at
building a bridge between the two sets of interest. Other papers which reflect such
bridge building are Afdal (2012), and Nerland and Karseth (2015), among others.
We are mindful and appreciative of this work, but do not engage further with it
directly in what follows; the opportunity will surely present itself in the future.

The difference in emphasis between the terms 'knowledge' and 'expertise' has resisted easy resolution, and this is critical when it comes to professions. This is so because professionals self-evidently have, and need, both specialized knowledge and practical expertise, 'know that' knowledge and 'know-how' knowledge. On the other hand, while all professions involve some 'practical expertise', you can be an 'expert' in all manner of activities without your expertise being associated with a profession – brilliant poker players and winners at Mastermind-type quiz shows are examples that come to mind. This distinction is sometimes referred to as similar to distinctions between 'abstract', 'pure' or 'theoretical' knowledge, and 'applied' knowledge, and between theory and practice, but as we will show, the parallel is one of many that obscures more than it clarifies.

A marker in this debate was put down in a particularly graphic way by the English philosopher Gilbert Ryle (1945). Ryle was conducting a pointed argument with what is known as Cartesian rationalism, the view that the essence of all knowledge lies in its propositional content, and in his wake have come many educators who have railed against the 'content only' curriculum, and against the perniciousness, as Gradgrind in Dickens' *Hard Times* so memorably had it, of 'facts, facts, facts' (see Taylor and Vinjevold 1999 for a discussion). The Rylean point was that propositions on their own are inert. The learner must also know *how to do* something with the propositions. In this way Ryle launched his famous distinction between 'knowing that' and 'knowing how', in the process complicating the distinction between knowledge and practice.

But what does it mean to 'know how' to do something with a proposition? What exactly is that knowledge and how should it be described? Christopher Winch (2010), in an important recent book, helpfully describes two kinds of 'know-how' knowledge, both of which, over and above propositional knowledge, he regards as integral to the 'systematically organized knowledge' which is the bedrock of school subjects and academic disciplines. They are:

- knowledge of the *inferential relations* between the propositions. It is not enough to know the propositions in themselves. Neophytes, to become adept, must also know what the reach and power of the propositions is, and how to make their way around and between them. This involves knowing which normative rules are non-negotiable and which admit of latitudes of discretion (are defeasible). This is facility with *existing knowledge*; and
- knowledge of the *procedures* in assessing, testing and acquiring new knowledge. For any field of knowledge this is knowing how warrants work; what their scope and limits are; and how to put them to work in judgements that produce something novel. This is facility with *new knowledge*.

In an influential contemporary branch of philosophy, this is known as making your way around the 'space of reasons' – knowing how to play the game of giving and asking for reasons. Conceptual knowledge in this account is that which can be offered as, and itself stands in need of, reasons. Understanding or grasping such propositional content is a kind of know-how, or practical mastery of the game of giving and asking for reasons. To be able to play the game is to be able to keep score on what you, and other players, are committed and entitled to. Evaluating a claim means understanding how it would change the score. The conceit of 'scorekeeping between players' usefully brings out the social nature of 'know that' and 'know-how' knowledge, and judgements based on them.

There is a position in philosophy – the intellectualist or Cartesian camp (see Stanley 2011; Stanley and Williamson 2001) – that maintains that all 'knowing how' is a kind of (or can be translated into) propositional knowledge, or 'knowing that'. On the other side of the spectrum, the 'fluency' theorists, like Hubert Dreyfus (2006) seem to be suggesting that all knowledge possessed by expert practitioners is embodied, tacit and exercised in a fluent way without passing through cognition at all; all knowledge for them is 'know-how'. Both intellectualists and fluency theorists have their defenders but are in the end not helpful for our specific problematic. That the Rylean position presents the midway position has been argued by Winch (2010). To sum up the discussion thus far: there are two kinds of knowledge, 'knowledge that' and 'knowledge how'. Both are more inter-related than previously thought and both must be accounted for in accounts of professional knowledge.

Winch has been persuasive that all three kinds of knowledge ('know that' and the two kinds of 'know-how') should be described in what he calls a (school) 'subject' (Winch, 2012). For Winch, a 'subject' is an example of 'systematically organized knowledge'. We can conclude that subjects are systematically organized ensembles of 'know that' and 'know-how'. This is helpful as far as it goes, but we will need another distinction when considering professional knowledge or the professional in contrast to the school curriculum. Professional education students need access not only to 'knowledge that', propositions of a subject, and 'knowledge how', how the propositions are used in a subject; they need knowledge of 'how' propositions may or may not be useful (or solve or suggest solutions to) specific problems in their sectoral 'field of practice' – a point we will return to.

In what follows, we will first redescribe the distinction usually referred as 'pure' versus 'applied' knowledge in order to establish an initial point of departure for considering the nature of professional knowledge. We are not interested here in a related but different distinction between 'theory' and 'practice'. The distinction we are interested in is an antecedent one concerning the kind of knowledge that forms the substance of what gets taught in the professional curriculum and what forms the cognitive substrate of all professional decisions and judgements. In the philosophy of technology, it is conventional (see Meijers 2009) to say that the 'pure'/'applied' distinction is too simple, which is easily granted. But how then should it be considered? We start with some theoretical clarifications:

1   According to Bernstein's (2000) schema, there are *two kinds of theoretical knowledge*. They are distinguished by the way that they *elaborate:* either 'hierarchically', that is say, by means of an expanding conceptual edifice, which projects true law-like predictions of ever greater generality and universality; or 'horizontally',

that is to say, by means of new theoretical languages which break off to form a new theoretical stem, parallel and usually antagonistic to the parent stem or stems. What Bernstein did not do is to say further how specialists develop concepts *within* each new theoretical stem, but we assume he thought this was obvious – they develop in principle in the same fashion as concepts do in hierarchical knowledge structures. (There may well be lateral filling out of conceptual implications, but this is embroidery rather than elaboration.) So, we may provisionally conclude that all attempts to make conceptual advances within knowledge structures are, in the Bernsteinian framework, *hierarchical* whether or not the knowledge structures are themselves hierarchical or horizontal. In what follows, we will not distinguish between conceptual cores that are more or less hierarchical; when we refer to 'conceptual cores', we include both kinds.

2   It is often asserted that professions are distinguished by their control over their knowledge base. From our point of view and, in light of the clarifications above, we distinguish *two principal kinds of specialized knowledge* that together make up a professional knowledge base. It is sometimes assumed that only conceptual knowledge codified in disciplines is specialized knowledge – and therefore that the practical or 'know-how' knowledge we referred to earlier is tacit and can be disregarded, another version of the misleading dichotomy we discussed above. But a moment's reflection shows that this cannot be the case. The craft guilds that pre-dated the science-based professions such as engineering and medicine were jealous guardians of knowledge traditions that were anything but unspecialized. When Galileo wished to demonstrate that there were moons around Jupiter, a prediction he arrived at theoretically, he could only show it, and make it open to testing, because he had available to him precision-ground optical lenses that were the result of lens grinders' specialized knowledge. Today lens grinding is a machine operation, an aspect of optical engineering that draws on scientific developments first initiated by Newton among others in the seventeenth century. If theoretical knowledge/conceptual edifices, as previously defined, could be regarded as knowledge specialized to conceptual generality, then lens grinding and other forms of medieval craft specialization and their contemporary equivalents can be regarded as knowledge specialized to purpose – to attain a specific end or solve a contextually specific problem. So, on the one hand, there is knowledge *specialized to develop conceptually*; on the other, there is knowledge *specialized to a contextual purpose*. Prior to the mathematicization of the sciences in the seventeenth and eighteenth centuries (Collins 1998), links between these types of knowledge as in the case of Galileo were rare. Yet this is the crux of the matter in the professions, particularly the science-based professions.

It is important to stress that this distinction between two distinct kinds of specialization foregrounds a particular feature of knowledges, namely, the way they elaborate – their telos or their 'epistemic destiny'. In answer to the question 'why elaborate the knowledge?', theoretical knowledge implicitly answers – to extend the generality and reach of the conceptual edifice; while for-purpose knowledge answers – to arrive at a more elegant or efficient solution to a technical problem.

These two forms of specialization joined common cause in the seventeenth century to create in part the conditions for scientific take-off that have been called the Scientific Revolution (Gaukroger 2006; Cohen 2010: see Chapter 11 above). Each side co-opted parts of the other to its own purpose – scientific knowledge adopted technological solutions to refine instrumentation; for-purpose knowledge absorbed theoretical knowledge to advance its quest for ever more sophisticated technical solutions; both led to new sub-branches of specialized knowledge, and to new forms of the division of intellectual labour. For our purposes here, this means that contemporary for-purpose 'professional' knowledge has, embedded in it, conceptual cores of different sorts; and likewise, much contemporary theoretical knowledge has roots in technical solutions, reached in advance of basic science, to explain it. It is this irreversible twist in the braid of contemporary specialized knowledges that seems to cause the greatest problem in conceiving of distinctive components of the professional knowledge base.

3   Reference is sometimes made to 'systematic knowledge'. When we use it here, we mean to denote the different components of specialized knowledge that go to make up a curriculum leading to a professional qualification. Winch refers to this as a 'subject', a useful term not to be confused with a school subject; it distinguishes between a 'discipline' – the parent knowledge structure which is usually one principal reservoir – from which the knowledge contents of the 'subject' are recruited, adapted, sequenced, and paced for learners. However, this does not distinguish either the different processes of recontextualization involved in developing school and university curricula and, more importantly for us, it does not distinguish the intra-subject recontextualization in say a physics curriculum from what we might call the professional recontextualization of physics involved in the engineering sciences, for example.

Whereas a subject such as physics or history involves 'know that' knowledge and, as Winch argues, two kinds of 'know-how', the systematic knowledge in a professional curriculum may, depending on the profession, require no less 'know that' knowledge, but, in addition, a new configuration of 'know that' knowledge *together with* practically derived and accumulated knowledge. This points to a far more complex recontextualization than the simplification of 'application' or 'applied knowledge' might suggest. We return to this below.

The important point is that curricular 'subjects' optimally include both kinds of specialized knowledge referred to earlier. In fact, as Winch goes on to show, we can usefully distinguish further among distinct sub-types of specialized 'know-how' that make up a curriculum. Nevertheless, there is also still an important sense in which 'subjects' making up a 'curriculum' – as a path towards a qualification that consecrates a particular blend of specialized knowledge expertise – can be said to be arranged according to either a conceptually or a contextually dominant *coherence principle* (Muller 2009). It is their dominant coherence principle that distinguishes between different qualifications like degrees, diplomas, and certificates: they are designed to specialize the knowledge base and the resultant expertise of neophytes for different purposes and create and limit opportunities both for further study and future employment. Any curriculum accordingly reflects a leaning either towards conceptual or contextual coherence (Muller 2009).

Having described in general terms some of the intellectual debates that underlie the field of professional knowledge we now move towards a closer consideration of the debates in the sociology of knowledge between those who favour a 'knowledge' point of departure and those who favour an 'expertise' or, as it is sometimes referred to, a 'practice-based' view. In order to stage this debate more graphically, we will contrast the views of Basil Bernstein and Donald Schön.

Donald Schön and Basil Bernstein; a comparative review

In contrasting two such different thinkers as Donald Schön and Basil Bernstein, it is important to note where they come from, and their very different projects. It is unlikely that many readers will be deeply familiar with the work of both. Schön became a Professor (at MIT) having spent the previous 15 years as a management consultant specializing in organizational learning. However, from the 1970s onwards, and following the publication of his book *Educating the Reflective Practitioner*, his work has had a profound and indeed increasingly global influence on professional development that extended from architecture and town planning to medicine, teaching and a range of other professions (Schön 1990). It is hard to come across a programme in initial or further professional development that does not somewhere mention Schön's idea of the 'reflective practitioner'. Whatever reservations we may have about his work, for our purposes in this volume there is no doubt that he grasped the predicament that neophyte members of any profession experience facing their first client, patient or student; they don't know what to do and nothing they have learned in their university degree seems to be of any help. It is a tribute to his insight that, despite only engaging indirectly with the question of specialized professional knowledge, his work forms an essential starting point for us.

With regard to Basil Bernstein, we can do no more than acknowledge his place (with Pierre Bourdieu) as one of the two outstanding sociologists of education since Émile Durkheim. However, his international reputation, which has grown rather than diminished since his death in 2001, is based primarily on his work on school knowledge, language, and pedagogy. It may therefore seem surprising that we should choose his work in establishing a sociology of professional knowledge. However, as we have already argued, the distinctive feature of professional knowledge is that it is specialized, and it is the sociology of specialized knowledge that was central to Bernstein's work, even if it was not until his last book (Bernstein 2000) that he linked this to the origins and future of professions. First, we examine the position of Schön.

Donald Schön's 'epistemology of practice'

Schön's starting point is that professional work is about judgement under conditions of uncertainty and complexity of modern society. He concedes that some
members of professions in every field succeed in coping well with these conditions
but argues that this is despite what he identifies as fundamental 'flaws' in the mainstream model of professional education. Schön summarises the traditional model of
professional education as including (a) an underlying disciplinary or basic science
component upon which professional practice is developed, and (b) an applied or
'engineering' component from which likely day-to-day procedures and problem-
solutions facing the profession are derived. What he refers to as this 'technical
rational' model will be familiar to many who have graduated in engineering or
medicine (Schön 2001).

Schön raises two questions about this model. First, 'is it the right model?' in
fields like engineering, where the conditions it assumes appear to, at least, broadly
apply. Second, he asks what happens to 'professions' such as education, city planning, and social work when the model is drawn on even though the conditions do
not apply? In such occupational fields there are rarely stable contexts or agreed-
upon systematic knowledge. Schön's alternative is developed in recognition that
even in engineering and other science-based professions, real-world problems are
rarely well formed; they are complex and ill-defined, and involve many different
types of factors which are mixed up with technical issues. In such situations, traditional 'problem solving' approaches do not apply and, Schön argues, professionals
have to act more like researchers and engage in forms of enquiry that they often
cannot explain or describe. Underlying Schön's alternative is what he refers to as an
'epistemology of practice' (ibid.). It draws on a combination of ideas drawn from
Dewey and Polanyi for whom, according to Schön, truth is tacit and located in the
everyday practice of 'reflecting in action' which is common to all human beings.
This position comes close to the anti-intellectualist stance that some derive from
Ryle that we referred to earlier. However, it could also be seen as a nostalgic return
to the practice of the medieval craft guilds but without their specialized focus. The
irony is that the only way the specialized knowledge of professions can be recognized in Schön's approach is through the element of professional education and
knowledge that his model excludes. He claims that while professional practitioners,
such as physicians, managers, and teachers, reflect-in-action as do we all, their
reflection is of a kind particular to the special features of professional practice.

The professional, for Schön, builds up experience of certain types of situations
and examples, and it is this store of experience that becomes the basis of their specialized knowledge. It is these stored experiences and the lessons to be derived from
them, rather than any codified specialized knowledge, that form the basis of the
professional's expertise and judgement. Progress or the development of new knowledge in such a model is limited to learning from one's mistakes – an attractive but
highly individualistic and in the end conservative approach to being a member of a
profession and one which had reached its limits with the craft guilds prior to the

emergence of the science-based professions in the early nineteenth century. One is reminded of the doctors in many Victorian novels where experience, a few somewhat dubious techniques, and little more was all they had to draw on. The most Schön will concede to the idea of professional knowledge beyond individual experience is when he suggests that 'aspiring practitioners learn to see, in the unfamiliar phenomena of practice, similarities to the canonical problems they may have learned in the classroom' (Schön 2001: 16). The specific case, in other words, for Schön, always takes precedence over the power of generalizable knowledge.

Where does Schön leave us in relation to our aim of conceptualizing professional knowledge? The enormous popularity of his work requires us to take it seriously and certainly his critique of the 'technical rational' model is persuasive. However, in relation to how we distinguish professional practice and judgement from everyday judgements, Schön has little to say. It is as if, despite the 'technical rationality' of the professional curriculum, some do become reflective professionals, even if we don't know exactly how. His form of judgement-based pragmatism has been superseded by Brandom and others and we are left with an experientialism without content or history. It is attractive because of its message that, underlying the good professional is the good and self-reflective human being, and there are certainly far worse values for a doctor, lawyer or teacher to live up to. However, the idea of 'reflection in action' as a moral rule offers the sociologist far less than Durkheim's account of professional ethics in which the idea of the professional as embodying society's morality is part of a theory of society. Part of the attractiveness of Schön's work is that it meshes with the anti-intellectualism of much that passes for research in the field of professional development. If reflection-in-action is generic to all professions, then professional developers do not need to worry about the specialist knowledge future professionals must acquire, whether they are engineers, actuaries, or teachers.

Schön's analysis is useful for reminding us that professions not only know things, they do things. However they do things in a different way from the rest of us, and this is because of their specialized knowledge. It is on account of having this knowledge that today's professions do more for us than of those of previous generations. Schön's unwillingness to go beyond experience and memory and to engage with the specialized knowledge that is the defining feature of professional work limits the answers he leaves us with. We turn therefore to our second thinker, Basil Bernstein, far less well known, if at all until recently, in the fields of professional education and professional knowledge.

Bernstein's 'regions'

It was in his last book, and almost as an aside, that Bernstein made the following cryptic comment: 'The construction of the inner was a guarantee for the construction of the outer. In this we can find the origin of the professions' (Bernstein 2000: 85). In one short sentence, parsed as 'inwardness and commitment shape(s) the terms of practical engagement in the outer world' by Beck and Young (2005: 7), he encapsulates, in characteristic elliptical fashion, what might be the starting point for a sociology of professional knowledge. Earlier in this introduction we introduced Bernstein's classification of types of theoretical knowledge. They are based on a prior differentiation between theoretical and practical (or common sense) knowledge, or in his terms, vertical and horizontal discourses; all theoretical knowledge being forms of vertical discourse. However, he recognized in his later work that these binary categories, though of heuristic value, were not adequate to grasping what are the increasingly dominant forms of knowledge in modern societies. Professional knowledge is both 'theoretical' (that is, general and unvarying) and 'practical' (that is, purposive and contextual). Contemporary professions are about doing things, but doing complex things that cannot rely on experience alone like crafts could for their expertise. Because professional practice is always in a context with a purpose outside itself, professional knowledge is always sectoral, not general, like the traditional disciplines; it relates to specific occupational sectors like health, transport, education. Although he does not explicitly say so, it may be for this reason that Bernstein introduces the term 'regions'; it is the activity, in Bernstein's terms, in a 'field of practice' within a society that shapes a profession's specialized knowledge. So it will be *regional* – applicable to some fields and not others; not *general* – like physics, which is applicable to all physical phenomena, or sociology (at least for Durkheim), which is applicable to anything social. But specialized disciplinary knowledge is differentiated into domains such as mathematics, chemistry and economics all of which have important roles in forms of professional knowledge such as chemical engineering and actuarial science. So Bernstein introduces another term, *singulars*, since each deals with a singular (separate and bounded) class of natural or social phenomena.

Singulars thus refer to knowledge relations that emphasize 'inwardness' (as in the first quote in this section). More familiarly, inwardness refers to 'knowledge for its own sake'; to the pursuit of truth when no external (regional or contextual) interests are involved. The nearest we get to the 'inwardness' of singulars are academic disciplines. In the terms we introduced earlier, singulars involve, as Winch has suggested, 'know that' knowledge and two forms of 'know-how'.

Regions are sources of current and future professional knowledge. First, they bring together, or 'recontextualize', several disciplines in relation to a field of practice like construction or medicine. They do this in ways that enable professionals to reconceptualize real world practices and processes in new ways related to new purposes. This means that professional knowledge will include 'know that' knowledge as the basis of the content to be selected from singulars (for example, engineers do not need to know all the content of physics) and the 'know-how' involved in bringing them together and in developing practically based 'know-how'. Second, regions also bring into play the past consecrated and canonized body of specialized professional knowledge which represents the stable reservoir gleaned from earlier 'applied' research which can, at times, augment not only the knowledge base of the profession, but add to new knowledge in one of the parent singulars.

This kind of specialized regional knowledge, which is not knowledge accrued from specific contexts, can, in stable professional fields like engineering, have its own proto-disciplinary form – for example, engineering science, with its own scientific literature and scientific communities that in the case of engineering, have global jurisdiction over the accreditation of engineers (see Hanhrahan 2010). So, for example, engineering students learn about thermodynamics in at least two different formats: first in the science singulars (physics and chemistry) as the nearest scientists have got to the truth about heat and its relation to energy and work, and then again in engineering science, where thermodynamics is recontextualized in relation to problems such as the heating of nuclear reactors (Smit 2012). It is this double movement in the professional curriculum requiring a shift, with the same scientific concepts, from a singular to a regional mode, which can cause such headaches for students.

Bernstein's innovation is to conceptualize an old problem, the relationship between theory and practice, in a new way that also enables us to characterize this relationship as lying at the heart of professional knowledge. In the process, he extended the familiar *binary* distinction between 'theory' and 'practice' into a three-*fold* distinction:

1   *Singulars*, which represent knowledge relations (or structures) oriented to inwardness – the rules, methods and boundaries that define a discipline (for example sociology or physiology);
2   *Regions* which combine disciplines, selecting, pacing and sequencing knowledge from them in relation to specific purposes in a field of practice (for example, combining parts of physiology and physics and stable contextually derived knowledge to form biomechanics which is part of the professional curriculum of physiotherapists);
3   *Fields of practice* which are the specialized practical contexts in which professionals practice – that is, exercise knowledgeable and reasoned judgements as professionals, by drawing on, often tacitly, their acquired stock of specialized professional knowledge (see also Stanley 2011: 184).

We can therefore analyse a profession's work, and the professional curriculum that aspiring professionals must follow to become qualified, as a region. Regions are never fixed and always 'face two ways' – towards their singulars and towards their field of practice. They will always express a tension between the demands of disciplines which are constantly searching for new, more general knowledge, and the demands of fields of practice which constantly face new, often more complex, practical problems. The latter may arise directly from clients or patients or customers; they may arise from, and become pursued in, sectoral research projects; they may also arise as demands from government to reduce the autonomy of a region and gain more control over its 'usefulness'. This is not to forget, of course, the 'interests' of the region, or the profession itself, which can, at least in the case of the mature professions, exercise considerable power.

The research tasks that Bernstein's approach points to are considerable if it is to be productive in developing a theory of professional knowledge, not least because it requires the sociologist to be familiar with the specialized knowledge of any profession to be studied to a competence which Collins and Evans (2009) call 'interactional expertise'. Bernstein's distinction between singulars, regions and fields of practice, together with that between his types of theoretical knowledge, are the basic building blocks for a theory of professional knowledge. A further step might involve a classification of types of professional knowledge along the two continua; the types of theoretical knowledge and the three types of relation to practice – singulars, regions and the 'real world' of specialized professional practice. It is clear to us that the task has only started.

REFERENCES

Abbott, A. (1983) 'Professional ethics', *American Journal of Sociology*, 88(5), 855–85.

Abbott, A. (1988) *The System of Professions: An Essay on the Division of Expert Labor*, Chicago: The University of Chicago Press.

Abbott, A. (1993) 'The sociology of work and occupations', *Annual Review of Sociology*, 19, 187–209.

Abbott, A. (2001) *Chaos of Disciplines*, Chicago and London: The University of Chicago Press.

Afdal, H.W. (2012) 'Knowledge in teacher education curricula', *Nordic Studies in Education*, 3–4, 245–61.

Allais, S.M. (2007) 'Why the South African NQF failed: lessons for countries wanting to introduce national qualifications frameworks', *European Journal of Education*, 42(4), 523–49.

Allais, S.M. (2009) 'Smokes and mirrors: what's really informing the growth of national qualifications frameworks internationally?', paper presented at UKFIET Conference, Oxford, 14–17 September 2009.

Allais, S.M. (2011) 'The impact and implementation of national qualifications frameworks: A comparison of 16 countries', *Journal of Education and Work*, 24(3–4), 233–58.

Allais, S. (2012) 'Claims vs. practicalities: Lessons about using learning outcomes', *Journal of Education and Work*, 25(3), 331–54.

Allais, S. (2014) *Selling out Education: NQFs and the Neglect of Knowledge*, Rotterdam: Sense Publishers.

Althusser, L. (1971) *Lenin and Philosophy and Other Essays*, New York: Monthly Review Press.

Apple, M. (1975) *Ideology and Curriculum*, London: Routledge and Kegan Paul.

Apple, M. (1993) *Official Knowledge; Democratic Education in a Conservative Age*, London: Routledge.

Apple, M. (2004 [1975]) *Ideology and Curriculum*, London: Routledge Falmer.

Arbee, A. (2012) 'Knowledge and knowers in the discipline of marketing at the University of KwaZulu-Natal', unpublished PhD thesis, University of KwaZulu-Natal.

Archer, M. (2013) *Solidarity and Governance*, Mimeo: Ecole Polytechnique Fédérale de Lausanne.

Azzouni, J. (1997) 'Thick epistemic access: Distinguishing the mathematical from the empirical', *The Journal of Philosophy*, 94(9), 472–84.

Bacon, F. (1620/1994) *The New Organon*, Book 1, Chicago: Open Court.

Bak, N. (1998) 'Organising learning in large group teaching' in W. Morrow and K. King (eds), *Vision and Reality: Changing Education Training in South Africa*, Cape Town: University of Cape Town Press, pp. 204–13.

Baker, D. (2009) 'The educational transformation of work: towards a new synthesis', *Journal of Education and Work*, 22(3), 163–93.

Baker, D.P. and LeTendre, G.K. (2005) *National Differences, Global Similarities: World Culture and the Future of Schooling*, Stanford: Stanford University Press.

Bakhurst, D. (2005) 'Il'enkov on education', *Studies in East European Thought*, 57, 261–75.

Bakhurst, D. (2012) *The Formation of Reason*, London: Wiley Blackwell.

Bates, A. and Poole, G. (2003) *Effective Teaching with Technology in Higher Education*, Indianapolis: Jossey Bass.

Becher, T. (1989) *Academic Tribes and Territories*, Milton Keynes: Open University Press.

Becher, T. (1994) 'The significance of disciplinary differences', *Studies in Higher Education*, 19(2), 151–61.

Becher, T. and Trowler, P.R. (2001) *Academic Tribes and Territories*, 2nd edn, Milton Keynes: Open University Press.

Becher, T. and Trowler, P. (2001) *Academic tribes and territories: Intellectual Enquiry and the Culture of Disciplines*, New York: McGraw-Hill International.

Beck, J. (2002) 'The sacred and the profane in recent struggles to promote official pedagogic identities', *British Journal of Sociology of Education*, 23(4), 617–26.

Beck, J. (2012) 'Reinstating knowledge: diagnoses and prescriptions for England's curriculum ills', *International Studies in Sociology of Education*, 22, 1–18.

Beck. J., Jenks, C., Keddie, N. and Young, M. (eds) (1977) *Worlds Apart: Readings for a Sociology of Education*, London: Collier Macmillan.

Beck, J. and Young, M. (2005) 'The assault on the professions and the restructuring of academic and professional identities: a Bernsteinian analysis', *British Journal of Sociology of Education*, 26(2), 183–97.

Bengson, J. and Moffett, M. (2007) 'Know-how and concept possession', *Philosophical Studies*, 136, 31–57.

Benn, M. (2012) *The Battle for Britain's Education*. London: Verso Books.

Benson, O. and Stangroom, J. (2006) *Why Truth Matters*, London: Continuum Books.

Berlin, I. (2000) *Three Critics of the Enlightenment: Vico, Hammann, Herder*, Princeton: Princeton University Press.

Bernstein, B. (1971) *Class, Codes and Control*, vol. 1, London: Routledge and Kegan Paul.

Bernstein, B. (1975) *Class and Pedagogies: Visible and Invisible. Studies in the Learning Sciences, No. 2*, Washington, DC: Organization for Economic Cooperation and Development.

Bernstein, B. (1996) *Pedagogy, Symbolic Control and Identity: Theory, Research, Critique*, London: Taylor and Francis.

Bernstein, B. (1999) 'Vertical and horizontal discourse: an essay', *British Journal of Sociology of Education*, 20(2), 157–73.

Bernstein, B. (2000) *Pedagogy, Symbolic Control and Identity: Theory, Research, Critique*, 2nd edn, Oxford: Rowman and Littlefield Publishers.

Bertram, C. (2008) 'Curriculum recontextualisation: A case study of the South African high school history curriculum', unpublished PhD thesis, University of KwaZulu-Natal.

Bertram, C. (2009) 'Procedural and substantive knowledge: Some implications of an outcomes-based history curriculum in South Africa', *Southern African Review of Education*, 15, 45–62.

Bertram, C. (2012) 'Exploring an historical gaze: A language of description for the practice of school history', *Journal of Curriculum Studies*, 44(3), 429–42.

Biggs, J. and Tang, C. (2007) *Teaching for Quality at University: What the Student Does*, Glasgow: Open University Press.

Bobbitt, F. (1918) *The Curriculum*, New York: Houghton Mifflin.

Boghossian, P. (2006) *Fear of Knowledge: Against Relativism and Constructivism*, Oxford: Oxford University Press.

Bohlinger, S. (2007) 'Competences as the core element of the European qualification framework', *European Journal of Vocational Training*, 42/43, 96–112.

Bolstad, R. and Gilbert, J. (2009) *Disciplining or Drafting? Rethinking the New Zealand Senior Secondary Curriculum for the Future*, Wellington: NZCER Press.

Bolton, H. (2006) 'Pedagogy, subjectivity and mapping judgement in art, a weakly structured field of knowledge', *Journal of Education*, 40, 59–78.

Bouder, A. (2003) 'Qualifications in France: towards a national framework?', *Journal of Education and Work*, 16(3), 347–56.

Boughey, C. (2003) 'From equity to efficiency: access to higher education in South Africa', *Arts and Humanities in Higher Education*, 2(1), 65–71.

Boughey, C. (2005) '"Epistemological access" to the university: An alternative perspective', *South African Journal of Higher Education*, 19(3), 230–42.

Bourdieu, P. (2004) *Science of Science and Reflexivity* (trans. R. Nice), Cambridge: Polity Press.

Bourdieu, P. (2011) 'The school as a conservative force' in S.J. Eggleston (ed.), *Contemporary Research in the Sociology of Education*, London, Routledge.

Bourdieu, P. and Passeron, J.C. (1990) (1st edn 1977) *Reproduction in Education, Society and Culture*, London: Sage.

Bourne, J. (2004) 'Framing talk: towards a "radical visible pedagogy"' in J. Muller, B. Davies and A. Morais (eds), *Reading Bernstein, Researching Bernstein*, London: RoutledgeFalmer.

Bowles, S. and Gintis, H. (1976) *Schooling in Capitalist America*, New York: Basic Books.

Bozalek, V., Garraway, J. and McKenna, S. (eds) (2011) *Case Studies of Epistemological Access in Foundation/Extended Curriculum Programme Studies in South Africa*, Cape Town: University of the Western Cape.

Brandom, R. (1998) 'Insights and blindspots of reliabilism', *The Monist*, 81(3), 371–92.

Brandom, R. (2000) 'Facts, norms, and normative facts: A reply to Habermas', *European Journal of Philosophy*, 8(3), 356–74.

Brandom, R. (2001) *Articulating Reasons: An Introduction to Inferentialism*, Cambridge, MA: Harvard University Press.

Breier, M. (2003) 'The recruitment and recognition of prior informal experience in the pedagogy of two university courses in labour law', unpublished PhD thesis, University of Cape Town.

Breier, M. (2004) 'Horizontal discourse in law and labour law' in J. Muller, B. Davies and A. Morais (eds), *Reading Bernstein, Researching Bernstein*), London: RoutledgeFalmer, pp. 204–17.

Brighouse, H. (2014) 'Equality, prioritising the disadvantaged, and the new educational landscape', *Oxford Review of Education*, 40(6), 782–98.

Brockmann, M., Clarke, L. and Winch, C. (2008) 'Can performance-related learning outcomes have standards?', *Journal of European Industrial Training*, 32(2/3), 99–113.

Brown, P. and Lauder, H. (1996) 'Education, globalization and economic development', *Journal of Education Policy*, 11(1), 1–25.

Burrage, M. and Torstendahl, R. (eds) (1990) *Professions in Theory and History: Rethinking the Study of the Professions*, New York: Sage Publications.

Burrow, C. (2014) Are you a Spencerian? *London Review of Books*, 36(21), 35–7.

Callaghan, R. (1964) *Education and the Cult of Efficiency*, Chicago, IL: University Press.

Canguilhem, G. (1989) *The Normal and the Pathological*, New York: Zone Books.

Canguilhem, G. (1990) *Ideology and Rationality in the History of the Life Sciences*, Cambridge, MA: MIT Press.

Carter, F. (2011) 'Pedagogic structuring of architectural knowledge: Principles for modelling the design curriculum', unpublished MEd dissertation, University of Cape Town.

Carter, F. (2014) 'On the cultivation of decorum: Development of the pedagogic discourse of architecture in France 1671–1968' in M. Young and J. Muller (eds), *Knowledge, Expertise and the Professions*, London: Routledge, pp. 128–42.

Case, J. (2011) 'Knowledge matters: Interrogating the curriculum debate using the sociology of knowledge', *Journal of Education*, 51, 1–20.

Case, J. (2013) *Researching Student Learning in Higher Education: A Social Realist Perspective*, London: Routledge.

Cassirer, E. (1943) 'Newton and Leibniz', *The Philosophical Review* 52(4), 366–91.

Cassirer, E. (1969) *The Problem of Knowledge: Philosophy, Science, and History since Hegel*, New Haven: Yale University Press.

Cassirer, E. (1996) (1st edn 1923) *The Philosophy of Symbolic Forms, Volume 4: The Metaphysics of Symbolic Forms*, (trans. J.M. Krois), New Haven: Yale University Press.

Cassirer, E. (2000) *The Logic of the Cultural Sciences: Five Studies*, (trans. S.G. Lofts), New Haven: Yale University Press.

CEDEFOP (European Centre for the Development of Vocational Training) (2008) *The Shift to Learning Outcomes*, Thessalonika: CEDEFOP.

Central Advisory Council for Education (England) (1963) *Half Our Future*, London: HMSO.

Charlot, B. (2012) 'School and pupil's work' in H. Lauder, M. Young, H. Daniels, M. Balarin, M. and J. Lowe (eds), *Educating for the Knowledge Economy? Critical Perspectives*, London: Routledge, pp. 211–23.

Chimisso, C. (2001) *Gaston Bachelard: Critic of Science and the Imagination*, London: Routledge.

Christie, F. and Martin, J.R. (eds) (2007) *Language, Knowledge and Pedagogy*, London: Continuum.

Cigman, R. (2012) 'We need to talk about well-being', *Research Papers in Education*, 27, 449–62.

Coffield, F., Borrill, C. and Marshall, S. (1986) *Growing Up at the Margins: Young Adults in the North East*, Milton Keynes: Open University Press.

Cohen, D. and Miller, G. (2010) 'You can't step into the same argument twice: Wittgenstein on philosophical arguments', *Cogency*, 2(2), 19–39.

Cohen, H.F. (2010) *How Modern Science Came into the World: Four Civilizations, One 17th-century Breakthrough*, Amsterdam: Amsterdam University Press.

Collier, A. (1994) *Critical Realism: An Introduction to the Philosophy of Roy Bhaskar*, London: Verso.

Collingwood.R.G. (1993) *The Idea of History*, Oxford: Oxford University Press.

Collins, H. and Evans, R. (2007) *Re-thinking Expertise*, Chicago: The University of Chicago Press.

Collins, R. (1998) *The Sociology of Philosophies: A Global Theory of Intellectual Change*, Cambridge, MA: The Belknap Press.

Collins, R. (2000) *The Sociology of Philosophies: A Global Theory of Intellectual Change*, London: The Belknap Press of Harvard University Press.

Commonwealth of Learning and South African Qualifications Authority (SAQA) (2008) 'Transnational Qualifications Framework for the Virtual University for the Small States of the Commonwealth Concept document', May 2008, at: http://www.col.org/resources/speeches/2007presentations/Pages/2007-09-22.aspx (accessed 19 May 2015).

Cooper, D. (2011) *The University in Development: Case Studies of Use-Oriented Research*, Cape Town: HSRC Press.

Cornwell, J. (2011) *Newman's Unquiet Grave: The Reluctant Saint*, London: Continuum.

Counsell, C. (2011) 'Disciplinary knowledge for all, the secondary history curriculum and history teachers' achievement', *Curriculum Journal*, 22, 201–25.

Crewes, F. (2006) 'Introducing follies of the wise', retrieved from: http://www.butterfliesandwheels.com/14/6/06

Dall'Alba, G. and Barnacle, R. (2007) 'An ontological turn for higher education', *Studies in Higher Education*, 32(6), 679–91.

De Sousa Santos, B. (2001) 'Towards an epistemology of blindness', *European Journal of Social Theory*, 4(3), 251–79.

De Sousa Santos, B. (2008) *Another Knowledge is Possible*, London: Verso.

Delors, J. (1996) *Education for the 21st Century. The Delors Report*, Paris: UNESCO.

Demaine, J. (1981) *Contemporary Theories in the Sociology of Education*, London: Macmillan Press.

Dempster, E.R. and Hugo, W. (2006) 'Introducing the concept of evolution into South African schools', *South African Journal of Science*, 102(3–4), 106–12.

Deng, Z. and Luke, A. (2008) 'Subject matter; defining and theorizing school subjects', in F.M. Connelly, M.F. He and J. Phillion (eds), *Sage Handbook of Curriculum and Instruction*, Thousand Oaks, CA: Sage.

Department for Education (2011) *The Expert Panel's Report on the National Curriculum*, London: DFE.

Department of Basic Education (2009) Report of the Task Team for the Review of the Implementation of the National Curriculum Statement: Final Report, Pretoria.

Derrida, J. (1981) *Plato's Pharmacy. Dissemination* (trans. Barbara Johnson), Chicago: University of Chicago Press.

Derry, J. (2008) 'Abstract rationality in education: From Vygotsky to Brandom', *Studies in Philosophy and Education*, 27(1), 49–62.

Dewey, J. (1908) 'What does pragmatism mean by practical?', *The Journal of Philosophy, Psychology and Scientific Methods*, 5, 85–99.

DFE (2011) Curriculum and Qualifications, available online at: http://www.education.gov.uk/schools/teachingandlearning/curriculum/nationalcurriculum (accessed 19 May 2015).

Dowling, P. (1998) *The Sociology of Mathematics Education: Mathematical Myths, Pedagogic Texts*, London: Routledge.

Dreyfus, H. (2006) 'Overcoming the myth of the mental', *Topoi*, 25(1), 43–9.

Dreyfus, H. (2007) 'The return of the myth of the mental', *Inquiry*, 50(4), 352–65.

Driver, R. (1982) *Pupil as Scientist*, Bletchley: Open University Press.

Durkheim, E. (1956) *Education and Sociology*, New York: Free Press.

Durkheim, E. (1964) *The Division of Labour in Society*, New York: Free Press.

Durkheim, E. (1977) *The Evolution of Educational Thought: Lectures on the Formation and Development of Secondary Education in France*, London: Routledge.

Durkheim, E. (1983) *Pragmatism and Sociology* (trans. J.C. Whitehouse and J.B. Alcock), Cambridge: Cambridge University Press.

Durkheim, E. (1993) *The Division of Labor in Society*, New York: Macmillan.

Durkheim, E. (1995/1912) *The Elementary Forms of Religious Life* (trans. K. Fields), New York: The Free Press.

Durkheim, E. and Mauss, M. (1967) *Primitive Classification*, Chicago: The University of Chicago Press.

Dworkin, R. (2013) *Religion without God*, Cambridge, MA: Harvard University Press.

Ecclestone, K. and Hayes, D. (2009) *The Dangerous Rise of Therapeutic Education*, London: Routledge.

Egan, K. (2004) *Getting it Wrong from the Beginning: Our Progressivist Inheritance from Herbert Spencer, John Dewey, and Jean Piaget*, New Haven: Yale University Press.

Elder-Vass, D. (2010) *The Causal Power of Social Structures: Emergence, Structure, and Agency*, Cambridge: Cambridge University Press.

Elman, B. (2009) *A Cultural History of Modern Science in China*, Cambridge, MA: Harvard University Press.

Elvin, M. (1983) 'Why China failed to create an endogenous industrial capitalism', *Theory and Society*, 13(3), 379–91.

Elzinga, A. (1997) 'The science-society contract in historical transformation: With special reference to "epistemic drift"', *Social Science Information*, 36(3), 411–45.

Ensor, P. (2006) 'Curriculum' in N. Cloete, P. Maassen, R.Fehnel and T. Moja (eds), *Transformation in Higher Education: Global Pressures and Local Realities*, Dordrecht: Kluwer Academic, pp. 179–93.

Entwhistle. H. (1979) *Antonio Gramsci: Conservative Schooling for Radical Politics*, London: Routledge.

Etzioni, A. (1969) *The Semi-Professions and their Organisation: Teachers, Nurses, Social Workers*, New York: Free Press.

European Commission (2009) 'New skills for new jobs', Draft Report Expert Group, Brussels: European Commission.

European Union (EU) (2012) *New Skills for New Jobs. Action now*, Luxembourg: Office of Publications for the European Community.

Evetts, J. (2006) 'Short note: The sociology of professional groups: New directions', *Current Sociology*, 54(1), 133–43.

Evetts, J. (2013) 'Professionalism: Value and ideology', *Current Sociology*, 61(5–6), 778–96.

Fine, B. (2001) *Social Capital versus Social Theory: Political Economy and Social Science at the Turn of the Millennium*, London: Routledge.

Fine, B. and Milonakis, D. (2009) *From Economics Imperialism to Freakonomics: The Shifting Boundaries between Economics and other Social Sciences*, London: Routledge.

Firth, R. (2011) 'Making geography visible as an object of study in the secondary school curriculum', *Curriculum Journal*, 22, 289–316.

Fitz, J., Davies, B. and Evans, J. (2006) *Educational Policy and Social Reproduction*, Oxford: Routledge.

Floud, J. and Halsey, A.H. (1958) 'The sociology of education: a trend report and bibliography', *Current Sociology*, 3(3), 66.

Fodor, J. and Lepore, E. (2007) 'Brandom beleaguered', *Philosophy and Phenomenological Research*, 74(3), 677–91.

Foray, D. (2011) 'Knowledge economy and services' industries–a case study of the educational sector' in B-J. Krings (ed.) *Brain Drain or Brain Gain?: Changes of Work in Knowledge-based Societies*, Berlin: Edition Sigma, pp. 33–52.

Foray, D. and Hargreaves, D. (2003) 'The production of knowledge in different sectors: A model and some hypotheses', *London Review of Education*, 1(1), 7–19.

Foray, D. and Steinmueller, W.E. (2002) *The Economics of Knowledge Reproduction by Inscription*, Paris: University of Paris, IMRI.

Foucault, M. (1977) *Discipline and Punish*, London: Allen Lane.

Foucault, M. (1991) *Remarks on Marx*, New York: Semiotext(e).

Frankfurt, H.G. (2005) *On Bullshit*, Princeton: Princeton University Press.

Fricker, M. (2007) *Epistemic Injustice: Power and the Ethics of Knowing*, New York: Oxford University Press.

Friedson, E. (2001) *Professionalization: The Third Logic*, Chicago: The University of Chicago Press.

Gamble, J. (2004a) 'Tacit knowledge in craft pedagogy: A sociological analysis', unpublished PhD thesis, University of Cape Town.

Gamble, J. (2004b) 'Retreiving the general from the particular: the structure of craft knowledge' in J. Muller, B. Davies and A. Morais (eds), *Reading Bernstein, Researching Bernstein*, London: RoutledgeFalmer, pp. 189–203.

Gamble, J. (2006) 'Theory and practice in the vocational curriculum' in M. Young and J. Gamble (eds) *Knowledge, Curriculum and Qualifications for South African Further Education*, Pretoria: HSRC Press, pp. 87–103.

Gamble, J. (2009) 'The relation between knowledge and practice in curriculum and assessment', report for UMALUSI, Pretoria.

Gamble, J. (2011) '"Approaching the sacred": Directionality in the relation between knowledge structure and pedagogy', University of Cape Town, Center for Higher Education Development.

Gaukroger, S. (2006) *The Emergence of a Scientific Culture: Science and the Shaping of Modernity 1210–1685*, Oxford: Clarendon Press.

General Medical Council (GMC) (2009) *Tomorrow's Doctors*, London.

Gewirtz, S. (2008) 'Give us a break! A sceptical review of contemporary discourses of life-long learning', *European Educational Research Journal*, 7(4), 414–24.

Gibbons, M. (1998) 'Higher education relevance in the 21st century', paper prepared for the UNESCO World Conference on Higher Education, October 1998, Paris.

Gibbons, M., Limoges, C., Nowotny, H., Schwartzman, S., Scott, P. and Trow, M. (1994) *The New Production of Knowledge. The Dynamics of Science and Research in Contemporary Societies*, London: Sage.

Giroux, H. (1983) *Theory and Resistance in Education: Towards a Pedagogy for the Opposition*, New York: Bergin and Garvey.

Gladwell, M. (2005) *Blink: The Power of Thinking without Thinking*, London: Little, Brown and Company.

Glazer, N. (1974) 'The schools of the minor professions', *Minerva*, 13(3), 346–74.

Goodson, I. (1987) *School Subjects and Curriculum Change*, London: Routledge/Falmer.

Gorbutt, D. (1972) 'Education as the control of knowledge: the new sociology of education', *Education for Teaching*, 89, 3–12.

Gorman, E.H. and Sandefur, R.L. (2011) '"Golden Age", quiescence, and revival: How the sociology of professions became the study of knowledge-based work', *Work and Occupations*, 38(3), 275–302.

Gould, J. (1977) *The Attack on Higher Education: Marxist and Radical Penetration*, London: Institute for the Study of Conflict.

Gove, M. (2009) 'Failing schools need new leadership', at: http://michaelgovemp.typepad.com/files/gove-2009-conference-speech-2.pdf (accessed 19 May 2015).

Gramsci.A. (1965) 'Editorial', *New Left Review*, 1 (1).

Guile, D. (2010) *The Learning Challenge of the Knowledge Economy*, Rotterdam: SENSE Publishers.

Haack, S. (1998) *Confessions of a Passionate Moderate*, Chicago: Chicago University Press.

Habermas, J. (2000) 'From Kant to Hegel: On Robert Brandom's pragmatic philosophy of language', *European Journal of Philosophy*, 8(3), 322–55.

Habermas, J. (2001) *The Liberating Power of Symbols: Philosophical Essays*, (trans. Peter Dews), Cambridge, MA: MIT Press.

Hacking, I. (1999) *The Social Construction of What?*, Cambridge, MA: Harvard University Press.

Hall, M. (2010) *Community Engagements in South African Higher Education*, Kagisano, no. 6, Pretoria: Council on Higher Education.

Hanrahan, H. (2010) 'Discussion of "forms of knowledge and curriculum coherence"', presented to the Launch Seminar of REAL, Education Policy Unit, University of the Witwatersrand.

Hardt, M. and Negri, A. (2000) *Empire*, Cambridge, MA: Harvard University Press.

Harrison, P. (2007) 'Religion, the Royal Society, and the rise of science', inaugural lecture, University of Oxford, 14 May 2007.

Hartman, N. (2014) *The Primary Health Care Approach and Restructuring of the MB ChB*, Saarbrücken: Lambert Academic Publishing.

Haslanger, S. (2008) 'Changing the ideology and culture of philosophy: Not by reason (alone)', *Hypatia*, 23, 210–23.

Hasselberg, Y., Rider, S. and Waluszewski, A. (2013) 'Introduction' in S. Rider, Y. Hasselberg and A. Waluszewski (eds), *Transformations in Research, Higher Education and the Academic Market: The Breakdown of Scientific Thought*, Dordrecht: Springer.

Herbert, M., Conana, C., Volkwyn, T. and Marshall, D. (2011) 'Multiple modes of epistemological access in physics' in V. Bozalek, J. Garraway and S. McKenna (eds), *Case Studies of Epistemological Access in Foundation/Extended Curriculum Programme Studies in South Africa*, Cape Town: University of the Western Cape, pp. 8–23.

Henkel, M. (2000) *Academic Identities and Policy Change in Higher Education*, London: Jessica Kingsley.

Hirst, P. and Peters, R. (1970) *The Logic of Education*, London: Routledge and Kegan Paul.

Hoadley, U. (2007) 'The reproduction of social class inequalities through mathematics pedagogies in South African primary schools', *Journal of Curriculum Studies*, 39(6), 679–706.

Hoadley, U. (2011) 'Knowledge, knowers and knowing' in L.G.M. Yates (ed.), *Curriculum in Today's World: Configuring Knowledge, Identities, Work and Politics*, New York: Routledge, pp. 143–58.

Hoadley, U. and Muller, J. (2010) 'Codes, pedagogy and knowledge' in M. Apple, S. Ball and L. Gandin (eds), *The Routledge International Handbook of the Sociology of Education*, London: Routledge, pp. 69–78.

Huntington, S.P. (1998) *The Clash of Civilizations and the Remaking of World Order*, New York: Simon and Schuster.

Illich, I. (1971) *Deschooling Society*, Harmondsworth: Penguin Books.

James, W. (1970) *Essays in Pragmatism*, New York: Free Press.

Jenks, C. (1977) *Rationality, Education and the Social Organization of Knowledge: Papers for a Reflexive Sociology of Education*, London: Routledge and Kegan Paul.

Jensen, K., Lahn, L.C. and Nerland, M. (eds) (2012) *Professional Learning in the Knowledge Society*, Rotterdam: Sense Publishers.

Jensen, P, Rouquier, J-P, Kreimer, P and Croissant, Y (2008) 'Scientists connected with society are more active academically', *Science and Public Policy*, 7(35), 527–41.

Jessup, G. (1991) *Outcomes: NVQs and the Emerging Model of Education and Training*, London: RoutledgeFalmer.

Johnson, K. (2010) 'Biology and its recontextualisation in the school curriculum: a comparative analysis of post-apartheid South African life sciences curricula', unpublished PhD thesis, University of KwaZulu-Natal.

Johnson, K., Dempster, E.R. and Hugo, W. (2011) 'Explaining the recontextualisation of biology in the South African life sciences curriculum, 1996–2009', *Journal of Education*, 52, 27–56.

Johnson, R. (1979) '"Really useful knowledge": radical education and working class culture, 1790–1848' in J. Clarke, J. Critcher and R. Johnson (eds), *Working Class Culture*, London: Hutchinson.

Jones, A. (2009) 'Redisciplining generic attributes: The disciplinary context in focus', *Studies in Higher Education*, 34(1), 85–100.

Karpov, Y.V. and Heywood, H.C. (1998) 'Two ways to elaborate Vygotsky's concept of mediation: Implications for instruction', *American Psychologist*, 53(1), 27–36.

Karseth, B. and Sivesind, K. (2010) 'Conceptualising curriculum knowledge within and beyond the national context', *European Journal of Education*, 45(1), 103–20.

Keddie, N. (1971) 'Classroom knowledge' in M. Young (ed.), *Knowledge and Control: New Directions for the Sociology of Education*, London: Collier Macmillan, pp. 133–60.

Keddie, N. (ed.) (1973) *Tinker, Tailor … The Myth of Cultural Deprivation*, London: Penguin.

Keeler, M. (2004) 'Using Brandom's framework to do Peirce s normative science: Pragmatism as the game of harmonizing assertions? in K. Wolff, H. Pfeiffer and H. Delugach (eds), *Conceptual Structures at Work*, Heidelberg: Springer, pp. 242–60.

Keen, A. (2007) *The Cult of the Amateur*, London: Nichols Breasley.

King, K. (2003) 'Education policy in a climate of entitlement: The South African case', *Perspectives in Education*, 14(2), 200–7.

Knapper, C. and Cropley, A. (2000) *Lifelong Learning in Higher Education*, London: Kogan Page.

Kotta, L. (2008) 'Affording or constraining epistemological access: An analysis of a case-based approach in a first year process and materials engineering course', unpublished MEd dissertation, University of the Witwatersrand.

Kotta, L. (2011) 'Structural condition and mediation by student agency: A case study of success in chemical engineering design', PhD thesis, University of Cape Town.

Kotzee, B. (2014) 'Expertise, fluency and social realism about professional knowledge', *Journal of Education and Work*, 27(2), 161–78.

Kress, G. (2008) 'Meaning and learning in a world of instability and multiplicity', *Studies in Philosophy and Education*, 27: 253–6.

Kronman, A. (2007) *Education's End: Why our Colleges and Universities Have Given Up on the Meaning of Life*, New Haven: Yale University Press.

Kuhn, T. (1962) *The Structure of Scientific Revolutions*, Chicago: Chicago University Press.

Kuper, A. (2005) 'Alternative histories of British social anthropology', *Social Anthropology*, 13, 47–64.

Lakatos, I. (1976) *Proofs and Refutations: The Logic of Mathematical Discovery*, Cambridge: Cambridge University Press.

Lakatos, I. and Musgrave, A. (eds) (1970) *Criticism and the Growth of Knowledge: Volume 4: Proceedings of the International Colloquium in the Philosophy of Science, London, 1965*, Cambridge: Cambridge University Press.

Lauder, H., Brown. P. and Brown. C. (2008) *The Consequences of Global Expansion for Knowledge, Creativity and Communication: An Analysis and Scenario*, unpublished, University of Bath.

Laugier, S. (2013) *Why We Need Ordinary Language Philosophy*, Chicago: Chicago University Press.

Lawn, M. (2006) 'Soft governance and the learning spaces of Europe', *Comparative European Politics*, 4, 272–88.

Le Grange, L. (2010) 'Scripture and practices: a reply to Wally Morrow' in Y. Shalem and S. Pendlebury (eds), *Retrieving Teaching: Critical Issues in Curriculum, Pedagogy and Learning*, Cape Town: Juta, pp. 76–86.

Lecourt, D. (1980) *Proletarian Science? The Case of Lysenko*, London: NLB.

Lotz-Sisitka, H. (2009) 'Epistemological access as an open question in education', *Journal of Education*, 46, 57–79.

Luckett, K. (2009) 'The relationship between knowledge structure and curriculum: A case study in sociology', *Studies in Higher Education*, 34(4), 441–53.

Lukes, S. (1972) *Emile Durkheim: His Life and Work*, New York: Harper and Row.

Lundahl, E. *et al.* (2008) 'Curriculum policies of upper secondary education: the Swedish case', paper presented to ECER 2008 Gothenburg, 10–12 September 2008.

McDowell, J. (1996) *Mind and World*, Cambridge, MA: Harvard University Press.

McDowell, J. (2007) 'What myth?', *Inquiry*, 50(4), 338–51.

MacIntyre, A. (1981) *After Virtue: A Study in Moral Theory*, Notre Dame: University of Notre Dame Press.

MacIntyre, A. (2002) 'Alasdair MacIntyre on education: in dialogue with Joseph Dunne', *Journal of Philosophy of Education*, 36(1), 1–19.

McLaren, P. (1995) *An Introduction to Critical Pedagogy*, London: Longman.

Magalhães, A.M. (2008) 'Creation of the EHEA, "learning outcomes" and transformation of educational categories in higher education', University of Oporto, unpublished.

Malatesta, M. (2002) *Society and the Professions in Italy, 1860-1914*, Cambridge: Cambridge University Press.

Malatesta, M. (2005) 'Comments on Sciulli', *Current Sociology*, 53(6), 943–6.

Mangez, E. (2008) 'Curriculum reform in French-speaking Belgium', paper presented to ECER 2008 Gothenburg, 10–12 September 2008.

Markus, G. (2003) 'The paradoxical unity of culture: the arts and the sciences', *Thesis Eleven*, 75, 7–24.

Maton, K. (2010) 'Canons and progress in the arts and humanities: Knowers and gazes' in K. Maton and R. Moore (eds), *Social Realism, Knowledge and the Sociology of Education: Coalitions of the Mind*, London: Continuum, pp. 154–178.

Maton, K. (2010) 'Theories and things: The semantics of disciplinarity' in F. Christie and K. Maton (eds), *Disciplinarity: Functional Linguistic and Sociological Perspectives*, London: Continuum, pp. 62–84.

Maton, K. and Moore, R. (eds) (2009) *Social Realism, Knowledge and the Sociology of Education: Coalitions of the Mind*, London: Continuum.

Méhaut, P. and Winch, C. (2012) 'The European qualification framework: Skills, competences or knowledge', *European Educational Research Journal*, 11(3), 369–81.

Meijers, A. (ed.) (2009) *Philosophy of Technology and Engineering Sciences*, vol. 9, Amsterdam: Elsevier.

Menand, L. (1995) 'Marketing postmodernism', in R. Orrill (ed.), *The Condition of American Liberal Education: Pragmatism and a Changing Tradition*, New York: College Entrance Examination Board, pp. 140–4.

Mendick, H. (2006) 'Review symposium of Moore (2004)', *British Journal of Sociology of Education*, 27(1), 117–23.

Menter, I. (2013) 'The history of primary education and the curriculum' in D. Wise, V. Baumfield, D. Egan, C. Gallagher, L. Hayward, M. Hulme, R. Leitch, K. Livingstone, and I. Menter, with B. Lingard, *Creating the Curriculum*, London: Routledge.

Merton, R.K. (1973) *The Sociology of Science: Theoretical and Empirical Investigations*, Chicago: The University of Chicago Press.

Merton, R.K. (1992) (1st edn 1973) *The Sociology of Science: Theoretical and Empirical Investigations*, Chicago: The University of Chicago Press.

Merton, R.K. (1993) *On the Shoulders of Giants*, Chicago: The University of Chicago Press.

Merton, R.K. (2001) *Science, Technology and Society in Seventeenth-Century England*, New York: Howard Fertig.

Meyer, J. (1992) *School Knowledge for the Masses: World Models and National Primary Curricular Categories in the Twentieth Century*, London: Falmer.

Moore, R. (2004) *Education and Society*, London and Cambridge: Polity Press.

Moore, R. (2006a) 'Going critical: The problems of problematising knowledge in educational studies', *Critical Education Studies*, 48(1), 25–41.

Moore, R. (2006b) 'Knowledge structures and intellectual fields: Basil Bernstein and the sociology of knowledge' in R. Moore, M. Arnot, J. Beck and H. Daniels (eds), *Knowledge, Power and Educational Reform*, London: Routledge, pp. 28–43.

Moore, R. (2007) *Sociology of Knowledge and Education*, London: Continuum.

Moore, R. (2009) *Towards the Sociology of Truth*, London: Continuum.

Moore, R. (2012) 'Social realism and the problem of the problem of knowledge in the sociology of education', *British Journal of Sociology of Education*, 34(3), 333–53.

Moore, R. and Maton, K. (2001) 'Founding the sociology of knowledge: Basil Bernstein, epistemic fields and the epistemic device' in A. Morais, I. Neves, B. Davies and H. Daniels (eds), *Towards a Sociology of Pedagogy: The Contribution of Basil Bernstein to Research*, New York: Peter Lang.

Moore, R. and Muller, J. (1999) 'The discourse of "voice" and the problem of knowledge and identity in the sociology of education', *British Journal of Sociology of Education*, 20, 189–206.

Moore, R. and Muller, J. (2002) 'The growth of knowledge and the discursive gap. *British Journal of Sociology of Education*', 23(4), 627–37.

Moore, R. and Young, M. (2001) 'Knowledge and the curriculum in the sociology of education: towards a reconceptualisation', *British Journal of Sociology of Education* 22(4), 445–61.

Morais, A., Neves, I. and Pires, D. (2004) 'The what and how of teaching and learning' in J. Muller, B. Davies and A. Morais (eds), *Reading Bernstein, Researching Bernstein*, London: RoutledgeFalmer, pp. 75–90.

Morrow, W. (1989) *Chains of Thought*, Johannesburg: Southern Book Publishers.

Morrow, W. (1994) 'Entitlement and achievement in education', *Studies in Philosophy and Education*, 13(1), 33–47.

Morrow, W. (2001) 'Scripture and practices', *Perspectives in Education*, 19(1), 87–106.

Morrow, W. (2003) 'Epistemic values in curriculum transformation' in P. Naudé and N. Cloete (eds), *A Tale of Three Countries: Social Sciences Curriculum Transformations in Southern Africa*, Lansdowne: Juta, pp. 2–12.

Morrow, W. (2007) *Learning to Teach in South Africa*, Cape Town: HSRC Press.

Morrow, W. (2009) *Bounds of Democracy: Epistemological Access in Higher Education*, Cape Town: HSRC Press.

Morrow, W. and King, K. (eds) (1998) *Vision and Reality: Changing Education and Training in South Africa*, Cape Town: Juta and Co.

Mortimore, P. (2008) 'Time for bold experiments', at: http://www.guardian.co.uk/education/2008/oct/07/schools.teaching (accessed 19 May 2015).

Muller, J. (2000) *Reclaiming Knowledge: Social Theory, Curriculum and Education Policy*, London: RoutledgeFalmer.

Muller, J. (2006) 'Differentiation and progression in the curriculum' in M. Young and J. Gamble (eds), *Knowledge, Curriculum and Qualifications for South African Further Education*, Cape Town: HSRC Press, pp. 66–86.

Muller, J. (2007) 'On splitting hairs: hierarchy, knowledge and the school curriculum' in F. Christie and J.R. Martin (eds), *Language, Knowledge and Pedagogy: Functional and Sociological Perspectives*, London: Continuum, pp. 65–86.

Muller, J. (2009) 'Forms of knowledge and curriculum coherence', *Journal of Education and Work*, 22(3), 203–24.

Muller, J. (2010) 'Social life in disciplines' in G. Ivinson, B. Davies, and J. Fitz (eds), *Knowledge and Identity: Concepts and Applications in Bernstein's Sociology*, Oxford: Routledge, pp. 39–53.

Muller, J. (2011a) 'Through others' eyes: The fate of disciplines' in F. Christie and K. Maton (eds), *Disciplinarity: Functional Linguistic and Sociological Perspectives*, London: Continuum, pp.13–34.

Muller, J. (2011b) 'The essential tension: An essay on sociology as knowledge' in D. Frandji and P. Vitale (eds), *Knowledge, Pedagogy and Society: International Perspectives on Basil Bernstein's Sociology of Education*, London: Routledge, pp. 211–23.

Muller, J., Davies, B. and Morais, A. (eds) (2004) *Reading Bernstein, Researching Bernstein*, London: RoutledgeFalmer.

Muller, J. and Gamble, J (2010) 'Curriculum and structuralist sociology: the theory of codes and knowledge structures' in P. Peterson, E. Baker and B. McGraw (eds), *International Encyclopaedia of Education*, 3rd edn, New York: Elsevier, pp. 505–9.

Nagel, E. (1961) *The Structure of Science: Problems in the Logic of Scientific Explanation*, London: Routledge and Kegan Paul.

Nagel, E. (1982) *The Structure of Science: Problems in the Logic of Scientific Explanation*, London: Routledge and Kegan Paul.

Nash, R. (2005) 'The cognitive habitus: its place in a realist account of inequality/difference', *British Journal of Sociology of Education* 26(5), 599–612.

National Education Policy Investigation (1993) *The Framework Report*, Cape Town: NECC/Oxford University Press.

Needham, J (1954) *Science and Civilisation in China*, Cambridge: Cambridge University Press.

Nerland, M. and Karseth, B. (2015) 'The knowledge work of professional associations: Approaches to standardisation and forms of legitimisation', *Journal of Education and Work*, 28(1), 1–23.

Newman, J. (1996) *The Idea of a University*, New Haven: Yale University Press.

Norris, C. (2000) *Deconstruction and the Unfinished Project of Modernity*, London: Routledge.

Norris, C. (2005) *Epistemology*, London: Continuum.

Norris, C. (2006) *On Truth and Meaning*, London: Continuum.

Nowotny, H., Scott, P. and Gibbons, M. (2001) *Re-thinking Science: Knowledge and the Public in an Age of Uncertainty*, Cambridge: Polity Press.

Nowotny, H, Scott, P and Gibbons, M (2003) 'Introduction: Mode 2 revisited: the new production of knowledge', *Minerva*, 41(3), 179–94.

Nozaki, Y. (2006) 'Riding tensions critically: ideology, power/knowledge, and curriculum making' in L. Weiss, C. McCarthy and G. Dimitriadis (eds), *Ideology, Curriculum and the New Sociology of Education*, London: Routledge, pp. 69–90.

Nussbaum, M. (1999) 'The hip defeat of Judith Butler: Professor of Parody', *New Republic*, 22 February 1999.

Nussbaum, M. (2013) *Political Emotions: Why Love Matters for Justice*, Cambridge, MA: The Belknap Press.

Nybom, T. (2013) 'Power, knowledge, morals: society in the age of hybrid research' in S. Rider, Y. Hasselberg and A. Waluszewski (eds), *Transformations in Research, Higher Education and the Academic Market: The Breakdown of Scientific Thought*, Dordrecht: Springer, pp. 21–37.

OECD (2005) 'Definition and selection of key competences: Executive summary' (DeSeCo), Paris: OECD.

OECD (2012) 'Literature review: Key competence development in school education in Europe' (KeyCoNet), Paris: OECD.

O'Halloran, K.L. (2006) 'Mathematical and scientific knowledge: a systematic functional multimodal grammatical approach' in F. Christie and J.R. Martin (eds), *Language, Knowledge and Pedagogy: Functional and Sociological Perspectives*, London: Continuum Press, pp. 205–36.

Ozga, J. (2009) 'Governing knowledge? Globalisation, Europeanisation and the research imagination', *British Journal of Sociology of Education*, 30(4), 511–17.

Payne, J. (2002) 'A tale of two curriculums', *Journal of Education and Work*, 15(2), 117–43.

Penrose, R. (2006) *The Road to Reality: A Complete Guide to the Laws of the Universe*, London: Vintage.

Perks, D., Sykes, R., Reiss, M. and Singh, S. (2006) *What is Science Education For?*, London: Institute of Ideas.

Perraton, J. and Tarrant, I. (2007) 'What does tacit knowledge actually explain?', *Journal of Economic Methodology*, 14(3), 353–70.

Phillips, D.C. (2000) *The Expanded Social Scientist's Bestiary*, Lanham, Maryland: Rowman and Littlefield Publishers.

Pickering, A. (1992) *Science as Practice and Culture*, Chicago: The University of Chicago Press.

Pinar, W. (1978) *Understanding Curriculum: An Introduction to the Study of Historical and Contemporary Curriculum Discourses*, New York: Peter Lang.

Polanyi, M. (1962) 'The republic of science', *Minerva* 1(1), 54–73.

Polanyi, M. (1966) *The Tacit Dimension*, London: Routledge.

Pring, R. (1972) 'Knowledge out of control', *Education for Teaching*, 89(2), 19–28.

Psillos, S. (2004) 'Tracking the real: Through thick and thin', *The British Journal for the Philosophy of Science*, 55(3), 393–409.

Psillos, S. (2011) 'Realism with a Humean face' in S. French and J. Saatsi (eds), *The Continuum Companion to Philosophy of Science*, London: Continuum, pp. 75–95.

Qualifications and Curriculum Development Agency (QCDA) (2009) The Aims of the Curriculum, at: http://curriculum.qca.org.uk/uploads/Aims_of_the_curriculum_tcm8-1812.pdf?return=/key-stages-3-and-4/aims/index.aspx (accessed 19 May 2009).

Raffe, D. (2007) 'Making haste slowly: the evolution of a unified qualifications framework in Scotland', *European Journal of Education*, 42(4), 485–503.

Ramognino, N. (2011) 'Reading Basil Bernstein, a socio-epistemological point of view' in D. V. Frandji and P. Vitale (eds), *Knowledge, Pedagogy and Society: International perspectives on Basil Bernstein's Sociology of Education*, New York: Routledge, pp. 224–40.

Rata, E. (2011) 'The politics of knowledge in education', *British Educational Research Journal*, 38, 103–24.

Rata, E. (2012) *The Politics of Knowledge in Education*, London and New York: Routledge.

Raven, D. (2011) 'What needs to be explained about modern science?', *The British Journal for the History of Science*, 44(3), 449–54.

Reckwitz, A. (2002) 'Toward a theory of social practices', *European Journal of Social Theory*, 5(2), 243–63.

Reeves, C. and Muller, J. (2005) 'Picking up the pace: variation in the structure and organisation of learning school mathematics', *Journal of Education*, 37, 97–125.

Review Committee (2000) *A South African Curriculum for the 21st century: Report of the Review Committee on Curriculum 2005*, Pretoria: Ministry of Education.

Roberts, M. (2012) 'The work of The Prince's Teaching Institute – insisting that established subjects matter to all pupils', *Education 3-13*, 40, 117–28.

Roberts, M. (2014) 'Curriculum change and control: A headteacher's perspective' in M. Young and D. Lamberts, with C. Roberts and M. Roberts, *Knowledge and the Future School: Curriculum and Social Justice*, London: Bloomsbury.

Robertson, S. (2007) *Teachers Matter ... Don't They? Centre for Globalisation, Education and Societies*, Bristol: University of Bristol.

Rosen, C. (2012) 'Freedom and art', *New York Review of Books*, 9(8), 10 May 2012.

Roth, P. (1984) 'The art of fiction', *The Paris Review*, no. 84, quoted by C. Simic (2008) *New York Review of Books*, LV, 4.

Royal Society for the encouragement of Arts, Manufactures and Commerce (RSA) (2006) Opening Minds Framework at: http://www.thersa.org/projects/education/opening-minds-old/opening-mindsframework (accessed 19 May 2009).

Russel, B. (1967) *An Inquiry into Meaning and Truth: The William James Lectures for 1940 Delivered at Harvard University*, Baltimore, MD: Penguin Books.

Ryle, G. (1945) 'Knowing how and knowing that: The presidential address', *Proceedings of the Aristotelian Society*, 46, 212–25.

Scanlon, T. (2004) 'Why does equality matter?', paper presented to the John F. Kennedy School of Government, April 2004.

Schmaus, W. (1994) *Durkheim's Philosophy of Science and the Sociology of Knowledge*, Chicago: The Chicago University Press.

Schön, D. (1983) *The Reflective Practitioner: How Professionals Think in Action*, London: Temple Smith.

Schön, D. (1990) *Educating the Reflective Practitioner: Towards a New Design for Teaching and Learning in the Professions*, San Francisco: Jossey Bass.

Schön, D. (2001) 'The crisis of professional knowledge and the pursuit of an epistemology of practice' in J. Raven and J. Stephenson (eds), *Competence and the Learning Society*, New York: Peter Lang.

Sciulli, D. (2005) 'Continental sociology of professions today: Conceptual contributions', *Current Sociology*, 53(6), 915–42.

Scott, I. (2009) 'Academic development in South African higher education' in E. Bitzer and M. Botha (eds), *Higher Education in South Africa. A Scholarly Look Behind the Scenes*, Stellenbosch: Africa Sun Media, pp. 21–50.

Searle, J. (2009) 'Why should you believe it?', *New York Review of Books*, 24 September, 88–92.

Sfard, A. (1998) 'On two metaphors for learning and the dangers of choosing just one', *Educational Researcher*, 27(2), 4–13.

Shalem, Y. (2010) 'How does the form of learning affect systemic learning?' in Y. Shalem and S. Pendlebury (eds), *Retrieving Teaching: Critical Issues in Curriculum, Pedagogy and Learning*, Cape Town: Juta, pp. 87–100.

Shalem, Y. (2014) 'What binds professional judgment; the case of teaching' in M. Young, and J. Muller, *Knowledge, Expertise and the Professions*, London: Routledge.

Shalem, Y. and Slonimsky, L. (2010) 'Seeing epistemic order: Construction and transmission of evaluative criteria', *British Journal of Sociology of Education*, 31(6), 755–78.

Shapin, S. (1995) *The Social History of Truth*, Chicago: The University of Chicago Press.

Shapin, S. (1996) *The Scientific Revolution*, Chicago: The University of Chicago Press.

Shapin, S. (2008) *The Scientific Life: A Moral History of a Late Modern Vocation*, Chicago: The University of Chicago Press.

Sharples, M. *et al.* (2007) 'A theory of learning for the mobile age', in R. Andrews and C. Haythornthwaite (eds), *The Sage Handbook of Elearning Research*, London: Sage, pp. 221–47.

Shay, S. (2011) 'Curriculum formation: A case study from History', *Studies in Higher Education*, 36(3), 315–29.

Shay, S. (2012) 'Educational development as a field: Are we there yet?', *Higher Education Research and Development*, 31(3), 311–23.

Shay, S. (2013) 'Conceptualising curriculum differentiation in higher education: A sociology of knowledge point of view', *British Journal of Sociology of Education*, 34(4), 563–82.

Shay, S., Oosthuizen, M., Paxton, P. and Van der Merwe, R. (2011) 'Towards a principled basis for curriculum differentiation: Lessons from a comprehensive university' in E. Bitzer and M. Botha (eds), *Curriculum Inquiry in South African Higher Education: Some Scholarly Affirmations and Challenges*, Stellenbosch: SUNMedia, pp. 93–112.

Shinn, T. (1999) 'Change or mutation? Reflections on the foundations of contemporary science', *Social Science Information*, 38, 149–76.

Siedentop, L. (2014) *Inventing the Individual: The Origins of Western Liberalism*, Cambridge, MA: The Bellknap Press.

Siegel, H. (2006) 'Epistemological diversity and educational research: Much ado about nothing much?', *Educational Researcher*, 35(2), 3–12.

Singh. P, Sadovnik, A.R. and Samel, S (eds) (2010) *Toolkits, Translation Devices and Conceptual Accounts: Essays on Basil Bernstein's Sociology of Knowledge*, New York: Peter Lang.

Skidelsky, E. (2008) *Ernst Cassirer the Last Philosopher of Culture*, Princeton: Princeton University Press.

Slaughter, S. and Rhoades, G. (2004) *Academic Capitalism and the New Economy: Markets, State and Higher Education*, Baltimore: Johns Hopkins University Press.

Slonimsly, L. (2010) 'Reclaiming the authority of the teacher' in Y. Shalem and S. Pendlebury (eds), *Retrieving Teaching: Critical Issues in Curriculum, Pedagogy and Learning*, Cape Town: Juta, pp. 41–55.

Smit, R. (2012) 'Engineering science and pure science: Do disciplinary differences matter in engineering education?', presentation to the 23rd Annual Conference of the Australasian Association for Engineering Education, Melbourne, 3–5 December 2012.

Smith, J., Smith, B. and Bryk, A. (1998) 'Setting the pace: opportunities to learn in Chicago public elementary schools', Consortium on Chicago Schools research report, at: http://www.consortium_Chicago.or/publications/pdfs/p0d04.pdf (accessed 1 October 2001).

Sokal, A. (1998) *Intellectual Impostures: Postmodern Philosophers' Abuse of Science*, London: Profile Books.

Stanley, J. (2011) *Know How*, Oxford: Oxford University Press.

Stanley, J. and Williamson, T. (2001) 'Knowing how', *Journal of Philosophy*, 48(8), 411–44.

Stokes, D. (1997) *Pasteur's Quadrant: Basic Science and Technological Innovation*, Washington, DC: The Brookings Institution.

Tallis, R. (2014) *Aping Mankind: Neuromania, Darwinitis and the Misrepresentation of Humanity*, Abingdon: Routledge

Taylor, N. (2014) 'Knowledge and teacher professionalism; the case of mathematics teaching' in M. Young and J. Muller (eds), *Knowledge, Expertise and the Professions*, London: Routledge, pp. 171–84.

Taylor, N. and Vinjevold, P. (1999) 'Getting learning right: The report of the President's Education Initiative research project', Johannesburg: Joint Education Trust.

The Independent (2013) '100 academics savage Education Secretary Michael Gove for "conveyor-belt curriculum" for schools', at: http://www.independent.co.uk/news/education/education-news/100-academics-savage-education-secretary-michael-gove-for-conveyorbelt-curriculum-for-schools-8541262.html (accessed 26 February 2015).

Tiles, M. (1984) *Bachelard: Science and Objectivity*, Cambridge: Cambridge University Press.

Torstendahl, R. (2005) 'The need for a definition of "profession"', *Current Sociology*, 53(6), 947–51.

Turner, R.S. (1971) 'The growth of professorial research in Prussia, 1818 to 1848 – causes and context', *Historical Studies in the Physical Sciences*, 3, 137–82.

Turner, R.S. (1975) 'University reformers and professorial scholarship in Germany 1760-1806', in L. Stone (ed.), *The University in Society*, vol. 2, Princeton, NJ: Princeton University Press.

Turner, S. (2007a) 'Merton's "norms" in political and intellectual context', *Journal of Classical Sociology*, 7(2), 161–78.

Turner, S. (2007b) 'Social theory as a cognitive neuroscience', *European Journal of Social Theory*, 10, 357–74.

Turner, S. (2009) 'Many approaches, but few arrivals', *Philosophy of the Social Sciences*, 39, 174–211.

Turner, S. (2011) 'Collingwood and Weber vs. Mink: History after the cognitive turn', *Journal of the Philosophy of History*, 5, 230–60.

Turner, S. (2012) 'Whatever happened to knowledge?', *Social Studies of Science*, 42(3), 474–80.

Tyack, D.B. (1974) *The One Best System: A History of American Urban Education*, Boston: Harvard University Press.

Tyler, W. (2010) 'Towering TIMSS or leaning PISA? Vertical and horizontal models of international testing regimes' in P. Singh, A. Sadovnik and S. Semel (eds), *Toolkits, Translation Devices and Conceptual Accounts: Essays on Basil Bernstein's Sociology of Knowledge*, New York: Peter Lang, pp. 143–58.

Usher, R. and Edwards, R. (1994) *Post Modernism and Education*, London: Routledge.

Verene, D.P. (1969) 'Kant, Hegel, and Cassirer: The origins of the philosophy of symbolic forms', *Journal of the History of Ideas* 30(1), 33–46.

Weber, M. (1958) 'Science as a Vocation', *Daedalus*, 87, 111–34.

Weber, M., Baehr, P.R. and Wells, G.C. (2002) *The Protestant Ethic and the "Spirit" of Capitalism and Other Writings*, New York: Penguin Classics.

Weinel, M. (2007) 'Primary source knowledge and technical decision-making: Mbeki and the AZT debate', *Studies in History and Philosophy of Science Part A*, 38, 748–60.

Weingart, P (1997) 'From "finalisation" to "mode 2": Old wine in new bottles"?', *Social Science Information*, 36, 591–613.

Weiss, L., McCarthy, C. and Dimitriades, G. (eds) (2006) *Ideology, Curriculum and the New Sociology of Education: Revisiting the Work of Michael Apple*, London: Routledge.

Wheelahan, L. (2007) 'How competency-based training locks the working class out of powerful knowledge: a modified Bernsteinian analysis,' *British Journal of Sociology of Education*, 28(5), 637–51.

Wheelahan, L. (2009) 'The problem with CBT (and why constructivism makes things worse)', *Journal of Education and Work*, 22(3), 227–42.

Wheelahan, L. (2010) *Why Knowledge Matters in the Curriculum: A Social Realist Argument*, London: Routledge.

Whimster, S. (2004) *The Essential Weber: A Reader*, London: Routledge.

White, J. (2007) 'What schools are for and why?', Impact Paper, Philosophy of Education Society of Great Britain.

White, J. (2012a) 'An unstable framework – Critical perspectives on the framework for the National Curriculum' and Young, M. (2012) The curriculum – 'An entitlement to powerful knowledge: A response to John White', both at: http://www.newvisions-foreducation.org.uk/2012/05/03/the-curriculum-%E2%80%98 (accessed 26 February 2015).

White, J. (2012b) 'Powerful knowledge: too weak a prop for the traditional curriculum', at: http://www.newvisionsforeducation.org.uk/2012/05/14/powerful-knowledge-too-weak-a-prop-for-the-traditional-curriculum/ (accessed 19 May 2015).

Whitty. G. (1974) 'Sociology and the problem of radical educational change' in M. Flude and J. Ahier, *Educability, Schools and Ideology*, London: Croom Helm.

Whitty, G. (2009) 'Evaluating "Blair's educational legacy?": Some comments on the special issue of Oxford Review of Education', *Oxford Review of Education*, 35(2), 267–80.

Whitty, G. and Young, M. (1976) *Explorations in the Politics of School Knowledge*, Driffield, Yorks: Nafferton Books.

Winch, C. (2009) 'Ryle on knowing how and the possibility of vocational education', *Journal of Applied Philosophy*, 26(1), 88–101.

Winch, C. (2010) *Dimensions of Expertise: A Conceptual Exploration of Vocational Knowledge*, London: Continuum.

Winch, C. (2012) 'Curriculum design and epistemic ascent', *Journal of Philosophy of Education*, 47(1), 128–46.

Winch, C. (2013) 'Curriculum design and epistemic ascent', *Journal of Philosophy of Education*, 47(1), 128–46.

Winch, C. (2014) 'Know-how and knowledge in the professional curriculum' in M. Young and J. Muller (eds), *Knowledge, Expertise and the Professions*, London: Routledge, pp. 47–60.

Winch, P. (1958) *The Idea of a Social Science and its Relation to Philosophy*, London: Routledge and Kegan Paul.

Williams, B. (2002/2010) *Truth and Truthfulness: An Essay in Genealogy*, Princeton: Princeton University Press.

Williams, R. (1961) *The Long Revolution*, London: Chatto and Windus.

Willis, P. (1977) *Learning to Labour*, England: Saxon House.

Wittgenstein, L. (1953) *Philosophical Investigations* (trans. E. Anscombe), Oxford: Basil Blackwell.

Wolf, A. (2014) *Review of Vocational Education*, London: Department for Education.

Woodhead, C. (2002) *Class War: The State of British Education*, London: Little Brown.

Woodhead, C. (2009) *A Desolation of Learning: Is this the Education our Children Deserve?*, London: Pencil Sharp Publishing.

Yandell, J. (2014) 'Classrooms as sites of curriculum delivery or meaning-making: whose knowledge counts?', *FORUM*, 56(1), 145–55.

Yates, L. (2013) 'Revisiting curriculum, the numbers game and the inequality problem', *Journal of Curriculum Studies*, 45(1), 39–51.

Yates, L. and Collins, C. (2010) 'The absence of knowledge in Australian curriculum reforms', *European Journal of Education*, 45(1), 89–102.

Yates, L and Young, M. (2010) 'Editorial: globalisation, knowledge and the curriculum', *European Journal of Education*, 45(1), 4–10.

Young, M. (ed.) (1971) *Knowledge and Control: New Directions for the Sociology of Education*, London: Collier Macmillan.

Young, M. (1998) *The Curriculum of the Future*, London: Falmer.

Young, M. (2006) 'Review of Weiss et al. (ed.) (2006)', *London Review of Education*, 4(3), 306–8.

Young, M. (2007a) *Bringing Knowledge Back In: From Social Constructivism to Social Realism in the Sociology of Education*, London: Routledge.

Young, M. (2007b) 'Qualifications Frameworks: some conceptual issues', *European Journal of Education*, 42(4), 445–59.

Young, M. (2007c) 'Structure and activity in Durkheim and Vygotsky's social theories of knowledge', *Critical Studies in Education*, 1(1), 43–53.

Young, M. (2008) *Bringing Knowledge Back In: From Social Constructivism to Social Realism in the Sociology of Education*, London: Routledge.

Young, M. (2009a) 'NVQs in the UK; their origins and legacy', report prepared for the International Labour Organisation's Implementation of National Qualifications Research Project.

Young, M. (2009b) 'Curriculum theory and the problem of knowledge: a personal journey and an unfinished project' in L. Waks and E. Short (eds), *Leaders in Curriculum Studies; Intellectual Self Portraits*, Rotterdam: Sense Publishers.

Young, M. (2011a) 'National Vocational Qualifications in the United Kingdom; their origins and legacy', *Journal of Education and Work*, 24(3–4), pp. 259–82.

Young, M. (2011b) 'The return to subjects: a sociological perspective on the UK coalition government's approach to the 14–19 curriculum', *The Curriculum Journal*, 22(2), 265–78.

Young, M. (2011c) 'The future of education in a knowledge society: the radical case for a subject-based curriculum', *Journal of the Pacific Circle Consortium for Education*, 22(1), 21–32.

Young, M. (2011d) 'Knowledge matters' in L. Yates and M. Grumet (eds), *Curriculum in Today's World: Configuring Knowledge, Identities, Work and Politics, World Yearbook of Education 2011*, New York: Routledge.

Young. M. and Allais, S.M. (2010) 'Conceptualising the role of qualifications in educational reform', ILO Discussion document, unpublished.

Young, M. and Allais, S. (eds) (2013) *Implementing NQFs Across Five Continents*, London: Routledge.

Young, M. and Lambert, D. with Roberts, C. and Roberts, M. (2014) *Knowledge and the Future School: Curriculum and Social Justice*, London: Bloomsbury.

Young, M. and Muller, J. (2013) 'On the powers of powerful knowledge', *Review of Education*, 1(3), 229–50.

Young, M. and Muller, J. (eds) (2014) *Knowledge, Expertise and the Professions*, London: Routledge.

Young, M. and Whitty, G. (eds) (1977) *Society, State and Schooling*, Falmer: Falmer Press.

INDEX